I Was Born Greek

MELINA MERCOURI

I
Was Born
Greek

Doubleday & Company, Inc., Garden City, New York 1971

I Was Born Greek

Chapter One

What I love most in the world is Greece, but the Greek sea, the Greek hills, the Greek sun, the reflection of the sun on the Greek hills are not for me to see. I am not permitted to return to Greece. That is why I am writing this book.

The story is about me and people I know. It's about Greece and its politics, about the repeated frustrations of my people to obtain independence from foreign domination and the lousy Greek politicians who served those powers.

I shall not write with modesty or reserve because I am neither modest nor reserved. And if at one moment I seem to be an unbridled hedonist and the next moment Joan of Arc, it is because I am a hedonist and I am Joan of Arc. I must add, quickly, that I have been Joan of Arc only since 1967. That was the year that Greece was afflicted with the curse of the colonels. Joan is a role that suits me poorly. In the theatre and films, where I earn my living, it would be called "weird casting." But it is a role that was thrust upon me, and such is the nature of our times that a similar role could be thrust upon any one of us.

Men. Let's start with men. I am now bound in marriage. It is a damned good one, as marriages go, and to my amazement, I have been faithful to my husband for fourteen years. But before I met him I knew other men and there is not one of them that I was not happy to have known and loved.

The first man I loved was called Spiros. He was extremely handsome, extremely seductive. His mouth smelled sweeter than any man's I've ever known. I adored his embrace, an embrace scented of rosewater and basil. He was strong. He was tall. He loved his wife and cheated on her. He loved his sons and took care of them. He had a passion for me. It made my childhood a very happy one. Spiros was my grandfather. He was also mayor of Athens for thirty years.

His son, Stamatis, my father, was also destined for politics. But even when he married at the advanced age of twenty-two a girl who was twenty-one, he continued to live in the house of Big Spiros and to be dominated by him. Spiros was the supreme authority. We were all slaves to him, but it was a slavery that was sweet.

He was elegant, he was fastidious, he was hygienic to the point of mania, never sleeping twice in the same sheets and washing his hands twenty times a day. His hair and beard were white but I didn't think him old. I thought him eternal. At the age of eighty-five he never wore glasses and not a tooth in his head was false. There could be no concessions to age, weakness, human frailty, the climate. Even in the coldest weather he refused to wear an overcoat. This is also true of my brother Spiros. There is something about baring his chest to the wind that makes him feel very Greek, very male, very much my grandfather.

To be mayor in those days meant being more powerful than anyone in parliament or even a minister to the Crown. To illustrate:

In 1832, a Bavarian prince, Otto, was made King of Greece by our foreign protectors. (He was not the last.) Despite the fact that poor Otto could not speak a word of Greek, he took it into his head to go out and meet his people. So with panoply, laurel carpets, tolling church bells and an interpreter, he set forth. In one village a peasant came forward to wish Otto well. Addressing himself to the interpreter, he said: "Please tell His Majesty, good luck, good health, and may he one day become the mayor of Athens."

Governments rose and fell, kings came and went, but Grandfather's rule went on and on. He was unassailable because he was loved. He was loved because he loved. He cared about everyone in Athens. Not from behind a desk but actively with direct concern. If someone's rubbish bin was not emptied by the sanitation services, he knew about it and saw that it was done. He knew which child of which constituent had diarrhea and brought him a doctor, and woe to the doctor who made a wrong diagnosis; Big Spiros had studied medicine and only chucked his doctorship to enter politics. He was counselor, lawyer, midwife, and redresser of wrongs. He was godfather to literally hundreds of Greek children, and knew exactly how each godchild was faring. And he actually remembered each one of them by name. Truly he was a tribal chief.

He was available to all. His door was never closed. The dining-room table was kept laid from noon to three o'clock ready for anyone who might come. And they came in great numbers. Whoever they were, ordinary voters, merchants, or ministers, they all received the same greeting from my grandfather: "*Yiassou matia mou.*" Health to you, my eyes.

I'll never know how we fed all those people. We had no money. But often we needed none. People would come and bring cheese or eggs or vegetables. A peasant might bring a lamb. But he would want just a little taste of it. So at once it was cooked and prepared, and at four o'clock in the afternoon, everyone present sat down to taste his lamb—the peasant, the minister, and the poet. Athens was that kind of big village. It was unaffected. It was simple. Because I grew up in that atmosphere, I've never been able to tolerate the division of society into classes. In our household it was unthinkable.

3

Grandfather's re-election and re-election became a matter of course. In Greece they voted for the man, not the party or the platform. It was all wrong of course. Too often, paternalism substituted for government. Solid political structures are not built that way. Big Spiros was a scrupulously honest mayor, so much so that sometimes people lost patience with him, as they did with another Greek before him; he was too honest. In Greek thinking, a man who is too honest is not to be trusted. It's inhuman to resist all temptation. Big Spiros was the man who decided where new roads should be built. Had he been just a wee bit dishonest, he could have amassed one of the greatest fortunes in Greece, and Big Spiros owned nothing. An astonishing number of people offered him gifts of land, with small suggestions about where new roads should go. Big Spiros was incorruptible, and his heirs have no land. But there is a street that bears his name in Athens, a street in which his statue stands.

Despite all the time and energy he gave to his political duties, my adored Big Spiros nevertheless found time and energy for the ladies. My father was a pretty good hand at that too. In Greece this was not and is not considered reprehensible. On the contrary, this was and is considered proper to the conservation of masculine honor.

Sometimes perturbations and protests would be made by the women in our house but only as a matter of form. They, of course—my mother Irene and my grandmother Amalia—were confined to the hearth and the joys of needlepoint. If ever they even stole a furtive glance at a man, they were menaced with strangulation and/or expulsion. Besides, no Athenian of sane mind would have dared to approach a woman of our family. Big Spiros had pistols in the house. That was well known. And my father, not only for an impressive list of infidelities, but for his reckless courage as well, was named D'Artagnan.

Even as a child I recognized the injustice of these double

standards. There were many D'Artagnans in Athens, but not enough miladies. I decided to be milady or Lady Hamilton or Catherine the Great, but certainly not to accept the life of my mother or grandmother. In short, I wanted to change the times. I doubt whether it was I who was responsible, but the times have changed.

My childhood was blissful. Grandfather protected me. He took me with him wherever he went. Everything amused us and everyone was jealous of us. I was his favorite and to be the favorite of Athens' favorite son was paradise. Especially in carnival time. On Sundays in carnival time he drove through Athens in an open horse-drawn carriage, the father of the city meeting his people. And it was I who sat beside him. But first, a little rehearsal. Sit up straight, dignified, assured. Bow gracefully, to the right, to the left. Very good! Off we go.

We were going to the Dardanelles, a narrow street near Constitution Square, which separated the Yannakis and the Doré, the two most fashionable cafés of the day. Just before reaching this point, Big Spiros got down to walk beside the carriage, making his way slowly through innumerable greetings and handshakes, while I stayed in the carriage bowing and smiling in a daze of reflected glory.

After the parade we went home to the midday meal. On the dining-room sideboards the *cremes au canelle* would be cooling in their dishes, filling the house with the smell of cinnamon. It was my joy to spit secretly into each dish. One day I was caught and beaten. (I have been much beaten in my life.) Grandfather refused to be shocked. Mock-severe, he looked from me to the blancmanges.

"So she spat. But with style, like an aristocrat."

He was always on my side and I knew how to take advantage of it. When my mother raised her hand to me, I would check the blow with an immediate resort to blackmail.

"I'll tell Big Spiros you beat me!"

Very often it worked.

5

We lived in Big Spiros' big house. It wasn't splendid or rich. There was no garden. It opened directly on to the street, and Big Spiros would have it no other way: he liked his door opening directly on to Athens. We were on the first floor, Big Spiros, Grandmother Amalia, and their son George on the second floor. In winter the house was icy cold and in summer it was always dusty with the footprints of all the people who trooped in and out. There was an eternal coming and going and rushing up and down the staircase. If ever there was a moment's calm, you could count on an imminent eruption for political reasons, for domestic reasons, or for reasons *passionnelles*. No child could hope for a more perfect disorder.

Let me not forget Grandfather Spiros' bodyguards. They were marvelous and they were useful. (Greece, thank God, was always a hot country and Big Spiros' constant re-election earned him some enemies.) His bodyguards were my first playmates. They let me handle their pistols and wear their brass knuckles. They were not mercenaries, no, nothing like that vulgar breed that flourishes today. They were people totally devoted to my grandfather. They were ready to die for him. They were ready to die for my grandmother, my mother, my Uncle George, for me and for Grandfather's dog. My favorites among them were named Mimis and Kostas.

It was much later, with the aid of Mimis and Kostas, that the greatest fraud ever perpetrated against an educational institution was accomplished. I refer to my passing my high school exam.

If I have no other record of achievement, I have one record that will stand forever. No child in any school system, anywhere, could possibly compile a greater number of zeros in a school career than I did. It was not that I was completely stupid. School was a never ending agony. It was an adult plot designed to place me by sheer force into a group of other captive children for no other purpose but to pound me on the head with things that bored me to death. Nobody went to more schools because nobody was kicked out of more schools. I could never pass an exam. Never. In the end my teachers all adopted the same tactic. Out of love for my grandfather or for the desperate need to get rid of me, they kept promoting me to higher classes as quickly as possible. But to graduate, I was confronted by the final exam.

It was a catastrophe. I knew absolutely nothing, and the examiner knew that I knew nothing. I kept looking up from a blank sheet of paper to the examiner and back to the blank sheet of paper. After a solid hour the paper was still blank. I laid down my pencil and held my hands up in a signal of surrender. Strangely, the examiner smiled at me in absolutely loving fashion. He approached me. He asked me a question about geometry. I told him I knew nothing. He looked away, then back to me, and his smile was more loving than ever. He asked me a question about Byzantine history. I told him his questions would get him nowhere. Again that look away and back with that adoring smile. Then in a flash I guessed what he was looking at each time he turned away from me. Sure enough, there framed in the glass panel of the door, stood Mimis and Kostas. With burning eyes and pistols drawn, they communicated the certain destiny that would befall the teacher if Melina were to fail her exam.

Dear Mimis, dear Kostas. They taught me the meaning of friendship. With hair slicked and wearing brilliant ties, they partook in the family celebration on the passing of my exam. So did the town hall band. When my elaborately framed certificate was hung on the wall, they broke into a stirring march. Mimis and Kostas watched me receiving congratulations from all and they didn't blink an eye. But as I said, that was later. I can't claim childish innocence. I collaborated in the fraud against the school system when I was fifteen. I knew what I was doing.

If I have conveyed that my childhood was all laughter and fun, let me correct that at once. There was also a sea of trou-

7

bles. My first encounter with despair came when I was three and a half. My mother announced that she was going to bring forth another child. I immediately recognized that this was a plot against my security and my favored position. My hatred and anger were not undeclared. I stopped speaking to my mother and father. Not good morning. Not good evening. Not a word. But I needed an accomplice. Who else but Grandfather Spiros? As could be expected, he understood perfectly. He suggested we apply Spartan law and asked me if I understood what that meant. I hadn't the slightest idea but looked him straight in the eyes and said I did. He nevertheless explained it to me. If the newborn were to be a girl (and that was what I feared most), then we would strangle it, drown it, in one way or another liquidate it. And if it were a boy, not to worry, he would only be kept for breeding purposes. Thus reassured, I resumed saying good morning to my mother.

As luck would have it, the child was born male and was thus preserved. He too was named Spiros. I accepted him. I had no choice. My mother loved him, my grandmother loved him, my grandfather loved him, the bodyguards loved him, my Uncle George loved him, and now as I look back on it, I am sure that my father loved him even though he was not around when his son arrived. No, that was misfortune number two.

My father Stamatis, D'Artagnan, during the full bloom of Mama's pregnancy, ran off with a charming actress who, next to me, had the most beautiful eyes in Athens. He was in disgrace in his father's house. No one was allowed to mention his name. But Grandmother Amalia paid him secret visits.

I recognized that Father's flight was serious, but the real calamity came when my mother, thus abandoned, chose to take refuge in her mother's house. I don't think I've ever known such intense misery as I did the day we left Grandfather's house.

Grandmother Lappas was a good woman, but she was severe and demanded order and silence. Her husband had died of asthma and during the long years of nursing him she became accustomed to staying indoors. She kept the shutters half closed. She was neurotic about money. Rather than buy clothes she rarely dressed. She moved through the silent dark rooms wearing an ancient peignoir and slippers. Going from Grandfather Spiros' house to hers was like leaving a carnival for a convent. Only Mama's compassionate decision to let me join Big Spiros for lunch each day kept me from nervous depression.

Then tragedy struck. Grandfather Spiros, the one and only, my passion, not to be outdone by his son, fell in love with another woman. Her name was Nana, like Zola's Nana, and she seemed to me a thousand times worse than Zola's Nana. A curious determination. I never read Zola. I never read anything. Nana was milk-white of skin. This in itself, in Greece, was an admission of bad faith. She was round, she was petite, not petite, downright small. But Spiros loved her and saw her beautiful.

My grandmother Amalia felt almost as betrayed as I did. That dear lady, who was lovable and gay, a marvelous storyteller, just couldn't cope with this horrible occurrence. Like most Greek women, she had learned how to make peace with her husband's infidelities. But this time he was in love. That was another matter. What to do?

There was a council of women. My grandmother, my mother, Grandmother Lappas, and me. It took place in Amalia's room. There we sat before rows and rows of wigs which she herself had made. It was her *violon d'Ingres*. The council unanimously expressed repugnance for Nana, for all men and above all, for Spiros. At his age, and in his position! After all he was the mayor of Athens! (Amalia never called him "Spiros," always "Mayor.") The council quickly reached a decision. There was only one person who, by depriving him

9

of affection and consideration, could make him suffer and bring him to his senses. That person was Melina, me.

It was voted that I would no longer lunch with him. Then this vote was modified. I was to lunch with him but not speak to him. Not a solitary word. Not until he gave up his harlot, Nana. Grandfather Spiros recognized the conspiracy at once. But he was of tough metal. He met my silence with his own. It was a contest of wills. There were weeks of daily lunches and not a word was spoken. At first I thought he meant to demonstrate that the women of the house could not dictate to him. Then I realized he was really deeply smitten by Nana. I was mad with jealousy.

One day, after the usual silent lunch, he took me firmly by the arm. He led me into the street and into a large automobile. Also present were a chauffer and the bodyguards, Mimis and Kostas. He gave the order to drive off. Only then did I realize that he was rather formally dressed. But I asked no question. We drove in silence. When we were miles from Athens, he announced that we were going to an official function. A brand new hotel was being inaugurated in Kifissia, a little outside Athens. I received this explanation with no comment—more silence. Then just before we reached Kifissia he revealed to me his darker purpose.

Nana was going to be at the ceremony and I was to greet her politely. I looked at him with hatred and demanded to be taken back to Athens at once. Big Spiros ordered the car to be stopped. He pointed to the road. His manner was so resolute, even the bodyguards said nothing. Getting out of an automobile is an awkward business at best. I managed it with elegance. Wordlessly I turned away and began a determined march back to Athens. I gave no thought to the many miles I would need to walk. I strode on, consumed by anger and jealousy. It was a long time before the car came back to fetch me. Mimis opened the door and pulled me back into the front seat.

The reception at Kifissia was a large one. Many notables attended. Some of them saw Nana, dressed to the nines, come to me and offer her milk-white hand. They also saw me turn to stone and stare her down until that hand was withdrawn.

All the way back to Athens, Spiros sat looking at me in the manner of a man who understands women. And I felt a delicious adult sensation. Without speaking he told me, "You're jealous and that's normal." And without speaking I told him, "You're angry with me and you have a right to be." And I took his wrist. I always loved to touch the fine blue veins in his wrist. He took me in his arms. And thus, at an early age, I had a brief vision of what love could be.

However, I am obliged to add he did not give up Nana.

Chapter Two

To be born Greek is to be magnificently cursed. To a surprisingly large number of people, it means you personally built the Acropolis, you created Delphi, the theatre, and you sired the concept of democracy. The truth is that you're poor, many of your people can't read, and the rare moments that you tasted of democracy and independence, foreign protectors and their Greek stooges snatched away from you.

It is infuriating to know how little the world knows about Greek history. Most people talk to you as if Pericles died only yesterday and as if Aeschylus is still writing plays. If now and then you meet someone who does know that in 1821, after four hundred years of Turkish occupation, the Greeks rose up against their oppressors, the chances are that that someone is English. And he happens to know about it only because Lord Byron came to fight at our side and wrote beautiful poems about us.

After six years of terrible struggle, the Turk was beaten and Greece was free. Free? A figure of speech. Because now was established a pattern that still exists today. The pattern of protective powers. Early in our struggle, France and England decided that Greece would fall into the Czarist grip because the Russian and Greek religions were similar. They decided that the best way to fight the Russians was to join them. And now all three powers would protect us. They took us into protective and suffocating embrace, all the while keeping a wary eye on each other.

The first Greek governor was a rather conservative gentleman called Jean Kapodistria, but the French and the English took it into their heads that he was a Czarist agent. In 1831 Kapodistria was assassinated. Let us not say that France and England engineered the assassination. Just let it be said that they shed no tears and that no flags were ordered to half mast. Followed, fifteen months of what is called political instability. Naturally it was for the trinity to put things in order. They decided what form of constitution was good for the Greeks. They decided that obviously the Greeks could not rule themselves. The solution? Greece needed a king. They checked the lists of royal unemployed, and by no apparent design plucked Prince Otto from Bavaria and dispatched him to the Mediterranean. He was the one who spoke no Greek and went out to meet his people accompanied by an interpreter. But Otto was only a fair-haired boy of seventeen, so he was girded round with a Bavarian council to run things. This Bavarian regency was a dedicated lot, dedicated to the principle that independence was not for the Greeks. In four years Otto was of age. He no longer needed the regency's help. To prove his manhood and to demonstrate that he could be just as tough as the council, he designated as traitors the two great heroes of the Greek revolution: Kolokotronis and Plapoutas. They were condemned to death. Twice during these thirty years the Greek people revolted and with the second revolution Otto was kicked out.

The protective powers made the obvious deduction. What Greece needed was a tougher king and a tougher regency.

Palmerston saw things very clearly. He summed things up thusly:

> Greece, as quickly as possible must become a people less dangerous and less active. Greece needs a considerable number of policemen.

Once more they made a tour of the royal palaces. This time they came up with George, a Glücksbourg from Denmark. He was more mature than Otto. He was a few months past seventeen. He was crowned George I, King of Greece. Since George owed his kingship to the suggestion made by an English banker named Harbo, it was perfectly fair that he ask the English to help him rule and keep the Greek people in hand. George stuck around for a long time—almost fifty years—until somebody in Salonika said: "Enough is enough," and poor George got a bullet in his head.

But George was fruitful enough to leave a son. His name was Constantine and he made a rather conspicuous debut. In 1912, he led a victorious Greek army against the Turks in Macedonia and liberated hundreds of thousands of Greeks. He became a hero. My grandfather loved and admired Constantine. That was enough for me. Nobody was more pro-royalist than I was. But Constantine had trouble with a Prime Minister who was just as popular as he was. Eleftherios Venizelos came from Crete, he was a brilliant man, and to complicate Constantine's life, he was a democrat. When World War I broke out, Venizelos thought that Greece's place was with the Allies. But Constantine didn't like this at all. After all, he was married to the Kaiser's sister. The enmity deepened. Twice in 1915, Constantine, regally indifferent to the Venizelos majority in Parliament, fired him from office. Greece was split down the middle—royalists against Venizelists.

In 1917, Venizelos got the upper hand. Constantine was ousted and departed the Greek shores. He left his throne to his son Alexander, but this problem was resolved by a monkey. He was Alexander's pet and in a playful moment took a bite out of the king who promptly died of blood poisoning.

The seesaw seesawed and back came Constantine, this time to lead Greece to disaster again. He led an army against the Turks. It was 1922. Greece was badly beaten. One million Greeks who lived for generations on the Turkish side of the Aegean were put out of their homes and flooded into Greece as refugees.

Now it was an army group that said enough is enough. Constantine got the point and abdicated. His son, George II, took over. But only for one year. In 1924 he got kicked out and wonder of wonders, Greece became a Republic.

All of this played havoc with my family. My father who was a royalist was clapped into prison. It was behind bars that he and my mother, both teen-agers, were betrothed. An old priest was permitted into the cell for the ceremony. "In the name of the Father, the Son and the Holy Ghost, the servant of God, Stamatis, is betrothed to the servant of God, Irene." He put rings on their fingers, then stepped aside for the guards who led my mother away. Afterward my father was exiled to the island of Mylos and that is where the marriage took place.

Then came news that stunned Athens. My father and Big Spiros were on different sides. My grandfather switched to the republicans. His friends and followers, all royalists, were aghast. They watched with horror when the photograph of Venizelos went up outside our house. It was shattering for me to hear my grandfather insulted. Yet I too, royalist to the core, was horrified that he could turn away from the monarchy. His voters abandoned him in droves, and yet Athens could hardly believe it when Spiros Mercouris lost the elections! We were all submerged in grief. All except Spiros. He said that the wheel would turn. He was ever the eternal optimist, a gift that he imparted to my father. I used to listen open-mouthed to my father rationalize a defeat when he himself ran for office.

He would take the figures that sealed his defeat and analyze them in such a way as to prove he'd won a tremendous moral victory. My brother Spiros is blessed with the same optimistic spirit. I am the only member of the family who is a confirmed pessimist. Till now I have concealed this from my small group of fans who insist that I represent the joy of life. No, to me every silver cloud has a dark lining. The fellow who said, "He could snatch defeat from the jaws of victory," was thinking of me.

Perhaps this pessimism came from knowing you could go to prison for your beliefs. My mother, even more than most Greek women, talked to her children about things adult: life, men, love—and politics. "War," "prison," "exile" were words I heard a lot.

My grandfather's desertion of the king caused a rift between us. I did not conceal my anger and my disappointment. One day he had the effrontery to tell me that he was taking me to visit Venizelos. With all my strength I refused. With all his strength, he insisted. I went. Today I know that Venizelos was a progressive man. He reorganized the state. He created the "Greece of the two continents and the five seas." He restored pride to Greece. But at that time I considered him a monster. He always wore a black forage cap. Some said it was because he was bald. Others, who knew better, said that his cap concealed a pair of devil's horns, that he wore his cap even in bed so as not to terrify his wife. This demon took me on his knees and kept me there all the time he was talking to my grandfather. As soon as I got home I washed my hair and drenched myself in eau de cologne.

But alas, the Republic was short-lived, eleven years. In 1935, with England in the wings, there was a royalist putsch managed by a General Kondylis. We got a king again. George II was dusted off and brought back from exile. In a matter of months George bowed low and handed the country over to General Metaxas. Greece became a dictatorship. Metaxas proclaimed himself "first peasant of Greece" and "first worker" and "first airman." He said his mission was to resurrect the noble "civilization of ancient Greece and Byzantium."

(Oh, those dreadful, dreary incantations! Today's Colonels are creating the "Greek Christian Civilization." But by whatever name, they all smell as bad, and they all use the same methods: imprisonment, deportation, torture, censorship and secret police.)

My royalist but anti-fascist father, Stamatis, in exile; my republican grandfather, Spiros, out of office. Joy did not reign in the Mercouris family. Sometimes we were permitted to visit my father. D'Artagnan had changed. Ever strikingly handsome, ever ready to spot a pretty skirt at a hundred meters, yet matured, developed. Time was given to reading and study. He hadn't taken it too seriously when at the age of twenty-two he was elected the youngest deputy in Greece. But now he began to understand Greece, its qualities and its agonies. D'Artagnan was becoming a responsible citizen. In his reading habits, he was in his Russian phase. We brought him books by Lermontov, Chekhov and Tolstoi. All books had to pass the censorship of the guards. Stamatis' guard considered anything Russian as bolshevik. He made it his business to know who was Russian and who was not. All it needed was the name to end in "ov."

"Lermontov, Russian. No."

"Chekhov, Russian. No."

"Tolstoi, okay."

Metaxas was a mean bastard, but the workers' movements and the left wing he tried to strangle just wouldn't die. All of this had little meaning to me. I stood my royalist ground despite my grandfather's designation of George II as a stinker. It was only when Metaxas created a youth movement akin to the Hitler Jugend that I was forced into opposition. If the reasons were more sartorial and aesthetic than political, they were nonetheless passionate. To my disgust I was forced into an ugly blue military uniform and asked to parade with other girls of my age who were half my size. To make matters worse I was appointed flag bearer. I stuck out like an elongated asparagus. At the age of eleven, I became a confirmed antifascist and a doubtful royalist.

Chapter Three

Oh, those God damn Greek islands! Everything you ever heard about them is true. I have traveled. I have seen beauty on this earth. But, oh, Greek islands, my islands. I wept at your loveliness when I was with you. And today I weep for longing of you. I tell people, don't go to Greece, don't bring tourist money to support the colonels' regime, but when they heed me, I feel a pain. I have deprived them of something lovely.

Our family island was Spetsai. We spent our summers there. Spetsai is one of the few islands that is green. The houses are white. Some are splendid. But even the poorest fisherman's house has elegance, style and is imaginatively decorated. There are no cars, even today. There are hosts of carriages drawn by slightly crazy horses that trot up and down lovely tree-lined lanes. And there are the Spetsai donkeys. No animal, or human, has more beautiful eyes than the Spetsai donkeys. I swear it. And one of the images that stays with me always is that of a Spetsai fisherman lightly perched on a plodding donkey—reading Proust.

Spetsai is where I first noticed that Greek men sent languid courting looks toward my mother. She was now an attractively vulnerable divorcee.

I adored my mother. She was young. She was beautiful, and marvelous company. People who know me really know that I've been imitating my mother all my life, and especially in the way she laughs. I adored lying in the sun after swimming, close to her. The special treat was to lick the salt drying on her arms. I didn't want to lose her to anyone else, so with my grandmother I plotted to keep her heart-free and at home. In the end, despite our vigil, she did find another man and married him, a fine and kindly man named Leonidas. But at Spetsai no suppliant could pass our guard.

My mother's future was the only cause which could put Grandmother Lappas and me on the same side of the barricades. In all other matters the adults of the house were allied against me. I was the rebel, the potential milady and needed constant surveillance.

Spiros, my brother, was the favorite. Only I could see that he was a wily little bastard and was infuriated at the ease with which he wound them around his little finger. When very occasionally, they beat him, he kissed their hands and shouted, "No, no, don't! It will hurt you!" And their hearts would melt.

One afternoon they let me go to the cinema. Alone in the house, Spiros brought in his friends, organized a game of football, and contrived to break a glass door in the hall. Grandmother Lappas was waiting for me when I got back. When I came into range, I was met with two staggering blows.

"If you hadn't gone to the cinema, your brother wouldn't have been left alone! And if he hadn't been left alone, he wouldn't have brought in his friends! And if he hadn't brought in his friends, the door wouldn't have been broken!"

It seemed to me that I was continually punished for what Spiros did and for what I didn't do. But as for the incident of my public chastisement in Spetsai, that was of my own making, or more precisely that of the theatrical microbe which had been gnawing at me with increasing appetite.

I was ten. I donned my mother's clothes and strutted into a forbidden café. I danced. I danced for the people. Mysterious island telegraphy summoned my mother in a matter of minutes. I received a majestic, monumental slap. But it was of little importance. All that counted was that people had applauded me. That I made them smile, that they liked me and their applause warmed my heart. From that moment I wanted to please them always and to ask for no reward but their applause.

Grandfather Spiros was an addicted theatregoer and in me he found an enthusiastic companion. He loved the theatre in all its forms. From Greek tragedy to music hall revues to Karagyozis. The Karagyozis is a form of puppet theatre, projected in shadow upon a screen. The puppets are all fixed characters and the theme was always the same: the Greek resistance against the Turks. The theatre is named after its most appealing character, Karagyozis. He was an ugly, beautiful hunchback. He was ever in the clutches of the wicked Sultan and his cruel guards. But in the end, Karagyozis would emerge victorious in each situation by Greek cunning, by wit, and by cheerful invention.

Traveling troupes played in courtyards and in parks. Sometimes the puppets were primitive. Sometimes they were fashioned with great art. Another character I loved was Katsantonis, a hero of the revolution. Ali Pasha would have him put in irons and the Turkish executioner would break his bones, one by one! I used to groan and sob and close my eyes to the terrible shadows on the screen. But Grandfather would lift my head with a finger and say: "Don't cry and don't ever close your eyes."

When I was older, he took me regularly to the satirical revues, a speciality of Athens. There was singing and dancing, but the heart of the Greek revue was political satire. It was an extension of Aristophanes. In all its history the Greek revue has been censored only three times: by the Metaxas dictatorship, by the Nazi occupation, and naturally by our ugly present-day colonels. Aside from these three afflictions, the revue always had total liberty to mock Greece, its institutions, its politics and its politicians. No one was immune, not even my grandfather. A very funny actor, wearing the same dapper hat that Grandfather always wore, presented a devastating caricature. No holds were barred. Big Spiros took many a ribald roasting. The audiences rocked with laughter but no one laughed louder than my grandfather. (In 1965, when I was a sort of unofficial ambassador for Greek tourism, I was the subject of a satirical sketch that I blush to remember. It was screamingly funny, but they flayed me alive.)

Sad to say that after the war, the high standards of Greek revue declined. Wit was sacrificed to tinsel effects. But in the 1930s the revues were marvelous. I have seen all kinds of theatre on the world stages, but I have never seen funnier improvisation, keener observation or more perfect sense of timing, than I saw in those revues. (When I saw Laurence Olivier's extraordinary performance in a London presentation of *The Entertainer,* part of the pleasure I felt came because he evoked for me actors of the Greek revue.) There was one immense talent that comes to mind, Anna Kalouta. She sang like a bird, she danced, she was a splendid actress, she was an acrobat. There was nothing she couldn't do. She and her sister started on the stage as children and dominated the Greek revue for generations after. Wherever you are, Anna, I loved you. You were great.

From the beginning, theatregoing was a delight and once bitten by the applause microbe in Spetsai, I was sure that there was no other life for me but the life of an actress. No sacrifice would be too great. No slap or series of slaps from my mother could have a discouraging effect. No reprimand stopped me. I took to painting my face. This made life difficult for my brother Spiros. When his sister paraded through Athens streets outlandishly made-up with Vaseline and lipstick, it was inevitable that her morality be seriously questioned. Spiros had to leap into the breech with his fists. It was a matter of tradition. The Greek brother had to defend his sister's honor. I kept him pretty busy. When, at the age of twelve, I tried mascara on my eyes, my very virginity was questioned. Spiros returned to the house bruised and bleeding, but victorious. My honor was safe.

I was nearing fourteen when my grandfather took me to the first night of a French melodrama called *L'Epervier*. It was in the theatre of Marika Kotopouli. She was the first lady of the theatre, a supreme artist. That night, I didn't even see Marika because on the stage was Giorgos. The moment he made his entrance, I fell in love. There was a burning in my cheeks. I was sure that the pounding of my heart could be heard all over the theatre. There was no return. I was desperately, definitely in love.

I went back to see the play for the fifteen following nights. And that took some doing. To get out of the house, I lied, I cheated. I invented catastrophes, friends in need, special studies. Nothing was beneath me. I had to get to see Giorgos each night, or expire. The problem of raising money to purchase theatre tickets (first row, mind you) was resolved simply. I begged in the streets. I would rush up to a poor passer-by and tell him that I had lost my purse and a train was leaving. I had to be on that train for a vital family mission. Another would be told that I was starving, another that I was a diabetic and needed immediate insulin. If I was recognized, I took advantage of that. If I was unknown to the passer-by, I assured him that I was of good family and that my mother would reimburse him the following day. The good Athenian people believed me. I was rarely refused. One lady who clearly did not believe me was the most generous. She must have known that at fourteen one was always in love and needed help.

23

Giorgos was tall, strong of feature, mysterious. He had beautiful hands. He had a deep voice. He was thirty-five. In short, he had all that was needed to make a fourteen-year-old virgin tremble. And tremble I did, for fifteen nights in a row. At first it was the actors on stage who took note of my nightly presence. They began to snicker at the sight of me. There were winks and nudges of elbows. One of the actresses in the play who was in love with Giorgos sent poisonous looks across the footlights at this maniac who sat staring and whose lips were now unconsciously mouthing the words of Giorgos' text. Then the ushers and the theatre personnel began to greet me with knowing smiles. It would only be a question of time before the news reached my family. This mattered not to me. Sure enough, the Athens gossip machine began to function, and that machine, from the days of Socrates on, has been well oiled.

Here was food for scandal. Melina, fourteen, virgin, granddaughter of Mayor Spiros, in the clutches of Giorgos, the most notorious heartbreaker in Greece. Most women in Athens were in love with him, many in secret, some admittedly. I had a dear friend whose name was Maria. She warned me of the gathering storm. She herself had heard of someone planning an anonymous letter to my grandfather. Maria's warning had no effect. There was no force on earth that could make me renounce my love.

And then it happened. I met him. And Maria was there. We were looking into a bookshop window. I felt someone watching us. I turned around. It was he. Giorgos in the flesh, and so handsome I came near swooning. I rushed for shelter into the bookshop. Maria followed. When we came out, he was still there, smiling at us. I left Maria to walk quickly away. And then, oh God, he spoke to me, his manner most proper and polite.

"I see you like the theatre."

I nodded spastically, somehow remembering to keep my

lips tightly pressed so that he would not see the ugly brace I wore to correct protruding teeth.

"Would you like me to teach you things about the theatre?"

More spastic nodding.

"Shall we meet tomorrow at the Zappeion Gardens?"

"Yes," I screamed silently, and fled to the dentist. "I can't stand the pain. Please remove this brace at once."

And the next day, with quickened heart and teeth free, I came to the rendezvous in the public gardens. He did not. I waited for hours. It began to rain. I began to cry. It rained harder. I cried harder. To no avail. He did not come to the rendezvous.

I did not yield to depression. I was going to win this man, come fire or flood. I made countless telephone calls, sent endless letters. I sent him flowers he did not know what to do with. I sent him little cream cakes which nauseated him. I made his life a hell. No human could long resist such pressures. He yielded. Rendezvous. The same park. The same bench. This time he was there before I was. At the first opportunity I told him I was past sixteen. I thought he believed it. We went by taxi to a little café at the foot of the Acropolis. I made easy talk about cigarettes and whisky, but Giorgos—*quelle humiliation!*—ordered an ouzo for himself and an ice cream cone for me. But when he took me home in the taxi, he kissed me. He kissed me! Like a sprinter released by a gun, I raced to Maria's house.

"He kissed me."

Then for days I couldn't get to see him. Impassioned notes, hysterical phone calls. No good. But there was no stopping me. I went to his house. I knocked at his door. It was opened by his mistress!

"Who are you?" Very hostile.

I gave a false name. I said I had a letter for Giorgos.

"You can leave it with me."

I said I was asked to give it to him personally.

25

"Open your mouth. Let me see your teeth."

The game was up. My teeth braces now back in place, were enough to betray me. For a moment, nothing. Then I snarled. I bared my teeth in defiance. I rushed down the stairs. She rushed to telephone my mother.

When I arrived home the clan was already there, grimly united. There was Grandfather. My mother and her new husband, Leonidas. Even my father, back from exile and remarried, was summoned. The one who struck me was my Uncle George. That was not the worst. They said I would be taken to a doctor to be examined. For the first time in my life I saw my grandfather crushed and weak. He came close to fainting. My father told me that the man who took my virginity was a notorious blackguard. Sobbing, I went to my grandfather. I swore it was all false, that Giorgos never touched me, that I was what was called intact. But he didn't believe me!

Much has happened to me since, but never a more profound pain than the loss of his confidence. I could think of no other way out but suicide. I gaily flung myself under an oncoming automobile. The driver's brakes were good. I found little satisfaction in some multi-colored bruises. Thus, at fourteen, I knew my first love and wanted to die. There were other loves to come, but I never again proposed to die for a man. I have a rather violent desire to live. That is why I could never forgive my grandfather for dying.

It happened a few months after the gathering of the clan to denounce me as a lost woman. I went mad with grief. For two weeks I laughed hysterically. No amount of injections could still that laughter. I destroyed every photograph of my grandfather I could find. He betrayed me. He made me feel that he was immortal and then he died. Nothing in his character or being ever seemed vulnerable to dying. There are people like that. They are so much of life, their deaths cannot be accepted.

I sought out Giorgos for consolation. He was patient, he

was kind. He taught me how to really read a play. He read the French poets to me—Verlaine, Rimbaud, Apollinaire. He did all he could to help. I appreciated it. I loved him, but something was broken. There was too much tragedy. And besides, poor Giorgos didn't quite know what to do with me. My age was a problem to him. There would be long periods when I didn't see him. At first I thought he was relieved. Then, when I stayed away too long, he decided he wanted me around. He proposed that I become his mistress. I was now fifteen. I refused, not really understanding why.

Summer came again. I went with my family to Spetsai. One day, a beautiful yacht arrived, and on the yacht was Pan Characopos.

Chapter Four

Pan was an attractive man, and the fact that he was a subject for scandal made him fascinating. His family was one of the oldest in Greece. He was what is laughingly called well bred. But he married a Romanian dancer who performed in nightclubs and thus struck a blow at the "best families" of Athens. By refusing to go out with the girls in high society, he offered a permanent passive resistance to bourgeois standards. Actually, he was a great, friendly, yet suspicious cat whose only ambition was to purr in the sun and to be left in peace, but I saw him as a revolutionary.

If this suggests the measure of my political judgment, it is simply that I gave no thought to politics except when a member of my family ran for election. If anything, I was conservative and to the right. Yet, somewhere, there was the gnawing notion that I was more to the right than I should be. I only felt this because of my brother Spiros, to whom I was now completely devoted. He was nearly twelve years old and had political notions more advanced than mine. I knew definitely that I did not trust the Communists without definitely knowing why. The fact that they were the bitterest enemies to the

Metaxas dictatorship, that thousands were jailed in their struggle against him, impressed me, but at the same time made me afraid of them. Perhaps the only clear understanding I had of anything was that Greece suffered because so many of our young men were leaving the country. Each year, thousands of them, unable to make a living in Greece, went abroad to find work. I knew then, as I know now, what a great loss this was to us.

Pan liked me at once and of course I knew it. He treated me like a woman and I led him on with wicked determination. A group of us were invited aboard his yacht. We went to swim at the myriad golden beaches that are the jewels of Spetsai. We danced. His wife preferred to play cards. She took no notice of the way I looked at Pan or the way Pan looked at me. Either she considered me a child or her passion for cards superseded all else.

Pan had studied at Cambridge. Because of it, or despite it, he had very good manners. He let me talk on and on of the theatre and was sympathetic to my ambitions. He stayed at Spetsai only a week. Then he sailed away to another island.

For the first time, a summer in Spetsai was long and irritating. I wanted to get back to Athens and take the theatre by assault. But Athens was inhabited by the ghost of Big Spiros. I could not accept that I, or even Athens should exist and not he. I was unable to recover from his death. Then one day, I understood that I must not try to recover, that I must go on thinking of him and go on loving him. I'm too much of a coward to take a clear stand on religion. I can get as far as, maybe yes, maybe no. But no one can tell me that my grandfather has stopped thinking of me or has stopped loving me.

The theatre: I read and I studied. A good deal of my study was given to producing tears. I developed this art with extraordinary facility. I rehearsed in front of a looking glass. I would make up a little scene. For instance, I, playing myself, asking my mother to buy me a gramophone, and also playing the role of my mother, refusing the request. I asked the mirror for the gramophone. Then playing my mother, I said no. At this point, I made my eyes glisten with tears but did not permit them to fall. Still the answer was no. Time to shed the tears. Tilt the head a bit. Let one, only one tear slide down the cheekbone. Hold it there. Wait. Now let it roll down, slowly, rhythmically. Great!

I employed this tactic of manufacturing tears to persuade my mother and Leonidas to let me become an actress. Not a chance. The false tears became true but they were unmoved and immovable. No theatre. No acting. My mother wanted me safely married. A life of solid values and the production of grandchildren for her to idolize.

Then a stroke of luck. Just at the time the Dramatic School of the National Theatre was auditioning, mother and Leonidas left Athens for a visit to Mytilene. I had made a friend with the unlikely name of Dimitris Horn. (Today, he's one of the pillars of the Greek theatre.) Takis, as everyone called him, was so highly regarded, even as a student, he was able to help me get an audition.

A huge room. A huge table. Behind the table, a row of examiners. Faceless. Just forms. I entered the room. The table seemed so far away I had the impression I was looking through the inverse side of a telescope. Silence. I knew that I had to do more than stand there. I knew I had to move forward. A long march. It was only when I reached the table that I could focus on the face from which came a friendly voice, suggesting, "Move back a bit, my dear." That was no ordinary face. That was no ordinary voice. It was that of Emile Veakis. To say Laurence Olivier to an Englishman, to say Raimu to a Frenchman is to say Emile Veakis to a Greek. The Great Veakis spoke to me. The Great Veakis told me to stand back a bit.

> "You are gone my Aris and all is lost with you.
> The gifts and furniture abandoned too."

That was my voice. It came from somewhere to speak a mournful poem by Kariotakis which Giorgos had taught me. All things come to an end. Even my poem.

Silence.

"I can say two other poems."

"That won't be necessary." It was Veakis.

"You may go. You will hear from us."

The long silent march out of the room, backward at first. In mid-course, I felt something like anger. I bowed to the long table and then made for the exit, head high. That's right, Melina. Maybe your poem was lousy but walk out elegantly. You know how to walk.

Three long days, three sleepless nights before the verdict came. I had passed! But the victory was dampened by doubt. I had been admitted to National Theatre Dramatic School, but how to resolve the problem of family opposition?

It was resolved by Pan Characopos.

He telephoned. A date. Another and another. Then with disconcerting ease, he arranged a divorce from his Romanian dancer. The Athens rumor machine had it that a great sum of money was a persuasive factor.

Another date.

"Forget the National Theatre. The real theatre is in France. Dullin, Renoir, Popesco, Jouvet, Pitoeff. Marry me. I'll take you to Paris."

And calmly spoken. Very English. Not a sign of emotion. It was so un-Greek, it was disarming. *Chez nous,* love, marriages were noisy, bustling, passionate affairs. Not with Pan. And there was no talk of setting up house. No talk of domesticity or raising a proper family. Talk of freedom. To do as I like. Talk of becoming a great actress. In a society where marriage implied a certain bondage, this was a marriage that offered liberation. Free. No one to keep me from the theatre, and away with the fierce guardians of Melina's chastity. Free. And a handsome man. A rich man. A man I liked.

31

We eloped. My family received a telegram "Marriage cele-brated." It was a lie. Unmarried we made our way to Nafplion. Off Nafplion, in the middle of the bay, is the tiny island of Bourzi, not much more than a naked rock. The only hotel was once an old Turkish prison. I sacrificed my virtue in one of the cells where prisoners used to wait for execution. At Pan's request, I wore a black lace nightgown. No bridal white for him. Did this in one way shock me? Not for a moment. I loved it.

We were married a week later in a small church in Kalamata, in the Peloponnese. The only witnesses were the daughters of the village priest. Pan was unshaven. The air was chill. I wore an old school coat which I'd so grown out of, the sleeves reached only halfway down my arms. Later it became a joke among my friends that I was married in my christening clothes. I permitted them this banter because I had a secret, my fan-tastic black nightgown. We came back to Athens and into a suite at the best hotel, the Grande Bretagne. I was married. I was free. I was sixteen.

Shortly after, we moved to "Pan's house." It was a large luxury apartment on Academias Street, near Constitution Square, with deep sun terraces from which you could see the mountains, the Acropolis, and the sea. "Pan's house," I always called it that. I lived there for many years but never felt it was mine.

When I married Pan, I posed one condition. Eleni must come and live with us. Eleni worked in my mother's house. Cook, nurse, housekeeper, confidante, she's one of the major loves of my life. Pan accepted with some reluctance, but it worked out well. Pan had a butler whose name was Michael. He was a good butler but he tippled a bit and had a way of wandering off. Michael fell in love with Eleni. He tippled less and wandered less. They eventually married but stayed on with us. Then, there was Anna. She came directly from the island of Tinos to work for us. She had never seen Athens before. Since then, Eleni, Anna, and I have been inseparable. Afterward, my life and work were to take me to many different countries. Anna always came with me. She learned four languages. She learned how to make me up for theatre and movies. She dresses with exquisite taste. She cooks for us at home and dines with us at Maxim's with equal grace.

In Greece it was embarrassing to use the word "servant". They were "the girls", daughters of the house, part of the family. Of course this made it easier to exploit them and in many instances to pay them slave wages. Yet it is true that in many homes they were received with affection and consideration. If any Europeanized matrons insisted that their girls wore little white caps and lacy aprons, they were immediately labeled "nouveau riche" and became the butt of Athens jokes. My mother used to buy the girls pretty dresses, weep at their misfortunes, and give them dowries when they married. And in big Spiros' house, the society was classless. No one would dare make it otherwise. And so it is with me. In my classless community, we do the jobs we're good at. I am a better actress. Anna and Eleni are better cooks. I trust them totally. No accounts are ever checked. And thank God that in this imperfect world they can count on my love and I have theirs.

Poor unsuspecting Pan didn't know at the time that with Eleni and Anna, I was only establishing a beachhead. The invasion soon followed. Next came Maria. Wisely distrusting my ability to run a house, she took over. And thank God she did. To this day I can't write a check. Then into the house came Spiros and with him hosts of friends.

If this outrageous invasion ever disturbed Pan, he showed it only in one way. He grumbled about the amount of money we were spending for food. He was enormously wealthy. He was one of the biggest landowners in the country. He had large shareholdings. My mother called him the Bank of England. And he complained, not about the annihilation of his privacy, but the food bills. That was my first understanding that I had married a miser. Pan was an out-and-out miser! But I never resented it. I even loved him more for it. I knew that he gave his first wife a fortune so that he could marry me. Now, seeing him wince with pain every time he parted with money made me appreciate the extent of his love for me.

With cruel insensitivity to his need for calm and privacy I turned Pan's house into a noisy kibbutz. There was coming and going, laughter, singing, dancing. I played bits of plays for my friends to loud applause or violent discussions. Everyone would speak at the same time. There is a talent that is uniquely Greek: Greeks can talk and listen at the same time. They can out-shout you and still hear every word you're saying. But Pan was by choice an Englishman. Quietly, every afternoon, Pan began to disappear between the hours of five and eight. I became worried and jealous. I confronted him. Where was he going every day between five and eight? He tried to make me believe that he went to the park or a café to read his newspaper. That it was impossible to read in the apartment and that from time to time he needed to catch up with world events. Of course, I didn't believe him and I put Maria on his traces like a detective. I wanted to know with whom he was being unfaithful to me. I already saw myself as the youngest divorcee in Athens. Maria returned with her report. She had followed him.

"Tell me at once."

"Pan went to the Zappeion Gardens to read his newspaper."

I was suddenly remorseful. The poor man. My kibbutz drove him to the public park to have a little peace. My remorse lasted only ten minutes and then I decided that this was all exceedingly English of him, and God damn it, he was Greek!

Not once did Pan speak a harsh word to me, ever. We became truly good friends. And that was fortunate because a few months after I came into his house our married relationship came to an end. By normal standards we should have separated. But neither of us wanted to. In a curious way the collapse of our marriage brought us closer together. Knowing Pan was to understand that he was a most conservative gentleman. In politics he was downright reactionary. He could find kind words to say for the dictatorship of Metaxas. Yet, at the same time, he gave not a hoot for public opinion. Maybe he was too rich to care. In any event, he accorded me perfect freedom. Never did he ask for an account, nor did he feel obliged to make any accounts to me. Pan was too English, too private for explanations. And that was good. Too much candor, after the Greek fashion, leaves scars. So, married but unmarried, we went on living together. He advised me, protected me, and gave me security.

Chapter Five

What has the month of April got against Greece? In April
of 1967, a band of gangster-colonels came like wolves in the
night to leap at our throats. In April 1941, the Nazi tanks
crashed through the Greek mountain passes and Stukas
bombed the port of Piraeus to bits. It marked the end of a
half-year's resistance to the Fascist army. On the mainland the
Greek army despite the lack of arms, transport or proper
clothes for mountain fighting drove the Italians out of Greece
and clear into Albania. It was the first Fascist defeat. Later
on, Cretan heroism against the Nazis was to inspire world
admiration. The Führer in what he considered praise for the
Greek soldier spoke of his "contempt for death." This is typical of dictator thinking. They equate love of liberty with contempt for death. Greeks know more about living than anybody.
They hate dying but they hate chains too. The Germans oc-
cupied Greece for three and a half years, and for three and a
half years they were harassed day and night by our resistance
forces. Mr. Papadopoulos remembers this well. That is why
his secret police has dug up the dossiers of every member of
the resistance groups against the Nazis. He knows who to be
afraid of and he's right to be afraid of them.

It is not in the province of this memoir to deal with events military or clashing armies. I don't know enough about that, but I know what many Greek people were like during the war and the occupation. I can tell about them. I can tell about me, even if it makes me shudder.

There were Greeks who collaborated. They were few, very few. There were Greeks who resisted. They were many. There were those who were corrupted by fear and the presence of death. There were those who decided to live each day to the fullest and to hell with anything else, including ideals and hopes for liberation. I was among them. I had no excuses; I knew what I was doing. I had too many examples close to me, not to know. My father had volunteered for front-line duty. He was made a captain of the cavalry and fought bravely. My brother Spiros, barely in his teens, joined a resistance organization called Epon. They believed that in the end we would win. I did not. I said there was no hope. Little Spiros, furious, threatened to go to the police and tell them that I was a defeatist. There are images that never leave you, that come back to you, years and years after the event.

An image: Athens deserted and shuttered. Not a soul in the streets and an endless file of Nazi tanks crashing over the pavement.

An image: The swastika rising slowly over the Acropolis.

An image: Late at night, a group of dark figures braving the curfew, running silently. They are led by a young boy. Quickly the group disappears into various houses. They were Greek Jews being hidden from the Nazis. Now only the boy in the dark street. For a moment he stands still, looking at the doors that quickly close. Then he turns and runs swiftly down the street.

37

Ellie: Today, a fine writer and a dear friend. Then, a school-girl. With friends she created a puppet theatre to play for children of poor families. The first performance, a fairy tale. A lovely princess saved from a witch by a young nobleman and the happy ending. Ellie, astonished when the children hooted the play out of the classroom. Ellie's collaborators weeping, unable to understand such a protest from small children. Ellie understood. She explained that these children, touched by the war, most of them hungry, could not be offered fairy tales. The next play was about two hungry boys who stole to eat. It was a huge success. Gradually, anti-German slogans got into the script. Ellie had developed the first underground theatre. For children! It wasn't long before the Germans got wind of the theatre. Orders were given to find Ellie. They didn't find her. The theatre, portable, mobile, went on performing.

One day, Ellie saw a young man shot down by German soldiers because he distributed clandestine newspapers. She returned to her home in a turmoil. To stop her hands from shaking she began to iron a dress. Her father arrived. He worked at a bank. The other workers were talking about creating a strike at the bank. He was nervously weighing the dilemma. The police would deal with him if he joined the strike. The partisans would deal with him if he did not. To relieve his tension he shouted at his daughter who, at such a moment, was so frivolous as to iron a dress.

"Don't you know there is an occupation?"

Ellie did know. Ellie's father did not know that a resistance group met at his house when he was away at work. He did not know that clandestine newspapers were hidden between the double springs of his bed, that each night he slept on dynamite.

Ellie's group, still of school age, were the messengers of the resistance. Messages and illegal propaganda were transported in their schoolbags. At night, they painted slogans on the

walls. "Down with the Nazis," "Resist," "S.S. shit." These slogans were written in green paint. One night a young man was
seen; he was shot at. In his haste to get away he upset the paint
over his shoes. They were his only pair. Covered in green paint,
they were too dangerous to wear. Ellie found a simple solution. She stole money from her father to buy him another pair.
Ellie talked to me and a friend. She said that in her mind,
anyone not working for the liberation of Greece was a traitor.
My friend said, "Melina is only seventeen." Ellie said, "I am
sixteen and I am one of the oldest of my group." After Ellie
left, my friend saw I was troubled. "Stop being silly," she said
to me. "Don't you know Ellie is a Communist?" I didn't know
that but I took refuge in the charge.

Anestis: Today, one of the most passionate opponents of
the colonels, a man with a price on his head and a dear friend.

Anestis was a *nom de guerre*. At the age of fifteen, an active
member of the resistance movement in Crete. He was caught
in a village and sentenced to be shot by a firing squad. His
mother and father were brought at gunpoint to witness the
execution. Anestis was marched to the wall, and the firing
squad took up position. Then something extraordinary happened. In that village lived a German woman, married to the
local doctor. She was distrusted by all. When the squad raised
their rifles, she appeared and rushed toward them. She wept,
she cursed them and then shamed them. She called them heroes of the master race waging war against boys. They spared
Anestis.

But they regretted it. He became a thorn in their flesh. He
knew no fear. From the British Secret Service, he got posters
and cartoons that attacked or insulted the Germans. Anestis
stuck them up on the German barracks, on the German tanks.
He organized a hold-up on a black market food shop and distributed the food to the hungry. He attacked German patrols,
stole their arms and got them to the partisans. The Germans
hunted him all through the war. When he was nineteen they

caught him again. Again he was sentenced to death and again
he was saved, this time by a group of partisans who broke into
his jail to rescue him. At the end of the war, he had become
one of the leaders of the resistance.

While I was working on this book, Anestis came to visit
me. My husband's daughter, Richelle, had just translated from
the Greek a marvelous poem by Ritsos. Iannis Ritsos is the
purest voice in Greece. He is a great poet. He was once listed
as a national treasure. The colonels fear such voices. Since
April 1967, Ritsos has been their prisoner. Richelle read to us.
She is American, and we were all touched by her sensitivity
to the nuances of Ritsos' very special language. When she finished reading, Anestis' eyes were moist with tears. This
clashed with my image of him as a steeled resistance fighter.
I asked him if he wept often. He thought for a while and then
said:

"Rarely."

Nobody talked. Anestis said:

"I'll tell you a story. In 1944, the Germans decided that they
preferred me dead. I was in jail awaiting execution. In the
next cell were two girls. I knew them. They were dressmakers,
both very young. They were not members of any resistance
group but worked with them. They were condemned to death
for hiding and caring for English soldiers. They were tortured
to reveal the names of people in the resistance. They did not
speak. They were condemned to be shot. They never de-
spaired. All day long, they would call out encouragements to
the other prisoners or sing Cretan songs. It was five days before their execution that a new German guard was assigned to
the prison. He treated the prisoners kindly. And then we
heard that, each day, up until the day of their execution, they
made love with the young German. A group of prisoners talked
about those girls. Some condemned them. They turned to me
and asked for my opinion. I burst into tears."

Mitsos: Today, a prisoner in the island of Aegina. He's an

automobile mechanic. I met him when he repaired an automobile that was used in a film I made in Greece. When he can, he writes to me.

Mitsos, during the occupation, received a tough assignment. The execution of a traitor. A Greek who worked for the German Security Services. He was responsible for the deaths of a number of resistance fighters. Mitsos accepted the assignment. He executed it in grim, if spectacular style. One afternoon, the traitor was walking down a main street. No one came near him, fearful of unseen soldiers who might be posted in windows of surrounding buildings. Then Mitsos appeared on a bicycle. He carried an ax sharpened to a razor edge. He cycled quickly toward the traitor and just as he passed him, he neatly sliced off the man's head. No one moved. No one made a sound. But Mitsos had dropped his cap. Calmly he turned his bike, went back to pick up his cap, wheeled again and sped away.

Manolis Glezos. In 1964, a deputy in Parliament. A friend of my father's. A friend of mine.

On the night of 30 May 1940, Manolis Glezos, a nineteen-year-old student and his student friend Apostolos Santas stood at the foot of the Acropolis. High overhead, mounted on a giant steel mast, the hated swastika flag streamed in a strong wind. German sentries were black against a moonlit sky. The two young men, armed with an electric torch, crept through the little pine wood on the north face of the hill. On the steep rocks that overhang the hill, they paused, waiting for the sentinels to pass. Then they dropped into the sacred area. They raced to the mast to pull the flag down. To no avail. The wind had snarled the ropes into tangles. The flag wouldn't move. First Glezos, than Santas climbed the mast to free the ropes. They pulled at the snarled ropes with their teeth and their nails. They saw the sentinels returning. Frantically, they pulled up the anchors which kept the mast steady and swayed the pole backward and forward until the ropes were freed.

The huge flag buried them as they fell to the ground. They gathered the swastika into folds and fled with it into the night. The next morning, the sky of Athens was beautifully free. The tearing down of the swastika has since been celebrated in poem and in song. At this writing Manolis Glezos is ill, held in the prison of the Island of Leros, by the colonels.

These were a few people I knew. There were many more. Some developed the first underground newspaper. Others joined the partisan fighters in the mountains, and some worked for the Germans. One of them was my Uncle George. Like a number of Greek royalists, he was a fervent Germanophile. He collaborated with John Rallis who was made Prime Minister in 1943. John Rallis was the man who organized "Security Groups." They were armed by the Germans and used those arms against the resistance forces. Rallis appointed Uncle George governor of the Bank of Greece. My brother Spiros, who was in Epon, my father, in a smaller resistance group called The Radical Organization, never spoke to him again. When George died of a heart attack, before the end of the war, they refused to attend his funeral.

The occupation was a scourge. Crops and cattle were confiscated by the occupation armies. There was famine. Water was scarce. It became a common sight to see people fall dead in the streets of starvation. Corpses were heaped in lorries and dumped in common graves. Deportation and firing squads took thousands upon thousands. And yet, from the first moment, spontaneous acts of heroism announced the will of the people to resist.

It took only five months for trade union groups, the Socialist Party, the Communist Party, the People's Democratic Party, to unite and create the National Liberation Front (EAM) and an arm of military resistance called the Greek People's Army of Liberation (ELAS). The EAM represented the large majority of the Greek people. Its power was made clear the following year, when in the teeth of the armed occupation, they organized massive demonstrations and strikes. They compelled the puppet government to declare to the Germans that there would be no forced labor battalions in Greece. The guerrilla forces became so strong as to tie down three German divisions and four Italian divisions. In 1942, their operation against the viaduct of Gorgopotamos was, according to Churchill himself, a distant prelude to the battle of El Alamein because the partisans cut the supply route from Greece to Rommel's troops.

All over Greece, people risked their lives in the struggle against the occupation. I risked mine too, but it was a private war. To eat, to feed my friends, to squeeze every ounce of pleasure out of life, to live it to the hilt while it lasted. Perhaps things would have been different had I not met Alexis.

Chapter Six

When an entire country is subjugated by a dictatorship, be it by its own military machine or by foreign troops, there is one constant. You live in humiliation. Your freedom is taken from you and you are degraded. But the greatest humiliation comes from your own fear. The very fact that you are afraid to take up a gun and shoot down your own oppressor makes you ashamed. Or, if you have the will and the courage to do so, you don't have the gun. It's the dictators who always have the guns. Your helplessness is humiliating. A Nazi soldier is billeted in your house. Something thick and twisted in him impels him to piss on your dining-room floor and to grin at you while doing so. You are silent and that silence diminishes you, kills you.

Some people, then many, found redemption in resistance. Others accepted passively, and became non-men. Others yielded to cynicism.

Alexis:

He hated the Germans because they were strong. He despised the Greeks because they were weak. He resolved the question of his own manhood by exploiting them both. Greeks who had ideals were to be ridiculed. Germans who had the guns and the tanks were to be outwitted. To outwit them meant to make money from them. To silence any possible voice of conscience meant to throw the money away. He recognized that in the end he could not win. He was twenty-six and said that before the war's end he would be killed. Life then had to be fun. Fun was risk. Risk was his own special kind of black market. Whatever the Germans wanted to buy he would find for them. But the game was really worthwhile if the goods he sold them were defective. The supreme satisfaction was to find and sell a great quantity of goods at exorbitant prices, then steal it all back and sell it all over again. The truth is the Greek collaborators were few. Some made huge fortunes. The money was sent abroad for safety. But Alexis, while earning enormous sums, never had a penny.

A nightclub full of people would see champagne brought to their tables. Champagne in wartime Greece! They would look up in amazement to the headwaiter. The headwaiter pointed to a corner table. At the table was Alexis who would bow and call out, "Drink while you can."

He always carried a loaded gun, ready to use it on Germans or on himself. This was the man who fell in love with me, and, God help me, I found him irresistible.

Pan's house now sheltered a host of my actor friends. Mattresses were everywhere. When food became impossible to find, Alexis' henchmen would appear carrying large stocks. During the entire occupation, when Greece was starving, I rarely went hungry. One evening, I found my bed covered with jewels. They were the jewels of a family called Davidov, refugees from bolshevik Russia. Alexis had bought them to impress me. Impressed I was, even though he took them back at once. He used them to buy some kind of machines which he sold to the Germans. It brought him a huge sum of money which he quickly lost at gambling tables. This troubled him little. He was too busy working on the next scheme.

And Pan? Pan withdrew from everything. He hated the Germans, but to him the resistance was Communist, and Communists had horns and tails. The Germans took his yacht and his car. German officers were billeted in his house. One of them was the brute who urinated all over the place to prove that he was a superior being. Another was the cliché seen in all the movies. He adored Mozart and knew well the history of ancient Greece. He would interrupt his instructions to a reprisal squad to speak about the perfect design of the Parthenon.

All of this broke Pan's spirit. There were really no problems about money. If time came when food was scarce it was because there was no food to buy. At such times, Pan caused provisions to be brought down from his estates in the North. He was the aristocrat who could not bear to see barbarians who were stronger than he was. He shut himself up in a back room of the house and played patience with a worn deck of cards. His fine house fell into decay and shabbiness but he spent most of the war and the occupation playing solitaire.

I asked nothing of him. He asked nothing of me. I had my friends, I lived dangerous, exhilarating hours with Alexis and that was fine with me. I knew it was ridiculous to defy the curfew. Too many people were shot that way. Yet I did so very often just for the hell of it. I knew that some days Nazi squads roamed the streets to pick up hostages. I would choose such days to walk to a friend's house just to show Alexis that my taste for risk was as strong as his. I was a parasitical, useless human being, and when I risked my life, I risked it for something as futile as a game of cards or an amusing evening. And Alexis approved. He thought that was the way to live. He approved when I stole money from him to give to my brother Spiros for the resistance. Not because he believed in the resistance but because I had the courage to steal from him.

My shield against the war was my ambition to be an actress, and the National Theatre School. There were no Germans in the school. There were only Greeks. From two to six each afternoon, there was no occupation, no fear, there was no Melina. There was Marguerite of *Faust*, there was Ophelia, there was La Locandriera, there was Electra. Dramatic school was heaven because you studied such a variety of parts and you felt you were in the best school in the world because your teacher was Rondiris.

My first year in the school was exciting. My teacher, Takis Mouzenides, gave me *belle femme* parts to play, and then and there I decided that boulevard comedy was the only interesting form of theatre that existed. I detested classical tragedy, the past, all things theoretical, and boring techniques like voice production. I was doing well, was much admired and enjoyed myself enormously. In my second year school became a passion because of Dimitris Rondiris. He was a genius. He was and is the supreme director of Greek tragedy. His staging of the Orestes trilogy in the Herod Atticus Amphitheatre is the single major theatre experience of my life. To be a pupil of his was conversion to a new religion. His students became his slaves. He demanded total commitment to the theatre and to himself. He was a genius but an egomaniac too. It was disloyal to see a play in another theatre. To talk of the cinema was absolute betrayal.

And he was a giant actor. In the heat of discussion of a role, he would suddenly begin to play the part. He was forty at the time, but with a turn of his body and a dimness he could give to his eyes, he would become old Lear, the next moment Horatio, and the next Ophelia. I've seen Ophelias in my time, but none came close to his, neither in madness nor in femininity.

Examinations were held on Mondays on the stage of the National Theatre. Rondiris would sit in the front seats, the rest of the class toward the back of the theatre. One Monday, an extraordinary thing happened. On the stage a young student was struggling with the part of Shylock. We, in the back, would watch, but with one eye on the shoulders of Rondiris and the back of his head. We could tell exactly what he was thinking. We saw that head begin to sway, the shoulders to hunch. His body tensed into a spring and suddenly he rose with a terrible cry. He was Shylock confronting his judges. He paced up and down between the seats, an animal caged, trapped, twisting, turning, looking for a way out. He did not play rage. He *was* rage. He was grief. He was the marrow of Shylock caught in the trap of injustice. We held our breath to watch him. The tears ran down our faces. At the end, our applause came in shouts and in sobs.

I wish the public could have seen him as an actor, but they knew him only as a great director. And not only in Greece. He had studied with Max Rheinhardt, the Austrian director whose exciting productions brought the world to his theatre before Hitler drove him away. When the Nazis came, Rheinhardt went to live and work in America. Rondiris returned to Greece. Just a few years later, he saw the Nazis again—this time in Athens. He shut himself up in his theatre. He drove himself in his work, so intensely that sometimes he managed to forget their existence.

Rheinhardt was tyrannical in his demands that an actor should have perfect control of voice and body. Rondiris brought this tyranny back to Greece. My first problem with Rondiris was on the question of voice control. I had always been impressed by Giorgos' voice on stage. It was deep. He kept it in the lower registers. What was good enough for Giorgos was good enough for me. Besides, Shakespeare himself wrote in admiration of low-voiced women. Rondiris was not impressed. He wanted my voice more flexible, the range expanded. And so those god damn breathing exercises. There I was, bursting with talent, dying to act, and all I kept hearing was abdomen-thorax-and one, two, three. Then the business of laughter. To me, sick with laughter is not just a metaphor. Rondiris had me laughing until I ached. For months a role from a Molière comedy—*la gamme du rire*. I once infuriated him by suggesting that voice and breathing lessons were deadly dull. He threw me out of the class.

When I was readmitted, another conflict. Rondiris had contempt for the boulevard theatre and my ambitions to shine in it. He insisted that I was meant for Greek tragedy, and put me to work on Electra. I admitted that Electra was the supreme tragic female role, but begged him to recognize that I wasn't Electra.

Then Rondiris talked to me. He talked about the glory of Greek tragedy, its poetry, its tradition, its deep meaning for the Greek people. All the time he was speaking, he became more passionate, more exalted. He converted me. I saw the light. From that moment he numbered me among his slaves. I admired him without reservation, without question. He was the Bible. To be taught by him was a religious experience.

So away with the boulevard, welcome the tragic muse. One day I was Medea, another, Antigone, and then on to Goethe. Private lessons at Pan's house. For months and months I knelt to declaim Marguerite's monologue in *Faust:* "My mother, the whore . . ."

Marguerite wore a hole in Pan's carpet.

When classes finished for the day in the drama school, the students often came home with me. We would talk late into the night. Then they stayed on. There was no point in risking the curfew, and there were mattresses spread all over the house. This was cheating a bit on the arrangement I had with Pan. It had been agreed that since I was studying acting, I should live like other students until I could earn money of my own. I still wore the coat I had grown out of, and my shoes were soled with wood as were most people's in those times of shortage. It was not part of the bargain that my fellow students should come to camp, and sometimes to be fed.

But even the dramatic school ceased to be the perfect refuge. It happened three times that the Gestapo suddenly erupted into the classroom and marched off a student whom we never suspected of being involved in resistance activities. There was a lovely girl, Aleka. She and I had been nicknamed "the two talents." Only after the war did we learn that she was an important member of the resistance.

There were times when I took a good look at myself. I didn't like what I saw. And the excitement, the school, the senseless flirting with danger, the company of Alexis, would stand exposed in its futility and nothingness. There were periods of deep depression. A few times I talked to Alexis about it. The answer would always be the same. "You're seventeen. Live."

But by the time the war ended, I was no longer seventeen. Occasional fits of depression were not treated compassionately by Alexis. Instead, he would burst into rages. "Go to the mountains. Join the maquis. After the war they'll be sold out, every one of them. I know Greece. You don't. After the war this country will turn into shit. I won't live to see it. You will. Wait and see."

After the German debacle in Stalingrad, we all knew that Hitler had lost. The Germans knew it too. They became uglier than ever. One afternoon, I went to join Alexis and two actor friends at a bar. It was not the best time to walk in the streets of Athens but that made for the excitement of the game. We sat at a small table talking. Alexis was drinking too much. And into the bar came three S.S. men with an Alsatian dog. Alexis started to tease the animal, taunting it in German. An S.S. man at the bar called out: "Since you speak German so well, come here and join us."

We ignored them. He called us again, louder, obscenely. He drew a revolver and with it waved us to the bar. We didn't move. Then another one of them drew his revolver and made the same gesture. First our two friends went to the bar. Then Alexis.

"You too," they called to me, "come drink with us."

I sat still. The gun was pointed at me.

"I will count three and then shoot. Ein . . ."

50

I was terribly frightened, but nothing would make me move.
"Zvei . . ."
An unfathomable stubbornness kept me glued to my seat.
"Drei . . ."
The glass at my elbow was shattered by a bullet. I leaped to my feet, blazing with anger.
"Pig! Pig! Pig!"
It just didn't occur to me that he could shoot again. Luckily, some German Military Police that the barman had the wit to summon were close by. They came in and took the S.S. men away.

We had the excitement we were looking for. I should have been pleased. It would make a good story to tell my friends. But that's not how I felt. I turned on Alexis and hit him in the face with all my might. At first, I didn't know why. Alexis was not a coward. He was capable of killing for me. Then I knew that I'd struck him because I was revolted by myself. People much younger than I was were dying so Greece could be free. I almost got myself killed to show off in a bar.

A few years ago, I read the announcement of a film to be made. Its title was *What Did You Do in the War, Daddy?* I never saw the film. I don't even know if it was made. Today, I am joined with those who would free Greece of the colonels. As of this writing, that fight is making slow progress. There are moments of despondency. Many of my friends are in the junta jails. I weep at the callousness of the so-called democratic countries. I weep that American policy is to support the junta. I despair that France competes with the United States to sell them jet planes, that England sells them tanks, that the Soviet Union has increased trade with Greece. But in these despondent moments, the phrase comes back to me: "What did you do in the war, Daddy?" And I find new resolve. During the war, I failed the test. Not now. I will fight the junta until I die.

Chapter Seven

October 12, 1944. Liberation.

There was an explosion of joy. Athens went wild. Forty-three months of shame, oppression, grief, were over. People poured into the streets. They wept, they laughed, they sang, they danced. Every bell of every church tower broke into a glorious chorus of chimes. From Athens to Piraeus, the cry rose, as at Easter, "Christ is risen," Christos Anesti. Greece was resurrected.

At the beginning it was all joy and love. Down from the mountains came the partisans to be wept over and embraced. The prisons were opened. Families were reunited. The Greek flag flew alone once more over the Acropolis. But soon, so soon, came a feeling of vague uneasiness. The partisan army had marched to Athens to join in the rejoicing, but outside the city it stopped. Why? And people began to look at each other with suspicion. Frightening questions were being asked.

"How is it that during the war you never went hungry?"

"You were seen in the company of the police. Why?"

"Where did you get the money?"

"Wasn't it you that I saw in a cabaret in the company of a German soldier?"

"What is this talk of the partisans wanting to take power?"

At first, the English troops that came to Greece, led by General Scobie, were hailed as liberators—now:

"Don't you understand that they're an army of occupation, no better than the Germans?"

Distrust. Suspicion. Calumny.

I was victim to it, and where it hurt most: my acting debut. Giorgos and I had always remained friends. We formed a troupe. We chose the play, *The Path of Freedom,* by a twenty-two-year-old playwright, Alexis Solomos. Of course, it was a play about the war. I played Irene. Irene's father became a traitor. My big scene was one in which I agreed with the resistance fighters that my father should be killed.

My first opening night, Athens, November 1944. And the audience persecuted me. Their hatred came to me in waves over the footlights. I was awkward. I acted badly. But it was palpable that their venom was not directed to the actress but to me personally. I looked too well. I was too well fed. I was the good-time girl during the war. My husband was too rich. I had a lover who was an underworld character. Anna, who was in the audience, heard all these things and more. She came backstage dissolved in tears. The critics slaughtered me too:

Too tall. Too young. Too blonde. Too awkward. No talent. There are deserving young actresses who need to earn a living. Why doesn't Miss Mercouri stay home where she belongs?

And yet the theatre was full every single night. Giorgos said, "I'm the star but they're coming to see you." I said that they were coming just to hate me, that they didn't forgive me for not dying of starvation during the war. And Giorgos understanding my own guilts, tried to help.

"Don't be ashamed of not dying. When you're young the blood runs quick. The sea is too blue. The men are too handsome, the dogs too affectionate."

There were two things that sustained me. One was the determination that the stage was mine and that no one could ever take it away from me. The other was that my hatred of the audience was equal to their hatred of me. These were not the partisans, down from the mountains, who might have had the right to judge me. Most of them were the bourgeoisie who played it safe. They were the same moralists, the same people of easy conscience who I held responsible for the death of my friend Maria. Maria died in the last year of the war.

I have spoken about Maria, my school friend who came to live with me when I married Pan. I loved her dearly. She knew all my secrets, all my hopes, all my anxieties. She was the heart of my house. Through all the good and the bad, she was there, close to me.

Maria had a lover during the war. She became pregnant. So strong was the fear of scandal and reprobation that she told no one. Not even me. Toward the end of her pregnancy she collapsed. An idiot surgeon cut out what he thought was a cancerous growth. She developed an infection. Antibiotics, all medicines were impossible to find then. She died a victim of bourgeois hypocrisy. And now those same hypocrites who had caused her death wanted to kill my spirit and take the theatre from me.

The play had run for a month when circumstances far beyond my poor performance closed the theatre on the third of December 1944 and ended my first painful experience of being a professional actress.

I was just entering the stage door when I felt the earth begin to tremble. Greece had known earthquakes. When I was a child, I had heard that if there was an earthquake, one should stand in a strong doorway. I raced to the Hotel Grande Bretagne, which was near the theatre. It was an earthquake, but man-made! The thunderous sound was made by marching feet. There was an army of people. As far as the eye could see. An ocean of clenched fists held high. And suddenly that great army broke into song. It was a song of the maquis. It was frightening, but infinitely beautiful. A man close to me held both fists high and shouted into my ear, "The voice of the people is the fury of God."

On and on they came. And this multitude had two voices. Those coming toward me singing the maquis song, and from those who had gone ahead, the cry came back: "Let the people rule."

The cry rolled back and back like an enormous wave until the two voices became one: "Let the people rule."

Athens shook with the sound of it. Then a new sound. Sharp. Staccato. The sound of bullets being fired. Later there was equivocation as to who gave the order to shoot into the crowd, but there were many wounded and twenty-eight dead. The nightmare of war and occupation had barely ended, when civil war began.

How to put together the pieces that led to that day?

From the beginning, the British Foreign Office expressed its distaste for the EAM. Too left. Its ELAS army, too strong. But the English are old hands at the power game. In this game, timing is important. The plan is simple. As long as the Nazis are in Greece, the ELAS army is needed, but plan for the day when the Nazis are out. The reds must never attain political power. But go easy. Don't try to do things all at once. The monarchy, even a too conservative government—they're for later. The first stage needs a political figure acceptable to the left, yet someone who, when the time came, could be used against the left.

The man they chose was George Papandreou. In the thirties he was Minister of Education. He earned respect for progressive reforms in the school systems. He was a brilliant orator. He had the popular touch. Best of all, he had a talent for exploiting the left and repudiating them at the same time. He was the ideal man for the job. Here's how the timetable worked.

55

April 1944

Six months before the Germans leave, Papandreou is brought to Egypt, the seat of the government in exile.

May

A meeting in Lebanon. All political opinions of Greece are represented. A coalition government is set up. The Communists will be part of the coalition. They are not promised any key posts, just enough to give them some illusions. So far so good. But the English already have it in their heads to send an expeditionary corps into Greece, just in case the country needs "to be protected from anarchy."

September

A month before the German defeat. The army of ELAS is persuaded not to enter and occupy Athens. They accept that the English march in as liberators. Moreover, with extraordinary naïveté, they agree to place themselves under the command of the English. (To this day the Communists refuse to admit they were duped. They say ELAS was still busy chasing Germans.)

October

The Germans are out, the English are in. A few days later, the government is back in Greece from exile and George Papandreou is Prime Minister. Damn clever, these English.

The commander of the English forces, General Scobie, goes into action. He has barely taken time to say "how do you do" before issuing the order that the partisans surrender their arms. This of course horrifies the EAM. They see that the same request is not made of the royalist army that is dominated by officers whose oppression they had known under the Metaxas dictatorship. The EAM leaders suggest that they'll turn over their guns if the royalist army does the same. "Ah no," says Scobie, "they are the regular army." Scobie is reminded that the EAM represents 70 percent of the Greek people. This impresses him not at all. He wants their guns. The EAM people get the point. Now they realize that they've been had. They resign from the government. Scobie sheds no tears over this. He sets a deadline. All arms are to be yielded up by December 10, or else.

This becomes the subject for passionate debate all over Greece. Kolonaki, the fashionable part of town where I lived is overwhelmingly pro-Scobie. (Kolonaki was then referred to as "Kolograd," which means arse town.) The arguments of Pan and his friends were direct and to the point.

"Yes, they fought against the Nazis, but they are reds and they want to take over. The hell with them."

The more moderate in Kolograd said it this way:

"Those crazy bastards have arms. Yes, they used them against the Germans for four years. In all decency, you can't reproach them for that. But the war is over. If they were reasonable people, they would hand over their guns, say 'thank you' for their use, and go back to their plows and their shovels."

The partisans didn't feel that way. They held on to their arms and to hold Papandreou to his promise of self-rule, they organized the demonstration of December 3 that left twenty-eight dead in the streets.

Less than two months after the Germans left, Greece was again a battleground. It became a country of hatred and horror. Nameless atrocities were committed on both sides. We saw Eleni Papadaki, one of Greece's leading actresses, dragged from her house and assassinated by the Communists because she had been a friend of John Rallis, the wartime quisling

Prime Minister. This act, and others of useless vengeance and cruelty cost the Communists sympathy and followers. But things just as bad, and worse, were done to them. It seemed to me that all Greeks had become savages.

One day a young man knocked at Rena's door. He told her that everyone must leave. The partisans needed to put a barricade across the street. They were going to dynamite the house next door. Result: Rena, her parents, her grandmother, find themselves crowded into a small flat that belongs to a friend. There were fifteen people in a three-room flat. And food? A cup of soup, morning and evening. After a week of this, Rena declares: "I've had it. I'm going to Pan's house."

This was easier said than done. Even though it was only a ten-minute walk to Pan's house, that day it took four hours. Rena walked down one street, machine gun bullets began to fly. She fled to another street. A barricade. Another street, held by the English: "Get out of here." Another street. More bullets. A young boy was killed just a few yards away from her. She ran on. Finally, in a state of panic and exhaustion, she reached the house and fell into my arms. Who is Rena? Stop the war. Hold still on the barricades. I'll tell you who Rena is.

I think the best way to introduce you to Rena is to introduce you to the word *kefi*. Kefi is a word so Greek, a spirit so Greek, that it's almost impossible to translate. It means panache, but more than panache. It means cocky, but more than cocky. Kefi is improvisation. Kefi is taking chances. Kefi is what leads you to the double or nothing. The grand gesture. That is Rena, Rena to the bone. She follows her kefi on the impulse of the moment and if it leads to disaster, "The hell with it; with tomorrow's kefi we'll start again."

I have known Rena Messolora as long as I have known myself. We grew up together. She was a fat, gay child. Suddenly, she's slim. She's sixteen. She's the liveliest spirit in Athens and she's married. His name was Salvago. He was twenty-six, ridiculously rich, and he carted her off to live in Alexandria. When she was gone, everybody realized that there was less laughter in Athens. In Alexandria all goes well until she meets her husband's uncle. Bang. Love at first sight. Scandal! The distracted husband flies back to Athens to consult with Rena's parents. Back to Alexandria. Threats. Virtual imprisonment. To no avail. Rena's heart belongs to Uncle. Another flight to Athens. This time the decision is to get her out of Alexandria. Rena resists. Finally, parental rage, the fear that her brother will come to Egypt to shoot down the uncle lover, makes her yield. All right, she'll go back to Athens. But now the war has come to Greece. Travel is a problem. It is worked out. And it could happen only to Rena. The English were sending a convoy of troops to Greece. Rena was part of that convoy.

No sooner off the convoy, she meets and falls in love with Mikas Pezas, a wild man, a penniless writer. Forgotten are uncle and nephew. She wants Pezas. He is the man in her life. She will defy the world to have him. He will be a Nobel prize novelist. She was born to love and inspire him. The husband turns up. In scorn he points out that Rena still wears the rich jewels that he showered upon her. Rena follows her kefi. In majestic silence she removes jewel after jewel and hands them over. There was a slight hesitation when she handed over a diamond ring, but only because it was a paste imitation. The original had gone to pay gambling debts. Yes, Rena was, is, always will be a gambler. The fact that she rarely wins is secondary. The thrill of gambling is more important than winning or losing. The extraordinary thing was the way she could lose at cards, even when dealt winning hands. In gin rummy, if she could "knock down" with two points on the very first hand, she'd wait until she got gin. When she got gin, she played for big gin. All the while knowing better! Rena is my closest friend, but even today a friction can come between us because of her gambling. Unfortunately, someone once gave her a biography of Dostoievsky. Whoever it was, I hate him. Since then, Rena tells me each time there is a crisis: "Dostoievsky was an incurable gambler. It was in his blood. Do you expect me to be better than Dostoievsky?"

And *she* gets angry at *me*. There was a time that Rena confronted me with her two-year-old son in her arms. "Give me a hundred drachmas to play cards, or I'll jump from this balcony with this innocent child in my arms. I know you don't care about me, but the death of this young boy will be on your conscience."

I said, "Jump." She didn't jump. But she never forgave me.

That's Rena. But no one has a bigger heart; no one is a truer friend. No one is more ready to serve or to love.

And Rena became part of the ever-increasing household. Pan's house was more and more crowded. We didn't have electricity, and could get water only every few days. We had to store it in a bath and measure it out by the cupful, staler and dirtier every day. Nor did we have enough to eat, although occasionally there were windfalls. Since Pan so much admired the British, it was normal to see a lot of them. Even more pro-British than Pan was his brother, who spoke better English than Greek and spent half of every year before the war in London. When General Scobie's troops arrived in Athens he soon made connections with the English officers. Some of us disapproved and felt justified in raiding his larder, which was full of British Army tinned food. We put people two in a bed, we gave them armchairs and sofas to sleep on. Others just slept on the floor. It was icy cold and it smelled bad because of the tallow candles, our only source of light, and because you can't keep a house clean without water.

There could be no other talk than that of the civil war. The atrocities continued and increased. We were horrified that we were capable of such things. Papandreou was called traitor and assassin. Things reached such a point that Churchill felt obliged to suspend all his other war duties and come to Athens himself. He and his advisers realized that Papandreou had to go. They looked for a replacement. Eventually they came up with a World War I hero. His name was General Plastiras. He was a kind of legend. He was nicknamed "the black horseman." Plastiras was to mark time till the English found it propitious to return George II to Greece. Before Churchill left, he had managed to arrange for a cease-fire.

Then in February, at a place called Varkisa, all sides reached agreement. The Communists finally turned over their guns. For a while we hoped for a spirit of conciliation and amnesty. The agreement said that no one would be pursued or punished, except common law criminals. Amnesty, my eye! The ink was not even dry on the agreement when the government began a reign of absolute terror. Taking advantage of the common law criminal clause, they started a wave of arrests, deportations, and executions. People left Athens by the thousands.

The next year civil war erupted again. Poor Greece. It was to last until 1949. In 1947 there was a change. The English announced that they were too tired and too broke to go on protecting Greece. We were handed over to the Americans. The Truman Doctrine was born. "The United States must help Greece safeguard her democratic regime." I have American friends who consider the Truman Doctrine a noble document, motivated by a concern for Greek democratic institutions. This to me is baloney. The American rulers don't give a damn about democracy in Greece; as a matter of fact they're against it. A democratic country is liable to think in terms of independence. It might even question the presence of American military bases and American troops on Greek soil. It might question the priorities given to American investment. How anyone can reconcile American concern for Greek democracy with American support of the present junta is beyond me. Let's call a spade a spade. The Americans fear a progressive or, God save us, a left government in Greece. The simple truth is, that after the war, Moscow and Washington staked out their zones of influence—the Americans claimed the right to protect Greece. They have been protecting us ever since—to the point of suffocation.

I should tell you what happened to Alexis, my wartime black-market friend. He was right. He did not live long after the war. The bullet he fired into his brain he had long prepared.

Chapter Eight

At that time, whoever worked in the Greek theatre had to be tough, physically tough. Other actors looked at you with mouth agape when they heard that you gave two performances a day —one at six o'clock, immediately followed by another performance at nine.

"Do you rest all day?"

"No. During the day we rehearse a new play. This is not Broadway. Here a long run is eight weeks."

But I loved it. The next years are given to work, to discipline, to becoming a professional.

Even though the fighting receded from Athens, the civil war raged over the rest of the country. I was growing as an actress and that was good, but with continuing news of bloodshed and atrocities, there were inevitable descents into melancholy. At one such time Rena Messalora Salvago Pezas came to me and said: "Too much is too much. You're leaving Greece. I'm taking you to New York."

"Where?"

"New York, U.S.A."

Rena got her Mikas Pezas. They were married. He had written a novel, *The Price of Liberty*. It was highly praised in the American press. They decided to go and make their lives in the golden land, and take me with them.

Oh, I was tempted all right. The idea was exciting and Rena had become important to me. I wanted to be where she was. But there were anchors in Greece. There was the basic need to be in that light, in that sun, near the Greek sea. There was the theatre. I was now accepted as part of it. There was Pan. If not quite the ideal husband, he was a dear friend. I loved him.

Rena persists.

"What would we live on, Rena?"

"I've got fifty dollars."

And she did go to America, fifty dollars in her fist and confident of a glorious future. But that was not the end of her campaign to get me there. She left behind her an active ally. George was born in Greece. He became an American. He returned to Greece as part of the American forces. He was downright beautiful. His nose was fine and straight. His eyes were green. He had a radiant American Colgate smile. George was beautiful, he was kind, and he said: "Melina, I love you. Marry me and come live with me in New York."

I thought hard. He offered me a new life. He was a man who exuded health. He was so balanced, so normal, that I thought he could rid me of all the guilts I accumulated during the war. I had a kind of fantasy marriage; he would give me a real one. He would take me away from the anguish and bloodshed of civil war. I meant to give George a responsible answer, so I was amazed to hear myself say: "Ask Pan."

George looked at me for a long moment, then said: "All right, I will."

Pan. Friendly, polite in his best Cambridge manner, tells George: "Let's look at this calmly. Yes, this is the way we shall proceed. You go back to America for six months. If, after that time, Melina is still tempted by this venture so contrary to her nature, why then she'll follow you. Of course, I shall try to dis-

64

suade her. I don't quite see her in an American kitchenette. Nor do I see her mothering green-eyed children in Washington, or in New York, or anywhere else for that matter. But perhaps I'm wrong. Good-by."

George went. I stayed, and Pan was right. It was to be a long time before I was to see America—but with another American. I shed a few tears when George left. Some were for him. Some were for Rena. The tears dried soon and Rena came back soon. America stubbornly refused to give of its gold and glory to Mikas Pezas. And there they were back in Athens, fifty dollars lighter, but undaunted. Rena was more cheerful and optimistic than ever. Of course they both moved into Pan's house.

Then nothing but work.

If Katerina, actress manager, took you into her company for the entire season, then you had to be taken seriously. If she gave you a leading role, your place in the theatre was assured. She cast me as Lavinia, in Eugene O'Neill's *Mourning Becomes Electra*. Melina Mercouri of Kolograd was a leading actress in a major company.

There was a critic in Athens to whom I was anathema. It was more than dislike, it was allergy. To make things worse, he was the critic whom the intellectuals respected. In the dressing room on opening night, Anna was helping me into my costume. She stopped. She had an idea. Just before curtain time, she would rush up to the critic. She would tell him to leave the theatre at once because his house was on fire. And she really meant to do so. It was not I who stopped her. It was my mother. Mother was always of the "Let her face the music" school.

The next day, thousands of Athenian eyebrows were raised when they read the critic's review. He praised my performance to the skies. What's more, he was right. I was good, pretty damn good. The audience agreed with me and the critic. It was celebration time. Rena took me in her arms and said: "Little horse, now you can run. Run."

65

Then another success. *Arms and the Man* by Bernard Shaw. Another—*Dangerous Corner* by J. B. Priestley. Three in a row! It went to my head. For the summer season, I had the arrogance to form a company of my own. This kind of arrogance was not particular to me. Too often in the Athens theatre, as soon as an actor gains a little prominence, he rushes to create his own company. He rents a theatre, chooses the plays, engages technicians and a troupe of actors, braving the adventure of being obliged to maintain those actors for the full season. I wish I could say that such companies are formed out of a need for independence—perhaps that could be the half-truth. The other half is certainly a yielding to ambitions for starism. But I told myself that my theatre would be different. It would be the purest, it would be collective in spirit, it would be young. I surrounded myself with the most talented who studied with the great Rondiris. Among them is Nikos Hadziskos, a rising young male star. We choose to do a play in verse. The author is Costas Palamas, the dean of Greek poets. The director is experienced and creative. Everything is in our favor. And we are a dismal flop. The one thing I remember of the reviews:

All right, perhaps la Mercouri has talent, but she does not look or act like a Greek.

Me!

To tell it briefly, we flopped all summer long. One catastrophe after another. I was just about reconsidering the kitchenette in Washington when I was summoned by Dimitris Rondiris. He had been named head of the Greek National Theatre and he invited me to join him! Balboa surveying the Pacific did not see wider horizons than I did when Rondiris made me that offer.

It was marvelous. The old intoxicating life of work and study with Rondiris. Fascinating discussions of how a role was constructed, what he called masonry and carpentry. All of this in a hypnotic atmosphere. With Rondiris, theatre was not just a profession. It was a dedication. You made vows. You took the veil. And again those private rehearsals that lasted until five o'clock in the morning. I studied. I studied and studied until I realized that I was only studying and not acting. Yes, said Rondiris, I was to be the great tragic actress but not yet. It had a familiar ring. I played a variety of parts but only for him. Never for an audience. This went on and on. I began to feel like a landscape that the painter refused to exhibit, like a marble that the sculptor would not sell. Perhaps it was complimentary. Perhaps it was not. In any case, I began to go "stir crazy" as the Americans say.

It did not help matters that Dora Stratou came to talk to me. Dora Stratou is the custodian of Greek culture. She has taped every folk song of Greece, from Athens to the last far-flung village. If she heard of a song that people sang in a mountain hamlet cut into rock, Dora would mount on muleback carrying toothbrush and tape recorder. She created the Greek dance company that toured the world. She had a built-in antenna that led her directly to any new composing talent. At the time she came to see me, she was the patron of a new theatre troupe. It was founded by Karolos Koun, who had come from Constantinople (we Greeks still cannot bring ourselves to call it Istanbul). Koun won an immediate following. Without Koun, Greece might never have seen the plays of Lorca, Genet, Ionesco, and Brecht. At the time Dora came to see me, he was preparing a play of Tennessee Williams. That was the point of her visit. Koun had dispatched her to ask me to play Blanche in *A Streetcar Named Desire*.

"Oh, my God," I said. "Blanche!"

"You must know Blanche," says Dora, and she stares at me because I'm crying.

"Know Blanche?" I sobbed. "I am Blanche. But I cannot play her."

"You cannot not play her," says Dora.

"Rondiris? He'd never forgive me."

"You'll never forgive yourself, if you don't."

"I cannot."

"You're a fool."

"I cannot."

And back I went to study. If my Marguerite from Faust resumed wearing holes in the rug, Blanche was eating at my heart. Then Pan was nice enough to break a bone in his leg. That broken bone eventually led me to play Blanche. Some surgery was needed. Pan chose to have it done in Lausanne. He asked me to go with him. I asked Rondiris to give me leave. He refused. I asked a second time, saying that once and for all I would finish my dental work. People who looked at me objectively always said I had a very wide mouth. Kinder people put it more delicately. They said I had a generous mouth, but they found no gentle way to describe my protruding teeth. A wide mouth with buck teeth was a little much. Rondiris said: "The Swiss have excellent dentists. Go have your teeth fixed. It will improve your diction."

A thousand miles away from the hypnotic glare of Rondiris, seated on a bench looking out on Lake Geneva, a soliloquy:

"You work backward, Melina." That's what Rondiris tells me. He says: "Think, search, analyze. The actress must find the precise image of the character. Then step by step (masonry, carpentry) she gradually grows toward that image. In manner, in speech, and in movement. It's a long, careful process. You choose and you reject. You rehearse. Finally, when you and the image become one, you have mastered the role."

Rondiris is right, but it doesn't work that way with me. I have to start from the outside and work my way in. If I can walk the character, sit as she sits, turn my hand as she does, the movements sink under the skin, down into the bone, and I meet the character that way. In rehearsals of Mourning Becomes Electra, *I floundered awhile. Then something an actor said made me turn my head slowly sideways and downward. At that moment I found Lavinia. That slow turn of the head was so cruel, so full of hate, it gave me the key to Lavinia. She was someone who extirpated from her being any sense of pity. Nothing can shake her from her purpose, nothing exists for her but the need for revenge. Well, Rondiris calls that working from outside in. I say: "If the point is to get in and I have to do it by climbing in through the window, what's the difference as long as I get there?" "Wrong, Melina, wrong." He warns against superficiality, against physical mannerisms. He says if you start from the surface, you stay there.*

"It's not surface. It simply helps me to be the clown if I put on his hat from the very beginning."

"A clown is for the circus."

"What's wrong with the circus?"

"Nothing. But you are not in the circus; you are in the theatre."

Is that why he keeps me locked in study and refuses to let me appear before the public? Is it true that I am so far from being ready? Can it be that I have to be the accomplished actress before I put foot on stage again? That's madness. The only way to develop is to work, to act before audiences. To grow from success, to learn from failure. He must know that. Why won't he let me act? Wait a minute. Maybe he's in love with me and love to Rondiris is possession. No, he's not in love with me. He's in love with Pygmalion. He needs his Galatea. I don't want to be Galatea. I want to be Blanche. There it is. You've said it. It's out. That's what this soliloquy is all about. It's not that you want to be free of Rondiris. You want to be free to play Blanche.

That's right, Melina. That's right, Mr. Rondiris. That's right, Lake Geneva. I want to play Blanche.

Pan's bone is mended. My teeth are straight. But Rondiris

69

is unchanged. When I timorously mentioned Blanche, he flew into a rage. The very idea is a betrayal of him. I will not play Blanche or anything else in the theatre of Koun. That theatre is a nest of serpents. What the hell does Koun care about the basic techniques of acting? The theatre should be a temple; with Koun it's the pursuit of success à la mode. Forget Blanche. Forget Koun.

And for the second time Melina tries to commit suicide. I race to fling myself under the oncoming tramway, Rondiris in hot pursuit. He catches me and holds me tight in his arms. A policeman and some passers-by gather around. They hear Rondiris say: "All right, Melina. You can play Blanche. But remember everything I taught you and play her well."

The theatre of Koun and that of Rondiris, two different worlds. Rondiris was the classicist, the perfectionist. He ruled the National Theatre like a despot. His was the only voice. His judgment was supreme. No one would dare to oppose him, to suggest a contrary idea. Koun, pioneer, innovator, was open to all people, to all ideas. He would readily consider a suggestion made by the stage electrician. Rondiris was austere and demanding. Koun worked in an atmosphere of warmth and fun. Love flowed from Koun to men, to women, to cats, to dogs. He had great appeal to the young and the new young talent of Greece was inevitably drawn to him. The new composer, Manos Hadjidakis, discovered by Dora Stratou, the poet Gatsos, who translated Lorca, the painter Tsarouchis, the designer Vachliotti, they all came to Koun.

The curtain fell on the opening night of *A Streetcar Named Desire*. There was a moment's silence, then a roar of applause. A standing ovation. There were cheers. Cheers for the poet, Tennessee Williams, for the director, Karolos Koun, for the composer of music, Manos Hadjidakis, and there were cheers for the actress who played Blanche. When the audience broke into a chant: Melina—Melina—Melina, I drowned the stage with tears. And through my tears I saw only one man, standing and applauding. It was Rondiris. Despite his hatred for "the serpent's nest," he had come to see me play Blanche. And now my tears flowed for all of mankind. Rondiris came to my dressing room. "You stole from Electra, but"—he nodded his head up and down three or four times—"but you were good. Very good."

Let me give you my definition of agony. Agony is the condition of an actress when she "breaks up" on stage. Breaking up on stage means laughing when you shouldn't. It is the actor's nightmare. And it hurts. You fight so hard to control the laughter that it ties you into knots. All your insides ache. This fear of breaking up haunts me. And, God help me, it has happened to me many times. It is a hysteria whose origins I remember. It began when my grandfather died and neither doctors nor their medicines could stop me from laughing. It has never left me. Françoise Sagan is one of the people I love most in this world. Once she was in a dreadful automobile accident. She lay unconscious in a field, pinned under a car. I rushed to the road to flag down oncoming motorists, shaking with sobs—and laughter. When the present-day colonels stripped me of my citizenship and declared me a non-Greek, I couldn't stop laughing, and not because it was funny—which it was.

The most insignificant thing can sometimes break you up. A garbled word, an unexpected glance, a sound from the audience, a delayed reaction from your partner on stage can be enough to set you off. Rondiris said it was lack of concentration. I swore it was not so. Koun once slapped me. I laughed harder.

So it was with panic that I met the actor who was cast to play opposite me in Philip Yordan's *Anna Lucasta*. His name was Lycourgos Kallergis. He was a fine actor, but his reputation as a "laugher" was equal to mine. We were introduced to each other in the wings of the theatre. He said hello and held out his hand. I saw a kind of flickering in his eyes. He saw my lips begin to tremble. That was it. We burst into laughter. Koun should have called off the whole thing right then and there. He was defying the gods to put us together on the same stage.

Rehearsals began. The usual procedure was the reading of the play, followed by discussion. Not this time. Koun had something to resolve first. In a severe tone he said: "Melina and Kallergis, go to the center of the stage."

We obeyed.

"Face each other."

We did, and fearing the worst.

"Melina, look into his eyes. Kallergis, look into hers. Now hold it. Don't make a sound. Just hold it."

We held it for five seconds. I prayed. Ten seconds. For some crazy reason an image came to me, that of milk boiling in a pan and coming to a rise. Fifteen seconds. Twenty. The milk ran over. The laughter came out of me like a whinnying horse. It came from Kallergis like the furious hissing of an overheated radiator. Koun was outraged. But the angrier he became, the more hopeless became our laughter. Sweat ran from my hands. I bit my lips till they bled. Now Kallergis was laughing and groaning with pain at the same time. He pressed both hands to his stomach and bobbed up and down like a Muslim in prayer. Koun was so busy insulting us, he did not notice that the contagion had swept behind him to the rest of the troupe. The fact that they turned away helped not at all. We didn't have trouble enough? We also had to deal with the spectacle of twelve pairs of heaving shoulders.

Singly and in pair we asked Koun to recast one of us. He was stubborn. He just said coldly: "You will not laugh during the performance."

He was wrong.

If Mr. Yordan, author of the play, had come to Athens to see our production, he'd have had the right to sue us all in a court of law. Had he seen it, he could have testified that the two principal actors never dared to look at each other. That in a scene when Kallergis asked my hand in marriage, he kept his eyes tightly closed. That in the big scene of dramatic confrontation the two actors stood back to back and that a sudden shriek of pain from Mercouri had nothing to do with the play. How could he have known that the hidden director jabbed this actress with a long needle to keep her from laughing?

It was astonishing how few people in the audience realized what was going on on that stage. The play was a success from the start. Such is the faith and trust of the theatregoer. But there was one man who saw it all. He came to see the play again and again. He was bastard enough to adore seeing us break up. But he was also kind enough to cover his face with a handkerchief so that his neighbors would not see him laughing. This cruel, kind bastard was my beloved Pyros, the most charming, the most fun-loving, the most attractive of men. I don't know why I've put off talking of Pyros till now. He was the first man to whom I gave my heart completely, with no doubts, no fears. His love, his companionship are of the treasures of my life.

There is a curious thing that sometimes happens to people. They meet, they know they have an affinity, but something unspoken, some strange rhythmic determination tells them— not yet, that they will meet later at the right time. That was true of Pyros and me.

I was still a schoolgirl when we first met. I had just left the school building when a group of naval cadets came toward me. The most handsome of them held up his hands in signal for them to stop. He looked at me for a moment, he winked at me, and then off they marched. The naval academy and my school were close by, so these chance meetings occurred quite often. The next time the wink was accompanied by "Hello, pretty." And from then on: "Grow up. I'll wait for you." And somewhere in the back of my schoolgirl head, I filed that away.

The name of the naval cadet, Pyros Spiromilios, was first heard in Greece in 1935. It was one of the rare moments when we were a republic. There was talk of a putsch from the royalists. Pyros played a part in the mutiny in support of the republic. In 1940 he was proclaimed a hero when he took on an Italian submarine. Pyros, in a small boat armed only with a machine gun, forced the submarine to dive for cover. There were a series of brave exploits during the war. At the liberation, Pyros was given the honor of leading the navy parade through Athens. I stood in the cheering crowd. I caught his eye. He marched head high, shoulders straight, and winked as he passed by.

Later on, he worked out an interesting style of regular visits. It was during that season of flops in the summer theatre. He came especially when we were doing the free verse play of Palamas. Most of Athens stayed away, but Pyros came often. Though not like an ordinary theatregoer, oh no. He would buy four seats: one to sit on; on another he stretched his legs; the third was for a bottle of ouzo and a bowl of ice; on the fourth, heaps of cucumbers and olives. The first time this happened, a fellow actress rushed into my dressing room. "There's a monster out there."

I ran to the wings to see the monster. There in an island of empty seats, he was sprawled out like a pasha. He caught me spying on him from the wings—and winked. To top it all, the bastard knew the play by heart, and was perhaps the only one in Athens who loved it.

Came the day when Pyros decided the right time had come. It was when Rena went to New York followed by my suitor. He began to pay assiduous court. I resisted him. I was surprised at the strength of my resistance, because in little time I was mad about him. I just could not accept that this man,

74

forward-looking in everything else, had the typical Greek reactionary attitude toward women. I couldn't believe that he subscribed to the same dreary pap:

"There are two kinds of women, wives and mistresses. Wives are responsible and dignified, mistresses are not. A wife who has a lover is a whore, but man is by nature polygamous and is free to take as many mistresses as he pleases, etc. etc."

Pyros, with what I called cowardly candor, could say to a woman: "I love you. Be my mistress, but I warn you that even though I love you, I'll despise you just a little bit because you are a mistress."

It was infuriating.

But after a year and a half of resistance, I succumbed. He was more irresistible than I was immovable. We loved each other for seven years. Seven beautiful, fun-filled years. Pyros was beautiful, and physical beauty matters to the Greeks. He went well with the sun. The paganism of Greece, surviving underneath the centuries of Christianity, came out in Pyros, in his appetite for life, in his optimism, in his sensuality. These gifts he gave me. It was Pyros who made me a woman; he taught me what pleasure is.

Karolos Koun used to buy cigarettes for all his cast. It was his way of making up for the high salaries he could not pay. Working with him was a joy, but we earned very little money. Sometimes we were too avant-garde to be commercial. And even when we were a hit, the theatre in those days could never pay high salaries. The price of admission was very low, and a full house did not necessarily mean big box office.

I never took any money from Pan, so with everyone else I looked forward to summer tours which were more profitable. We played the provincial towns such as Patras and Kavalla. We played in Salonika for which I have a special affection. We crossed the sea to play for the Greek communities abroad. We went to places of legend—Alexandria, made eternal by the

75

poems of Cavafy; Cyprus, Venus' island, and visions of Othello on the water's edge; Constantinople, known to all Greeks as "the city." Touring was hard work, but beautiful, and Pyros came to visit when he could. I was young, I was working, I was in love. Those were loving, lovely times.

Chapter Nine

Le ciel est bleu, la mer est verte
Laisse un peu la fenêtre ouverte.

Suzy Solidor was singing in Paris. And in the enchanted audience—Rena and I. Rena and I in Paris! Everybody in the world dreams of Paris. Everyone in the arts has a rendezvous with Paris. Fortunate are those who can keep the rendezvous. Partly because of an inferiority complex, partly because of unreasoning chauvinism, most Greeks refuse to be impressed by anything that is not Greek. That is not true of France. We sing French songs, we adore their poets, we copy their styles, we dream of Paris for our honeymoons and if we have a second language, it is French. I was in love with Baudelaire and Rimbaud when I was fourteen.

The first encounter with Paris literally goes to your head. It makes you dizzy. Wherever we went, Rena and I shed tears at its beauty. Tears in the Ile de la Cité. Tears at the Palais Royal. Tears on each of the thirty-two bridges that span the Seine. Tears were windblown on a privileged visit to the roofs of the Opéra. We were ridiculous. Rena and I are among those futile people who take a taxi to avoid walking four blocks. No one who knew us would believe the number of streets we tramped in Paris. We did so not only for their beauty, but also because of our delight in their names. One of the things I resented when I first saw New York was the way they named their streets. They have splendid broad avenues that they call: First Avenue, Second Avenue, Third Avenue, Fifth Avenue, etc. In France they are Rue Mozart, Rue Beethoven, Rue Goethe and Quai Voltaire. How can you not love a street that is called Rue de la Petite Musique? I am told that professional writers work in perpetual anguish. Well, believe me, so do amateurs. But for a moment, I'm going to work and enjoy it. I want the pleasure of writing down the names of Paris streets.

Rue de Cherche-Midi—Rue Paradis—Impasse des Trois Visages—Rue des Quatres-Frères-Peignot—Rue de Soleil—Rue de Repos—Boulevard de Bonne Nouvelle—Villa des Lilas—Cité Joyeux.

Rue des Artistes—Cour des Artistes—Villa des Arts—Rue de l'Ancienne Comédie—Square des Ecrivains Combattants morts pour la France—Cour d'Honneur—Rue des Camélias—Square Alice—Rue Capitaine Olchanski—Rue des Innocents—Rue des Fillettes . . .

Of course we went to the theatre every night. We went to the galleries, to the Louvre (Rena was angry that Winged Victory was in France and not in Greece), and we ate like gluttons, we even bought a pink picture hat in partnership. We were there for eight days. I don't remember sleeping. How did it come about, this first trip to Paris? This too, we owed to Pan's broken leg. It was on the way to Lausanne that Rena and I stole those eight days. And when we left Lausanne for Athens (Pan was still bedded down), we determined to steal a few more days in Paris. Those few days influenced my life and work for years.

We were lunching at the Petit Trianon in Versailles. There we saw a huge pair of horn-rimmed glasses. Our hearts leaped in excitement. The horn-rimmed glasses were famous in the

European theatre because behind them was Marcel Achard. He was the successful playwright. He wrote nothing but hits. His plays were filled with charm and wit. He was one of the most popular men in France. I looked good that day and I knew it. I was wearing the pink picture hat and it was a beauty. I willed Achard to look at me. He did. The great man sent a waiter to our table with a little note.

"Actress? Do I know you?"

I sent back a reply. "Actress, a little. Know me—impossible."

He came to our table. "May I join you for a few minutes?"

"Please sit down."

If that was not fairy tale enough, he told us that he was writing *La Petite Lili* for Edith Piaf, and would I like it if he'd write in a part for me? I was playing it rather sophisticated till then, but my mouth popped open and I gaped at him. When I found command of my jaw muscles, I closed my mouth. Behind his horn rims his eyes were laughing. He repeated the offer. I said, alas I could not, that I had commitments in Athens.

But Rena and I were back in Paris in the summer of the following year. We didn't feel like tourists this time. We were immediately plunged into the life and milieu of the artists and intellectuals of Paris. Achard introduced us to Marcel Pagnol, André Roussin, Henri Bernstein. There was a marvelous evening with Jean Cocteau. With three lines of a pen, he drew a Greek landscape on a paper napkin. With his fingers he built the Acropolis in the air. My God, he had extraordinary hands. We met Pierre Brasseur, the fantastic French actor; Jean Marais, who was so beautiful it was dazzling. One night we went to see Sacha Guitry. The Guitry manner. It was like being granted an audience by the Roi Soleil. But the touching thing was the timidity and deference with which Achard addressed him. Marcel Achard was on the top of the heap, but he behaved with Guitry like a schoolboy submitting his first poem. All of these people were fascinating, but the one who got right into my heart was Colette.

We knew that she was quite aged and that she would receive us in a wheelchair, so we were not prepared to meet someone so lovely, so intensely feminine, so coquette. Her famous curls were charmingly arranged. She was beautifully dressed. We spent most of the afternoon with her. She had such sweetness, so much mischief, and her regard was so penetrating that I felt she was going to put me into a novel. When she bade me adieu, she gave me a little poem. It ended: "Elle n'a qu'à lever les yeux et l'Acropole est là."

My first professional appearance in Paris was in Achard's *Le Moulin de la Galette*. The stars were the fabled Yvonne Printemps and Pierre Fresnay. Just to mention their names thrilled me. But it took only one meeting to see that they disliked me intensely, that they had decided to dislike me before we met.

To begin with, Achard offended Yvonne Printemps by dedicating his play to me. On the flyleaf was: "Pour Melina." I was honored, but soon came to curse the day he thought of it. Achard and I became targets for the French satirical papers. They were funny, but I didn't laugh. When the French put their minds to it, their wit becomes a scalpel. I had seen only smiles and charm. Now I saw fang and claw. Until then, in awe of the people I met, I spoke little and was happy to listen and learn. But now I felt the need to strike back. I expressed opinions. I made judgments. But it was no contest. I did not possess their arms. I used a mallet against the épée and the needle. I railed against my lack of sophistication. Someone wrote: "Picasso had his blue and pink periods, why could not Achard have his Greek period?" The phrase became "la néfaste époque grecque de Marcel Achard."

It was murder to rehearse in this atmosphere. Pierre Fresnay was austere and cold. So was everyone else. I was made to feel I was a young adventuress who had been imposed on the cast because I was Achard's mistress. Which I was not. I couldn't decide whether personal pride should make me quit or stay. I was working badly and knew it. I decided to stay and vowed with clenched teeth that by the play's opening my performance would be good. I was helped a little by the attitude of the stagehands and the electricians. They were friendly and encouraging.

My friends had no inkling of any of this. Proud of the Greek actress making her debut on a Paris stage, a delegation came from Athens to lend me support at the series of pre-premieres that are customary in the French theatre. Together with the Greek colony that lived in Paris, it amounted to an Attic invasion. They were exuberant, they had no doubts that I would be a success and, like all Greeks, they were critics.

My mother said I was too thin for the part. Someone else didn't like the way I spoke French. Pyros had reservations about some of the staging. In one thing they were unanimous. The plaid suit I wore in the second act just wouldn't do. So, with unpardonable naïveté, I rushed to the Greek dress designer Jean Dessès. Emergency. I needed a new dress that very night. Dessès rose to the challenge.

At the next preview, Pierre Fresnay on stage, expecting my usual entrance in the plaid suit, is startled to see an apparition in beige, veiled, hatted, and gloved. As the director, he was outraged; as the actor, this shocking entrance made him forget his lines. Splendid professional that he was, this was all concealed from the audience. But after the performance, all hell broke loose. His rage was terrible. And to make matters worse, the Greeks stormed backstage to loudly proclaim their approval of my new costume. But I knew that lightning would strike, that I had broken the discipline of the theatre like an idiotic amateur. I was preparing the text of my apology to the entire company, but chucked it when the hairdresser brought a note from Fresnay. It was cold. It was angry. Had he just criticized my lack of professionalism, I could have no complaint. But he acidly pointed out that the only reason I was in the play was because I had the favor of the author. I sobbed and stormed. The Greeks exploded. This was an insult to their national dignity. The place was in an uproar. Poor Achard rushed desperately from one dressing room to another. Pyros said he would close the theatre.

Yvonne Printemps was the only one who kept a cool head. With only three days to go before the first night, she knew that the only way to avoid catastrophe was by conciliation. She came to my dressing room. She caressed my cheek, murmuring: *"Ma pauvre petite."* My new costume wasn't that bad. Of course I could wear it. We just needed a special rehearsal for the rest of the cast to get used to it. With these kind words I broke down. All animosity was forgotten. You only had to stroke my cheek to make me cry.

Unlike most of Achard's plays, *Le Moulin de la Galette* was not well received by the press. I was sure that I would be slaughtered by the critics. To my surprise they were fairly gentle. No one declared I was a genius, but the faint praise I received was far more than I expected. There were to be other appearances in Paris, but less fraught with emotion, and not all in plays written by Achard.

The first actress of Greece was Marika Kotopouli. She was a superb craftsman. Her name was a household word. She was adored, imitated, and quoted. Her speech was a mixture of Shakespeare, Euripides, and imaginative obscenity. She was Greece's Mrs. Pat Campbell. She led and won the crusade for the language of the people, Demotiki, to be spoken in the theatre. She cast out the use of Katharevoussa, a bastardization of ancient Greek, that came into use in the nineteenth century. It's a phoney, affected language. It is consistent with the character of the present colonels' regime that Papadopoulos makes his public utterances in Katharevoussa.

In 1949 Marika was getting too old to act for a full season. Her husband and manager, Helmis, asked Koun to let me replace her. It was great for the morale, but I was realistic. If ever the day came when I could replace Marika Kotopouli, that day was far off indeed. But when the entire Koun company joined the Kotopouli theatre, I went along. Everyone expected that the Marika-Koun combination would bring a season of miracles. When Giorgos came to add his prestige to the company, there were no doubts possible. Well, the theatre has a way of rejecting the sure thing. The season was so disappointing that toward its end Helmis had to resort to a musical comedy to pull the theatre out of a financial mess. I took advantage of the hiatus to go to Paris to appear in a play by Jacques Deval. The play was *Il Etait Une Gare*. The action was set in a railroad station. I played a part that consisted of five monologues in the form of telephone calls and in the end a suicide. I liked the part, especially the suicide. Actors love to die in the theatre. This time the critics were generous, one or two even enthusiastic. With honor restored, I returned to Greece.

When I returned, things had changed. Koun had left the Kotopouli theatre. It was now directed by her nephew Dimitri Myrat. I also found myself installed as the leading lady. This theatre became my home for many years. The theatre prospered. I was delighted to be well paid. I played a variety of roles, among them: *Anne of the Thousand Days* by Maxwell Anderson, Pinero's *The Second Mrs. Tanqueray*, Gabriel Arout's *La Dame de Trèfle*, *The Lark* by Jean Anouilh, and my first comedy, *The Seven Year Itch* by George Axelrod.

It was at this time that I began to function as a citizen. This development was largely due to another actress in our troupe whom I shall call Sabina. Sabina had been a Communist before the party was made illegal. At the height of the "white terror" the police intercepted a letter she wrote. In it, there was the phrase: "Soon the song of the turtle will be heard in the land."

You can't fool around with the Greek police. They, of

course, recognized this sinister phrase as a slogan calling for a Communist takeover. Sabina was arrested. She was asked to sign things repenting that she was subversive. Not only did she refuse, she also told her jailers what she thought of them. Believe it or not, she was sentenced to death. To a number of people, among them Marika Kotopouli, this was considered slightly excessive. Marika interceded on Sabina's behalf. If an ordinary citizen couldn't fool around with the police, the police didn't dare fool around with Marika Kotopouli. She was too popular and her tongue was too barbed. No sooner was Sabina released than Marika took her into the company.

Since my first battles to be accepted into the Greek theatre, I had been always made conscious that I came from the right side of the railroad tracks. This gave me a complex. To compensate, I made it a point to be the first to come to the theatre and the last to leave. This then gave me time to talk to the backstage crew. Technicians in the theatre and in the cinema have my admiration and I've always been lucky in winning their friendship. I admire their special humor and the physical grace that so often goes with skill. Sabina came early one night to find me chatting and drinking coffee with the crew. Said she: "I didn't believe people from the right behaved that way."

She forgave me for laughing at her, and asked me to join a delegation of actors to make a protest.

"A protest against what?"

"A left-wing colleague who manages a theatre in the park has been dismissed."

"Why?"

"Because of his political opinions."

"Really?"

This time it was she who laughed, but she was surprised when I readily accepted to be part of the delegation.

Prime Ministers didn't last long in Greece. The longest term in this office was held by Konstantine Karamanlis. When I first met him, he was the Minister of Public Works. Public parks were in his charge. He was the man who received our delegation. He was already being referred to as the wonder boy of the right. I'll never understand how he felt comfortable on the right. It was a political wind that blew in the wrong direction. My liberal friends look at me with pity when, even today, I insist that he was born to be a man of the people, a progressive, and that somehow he got lost.

I spoke up when the delegation went to plead for the actor, but not right away. For a while I was rendered speechless by Karamanlis' good looks. He was a splendid hunk of man. He had the reputation of a man of action, and he looked it. He had won general applause, even from a begrudging left, when he took on an English company that had the tramway franchise. He had decided that the trolley was obsolete and had to make way for surface buses. He ordered the tracks removed. The English stalled. Karamanlis set a deadline. It was not met. Karamanlis took up pick and shovel, rolled up his sleeves, and hacked out some hundred meters of track. The English got the message.

He did not keep our delegation waiting. As soon as we arrived, we were admitted to his office. He heard us out. Normally, in this sort of situation, a secretary makes a few notes; the Minister assures that the matter will be studied; you are more or less politely dismissed, and that's the last you hear of it. Not so with Karamanlis. Within twenty minutes our colleague got his theatre back. Even Sabina was impressed.

From this beginning, I came to understand the need for trade unionism. I saw that the only way to reduce the killing work schedule in our theatres was by concerted action. I learned that the economics of the theatre left room for the actor to be better paid. I met actors who were too old and too tired to work, but had to continue because the pensions allotted to them couldn't keep them alive. I joined the actors' union. I began to read. This had always been a problem. Reading is such a solitary pursuit and I hate being alone. I'd rather be with someone I dislike than be alone. (I once told this to an American psychiatrist. He rubbed his hands in glee and actually licked his lips.)

At the time I joined the actors' union my reading had been confined to the major playwrights and everything I could find on the theatre. I realized it was more than time to explore other worlds.

Sabina and I became good friends, but there were differences. I thought that the Greek economy could be helped immensely by a tourist program. More hotels, art festivals, investment in better roads, anything that would bring visitors to Greece. Sabina hated the idea. To her a tourist was an American. We were already in the American grip and the more dollars that came, the more dependent we would become, and wasn't I afraid that a supermarket would be built under the Acropolis? No, I was not afraid, and as time went on, I became active in the development of Greek tourism. I called on help from French friends. I induced Jacques Deval to come to Athens and direct the Kotopouli company in "Ce Soir A Samarcande." Soon after, André Roussin agreed to come and direct *Hélène, ou La Joie de Vivre*. I had visions of brilliant foreigners coming to work in Greece, attracting thousands of tourists, who in turn would go home praising the beauties of Greece. Sabina said: "They will also talk of ugliness and injustice in Greece. They will talk about Glezos, the man who pulled the Nazi flag down from the Acropolis and who is now in prison. They will talk of Beloyannis. They will talk of Batsis."

Beloyannis. We first knew him by a picture of him. Police posted it all over Greece. Over the word "wanted," a high forehead, a smiling mouth and eyes of coal. He was a member of the central committee of the Communist Party. He was caught and charged with treason. The sentence demanded was death. It took little time to realize that Beloyannis was a special kind of man. When he spoke in his defense at the trial,

86

it was with culture, with humor and an extraordinary range of knowledge. And no one, whatever their political convictions, could deny this man's love and compassion for the Greek people. The trial attracted international attention. Committees, the world over, were formed in his defense. There was a detail that captured everyone's imagination. Somehow, every day of the trial, he appeared before his judges, wearing a red carnation. It inspired Picasso's famous etching. Beloyannis was condemned to death. But a second trial was ordered when the security police said they had found new evidence of espionage. There was no proof of espionage, but the court still ordered his death. The world outcry reached such a pitch that those who wanted Beloyannis dead became fearful that he might be saved. And something happened that dishonored our country. In the dark of night, on a Sunday, Beloyannis was taken before a firing squad. In the history of Greece no execution was ever permitted on a Sunday. The night was pitch black. How do you kill a man you can't see? The police were prepared. They brought large projectors. By the light of the projectors, Beloyannis was shot dead.

I had never met Beloyannis. I had never heard of him until his posters went up on the walls. But I had known Dimitris Batsis since I was twelve years old. Batsis shared the same cell with Beloyannis. He was shot by the same light. Dimitris Batsis was a man from a distinguished family. He was a leading lawyer and economist. One of his books on economics was a standard textbook. He was married to the daughter of a rightist minister. His father was an admiral of the navy. It was on a boat commanded by him that George II and his future successor, Paul, were returned to Greece (oh yes, we had a king again). No one could believe that Dimitris Batsis could be a Communist. Yet there he was on trial for espionage. He violently denied this charge, but to the general amazement, he admitted working for the left. The police now proceeded to break him down. They knew how. Finally they promised him freedom if he gave names. Batsis gave names. And then they sentenced him to death. It was his wife who revealed the broken bargain in letters to the press. The admiral petitioned King Paul to intercede for his son. He reminded His Majesty of his return to Greece on his boat. The petition was unanswered. A few days before the execution date, the head of the security police came to Batsis' cell.

"You gave us names we already knew. Give us more names and you will not be killed."

Batsis refused to be dragged down any further. He ordered the security man out of his cell.

They shot him with Beloyannis.

So many times have we become despondent. So many times have we been ashamed. But there is the sun and the sea, and the memory of all the good men who died for Greek freedom, to give us new hope. New hopes may bring new disappointments, but by sheer Greekness we'll find a way for hope to be born again.

Chapter Ten

Sabina says: "Two questions, may I?"

"Ask."

"First, in how many modern plays have you acted?"

"In this year of our Lord 1954, I count about sixty plays."

"How many of them were written by Greeks?"

"Four."

"No more questions."

We didn't need Sabina to remind us of this. It was the painful subject of endless discussion in our theatre. Sabina insisted on pointing out that it was a reflection of our political and social condition, that we would find the road to independence when we insisted on being Greek and vitally so in the arts. Some of our poets had found the way, and occasionally a novelist. Dora Stratou was fighting to preserve our dances, but our theatre was sterile and so was most of our music—until Manos Hadjidakis entered the fray.

How to start on the subject Manos Hadjidakis? His charm? I was slave to it from the first time we worked together, when he wrote the music for *Mourning Becomes Electra*. Since then we've worked together many many times. Plays, films, even a revue. I loved him and love him, even though there is a son-of-a-bitch side of his character that has more than once turned my love to fury. At the time of this writing, I'm trying to hate him, all the while knowing that it won't work or that if it does work, it won't last. As has happened before, confronted by his warmth and his charm, I'll fall into his arms; he will call me Agoraki (little boy) and I'll love him like crazy until the next exasperation. For the moment, then, let me confine myself to Manos' fight for Greek music. He made us listen to the bouzouki.

It was not an easy fight. He had to take on our middle and upper classes. They despised bouzouki music because its origins were Turkish and they were insistent on being Europeans. Their devotion to Athens was essentially phoney because they'd have preferred it to be London or Paris.

But Manos fought. His fight took him to obscure tavernas on the docks of Piraeus and the workers' sections of Athens and Salonika. Many of these were tiny. Some had only three or four tables. But all had at least one bouzouki player. Manos rushed to them with the fervor of an archaeologist on the verge of digging up a splendid ruin. He heard songs of the slums, the jailed and the drugged, songs of prison, songs of trouble with the police:

> Postman since you read my mail
> Tell my mother her son's in jail.

The songs had three essential themes: love, death, and the struggle to be free. The oldest strands in the music were the Taksimi, which came from Byzantine chant. They survived because succeeding generations of peasants used them as an expression of lamentation. These laments were of Turkish, Arab, and Balkan tradition. Each generation of Greeks contributed its modification. They mixed with Cretan improvisation, then with brighter rhythms of our island dances and gradually became Greek in character. They were sung in what amounted to a virtual clandestinity. The musicians and their instruments, the bouzouki, the sandouri, the baglamas, were ostracized by our "better people."

It's a sad society that permits a genius to languish in obscurity and poverty. If Manos had done nothing else but force our recognition of Tsitsanis, he'd have our gratitude forever. Tsitsanis eked out a living in a shabby café. He was a giant. The great artist is the one who uproots you and takes you into a world of his making. When I first heard Tsitsanis, I was in an absolute trance. I saw nothing else but that gaunt face and his fine, delicate hands. I heard only my own heartbeats and his tortured voice. His music—I don't know how to say it any other way—reached into your guts.

> My Sunday—melancholy. Cloudy
> Fog
> My Christ. My Virgin.
> There's fog in my heart.

And compassion, understanding of refuge in drugs, when he sang:

> There's no place but hell for you
> When you get there
> Ask the guys
> In your hell—do you get a crumb of hashish?

Tsitsanis could neither read nor write a note of music, but he created countless songs perfect in structure and musicality. He couldn't remember all the songs he made. Some he played only once—a moment's inspiration, then lost forever.

One day a record album of songs appeared. Most of them by Tsitsanis, all from these tavernas. Manos orchestrated them. The featured instruments were bouzouki, sandouri, and baglamas. Manos called the album *Six Images of the People.*

It was the breakthrough. It swept the country. Today that record album is part of our treasure. Then came torrents of songs from Manos, all faithful to the Tsitsanis tradition, but developed with Manos' own special magic, his charm and an inexhaustible gift of melody. He became undisputed king until he was challenged by Mikis Theodorakis.

Mikis was a different kind of man. From boyhood on, he was involved in Greece's political struggles. He was committed to the left. He fought in the resistance. During the civil war he was exiled. For years he was kept in the concentration camp of Macronissos. He was beaten. He developed tuberculosis. In short, the life of a Communist, or suspected Communist, in the democracy that the Truman Doctrine defended. When he was finally freed, he went to Paris to study and compose. His work was more classical in nature. He loved writing for the ballet. Then he came back to Athens; more, he came back to Greece. He put the people's bitter history into music. He gave song form to the poems of Seferis, Ritsos, and Elytis. His music was virile, often militant. His songs became political weapons. Mikis became so popular, he was elected deputy to Parliament by a great majority. He created a youth movement named after Grigoris Lambrakis, the popular liberal leader who was assassinated in Salonika. The exciting film Z, based on the book by Vassily Vassilikos and so ably directed by Costa Gavras, has made the story known everywhere. The actual murder is graphically restaged, the hired assassin rushing toward Lambrakis on a motorcycle, crushing his skull with a club, making his getaway with numbers of police nearby. The Karamanlis government was shaken by this murder. There were dark rumors that involved the royal family. I reveal no secret when I tell you that Queen Frederika could not win any popularity contests in Greece. She was disliked and distrusted. She assigned to herself vast political power. I don't want to say anything that would get me sued by Frederika. I don't like to be sued by ex-queens. I merely record, for those who are interested in judging the instinct of the people, that after the assassination, all over Greece, motorcycles were referred to as Frederikas.

The Lambrakis movement grew and flourished. And so did Mikis' political and musical prestige. He formed an orchestra that he took on tour with enormous success. The people loved his music and adored watching him conduct. Mikis is a great big man; he's almost six and a half feet tall, and when he conducts, he holds his arms as if he were a dancing bear. The colonels' junta has cut down the Lambrakis youth movement. They imprisoned Mikis for three years. But even at that time it was no bed of roses. More than once, organized hoodlums disrupted the recitals and the orchestra was stoned.

Manos and Mikis had respect for each other. But their mutual respect did not discourage the growth of two camps: those who swore that Theodorakis was the better musician— the others who upheld the banner of Hadjidakis. I kept switching back and forth to each camp. When I listen to the music of Mikis I'm thrilled, when I listen to the music of Manos, I'm seduced.

All of this talk of music leads me to "Stella." Stella sang in a bouzouki taverna. "Stella" was the name of the character I played in my first movie. I started late, but I got there. It's not that I had anything against the movies; on the contrary I was dying to act in a movie. I never dared to mention that when I was with Rondiris. He would have turned me out. And in Greece, till Michael Cacoyannis came along, most movies were impoverished productions that insisted that the main character again and again be the poor innocent girl seduced by a sophisticated villain. These films were rarely seen outside of Greece. It was in 1953 that I saw the first Greek film that did not embarrass me. It was *Springtime in Athens*, Michael Cacoyannis' first film. It had quality and talent. So before that, any thoughts of movies would make you look abroad. I tried. Alex Korda made a screen test of me in London—in black face! The character was an African. Korda and I saw the test together. We both burst into laughter. We agreed that I was ridiculous, and I went home.

"Stella" was born one day in the mind of Iacovos Campanellis. That day I was acting in a radio version of Anouilh's *Medea*. Campanellis had written the adaptation. I made quite an entrance into the broadcast studio. I had just cut my hair very short, like a boy. Campanellis said: "Melina, you are the most emancipated woman in Greece."

"Because of my hair?"

"No, not because of your hair. I'm going to write a play for you."

He wrote *Stella*. It never reached the stage. Cacoyannis read it and said he wanted to do it, but not as a play, as a movie. He came to see me and asked me to play Stella. I held up my wide mouth for him to see. But only for a second. He was a movie director, and if he didn't agree with everybody else that I could not be photogenic, who was I to quarrel? Before he could change his mind, I said: "We do it."

We flew into action. The first thing to do was to get leave of absence from the theatre. I told Helmis: "I'm not asking, I'm begging."

A long pause.

"Okay, on condition you play Lady Macbeth right after the film."

"I don't want to play Lady Macbeth."

"That's the condition."

"It's a deal."

Rush to Manos Hadjidakis to write songs and score. Rush to Denny Vachliotti to do the costumes. Rush to form the technical crew. It was Rena who said "Wait a minute, what about a contract?" I hadn't even thought of it. The contract was made. My salary, to star in the film, two thousand dollars. Do

94

I hear distant laughter from Hollywood colleagues? It doesn't matter. As trade unionist and actress, I could hold my head high. I broke a record. At that time, it was the highest salary ever paid to anyone to appear in a Greek film.

In those days in Greece, if a girl was unmarried at the age of twenty-one, she was an embarrassment to her family, she was wept over as an old maid. If this is an exaggeration, it's a slight one. Twist my arm and I'll make it twenty-two. So, to make a film about a girl like Stella meant exposing yourself to a good deal of wrath. Stella was a dissident. She was opposed to the very concept of marriage. She loves a man, she's happy to give herself to him, she finds great fun in his company. He wants marriage. She doesn't like that at all. Marriage is the surrender of freedom. Cacoyannis summed it up: "Stella is gay. She's vibrant. She's proud of her body. She's proud of her liberty. She loves and loves well, but does not accept the notion that marriage is security. Nor does she want the benediction of society. Anything that is blessed by society, she suspects."

Some of my Kolograd friends began to associate me with the character I was playing. Wasn't I going to the "bouzouki joints" in the name of research? What lady went to such places? Well, I did go for research. Often I would be the only woman present. Night after night of tavernas, of exciting music and the marvelous dancing of men. They danced, not to perform, but to respond to a need. It was fascinating. You watch a man seated at a table. His eyes are closed. He seems to be listening and waiting. Then comes the moment when the music lifts him out of his seat and he begins to dance, and the point is that he is removed and alone.

This usually happens to the music of the zeimbekiko. The zeimbekiko dance has no set figures. It has a contained rhythm that induces introspection and improvisation. It is entirely personal. It brings the man closer and closer to himself until he reaches a total solitude. It can become extremely sensual.

Often the man caresses his body. Most of the time his eyes are cast down and he dances in one spot as if held by a center of gravity; then suddenly, a sweeping gesture, a leap, an acrobatic turn. He's saying: I can explode. I can break chains. I can pull down pillars. You've tied me down to work and dogged obedience all week long, but this is Saturday night. I am free. I feel my body. I feel my strength. Don't push me around.

I saw a man so taken by the zeimbekiko that he went into trance. He was a man just released from prison. He seemed to dance in a state of hypnosis. There was one spasmodic gesture when he pierced his lips with a long needle. He didn't make a sound and not a drop of blood was spilled.

The bouzouki places, then, were not decorated. There were bare walls, a raised platform for the musicians and singers, tables and chairs, and nothing more. In the places where there was a woman singer, the thing that struck me most was the ease and sense of belonging. No man-woman stuff, just a relaxed, natural singing in harmony with the men and the ambiance.

Michael Cacoyannis had worked as an actor in the London theatre. He knew the actor's problems. He cared. He did not isolate us from the technical part of film making. He explained how it was there to serve us. He expected us to live the film with him, in its planning and in its growth. I had to be available to him at all times—and immediately available. The economics of making a movie demand that you be ready and sharp at all times.

Much has been said of the great difference in acting before a camera and acting before a theatre audience. I subscribe to few of the theories. Don't let anyone tell you that the audience doesn't exist when you work in the movies. Not only are they there, they are on top of you. That, to me, is the essential difference in the two forms—the terrible closeness of the audience in movies.

96

People speak of the sweep and scope of the cinema. The screen can contain the image of an entire city, of marching armies. But the real magic is the close-up. It brings the audience close enough to look into your heart. You cannot cheat. Sometimes in the theatre, inspiration does not come, concentration weakens; you're just not with it. But you can conceal it from the audience. You can get by with technique alone, which is a fancy way of saying you're lying. If you lie in close-up, you're immediately exposed. And the terrible thing is that it's there to stay. In the theatre you turn your shoulder. You speak words into the air. The next day the gesture can no longer be seen, the words no longer heard. The cinema is a letter that you have written and signed; if its contents are false, it stays to accuse you.

Cacoyannis permitted us to see the rushes. Some directors do not. They say that actors are too subjective to judge, that they watch only themselves, that they are too busy looking to see if the make-up is right or that the costume sits well. I assured him that I was able to be objective and detached. I did not confess that this was true only after having seen the rushes twice. The first time I looked only at me; the second time I was able to see the scene. As time went on, this objective sense developed until I began to refer to Stella as "she." I liked her. I liked her determination to be free. Once, at the rushes, I called out: "Good for you, Stella. Stand up to them."

Those were marvelous months. Friends came to spend the nights with us when we shot the scenes in the bouzouki place. Actors, technicians, friends, a tight little community, working, singing, dancing till the break of day. We were too happy to be tired. And there was the daily excitement of watching the rushes, seeing the story take form, the characters grow.

But don't let me make it sound like a picnic. We worked like dogs. And the cold! The action of the film was set in the summertime. We wore the lightest of clothes. But we were shooting in February, and in February, sunny Athens can turn into an icy bitch. When we spoke, we sent clouds of steam into the cold night air. They have a gimmick in the movies. They freeze your breath. They put an ice cube in your mouth so it will stop from steaming. My co-star was George Foundas, a fine actor and a beautiful specimen of man. I liked him, but try to look convincing when you're kissing a man in a passionate love scene with an ice cube in your mouth. I must mention that the film almost died at birth. There was a day that we still call the black Friday. The film began shooting on a Monday. Thursday night the producer, a Greek from Egypt, visited the card tables. The following morning, the black Friday, he announced to us that he had lost every penny he had, and that there was no more movie. Even Rena, forgetting Dostoievsky, cursed him. For three weeks we ran about trying to find money. Nothing. A rich acquaintance said he might be interested if, at the end of the film, Stella changed her mind and accepted the joys of marriage. We kept on looking. Nothing. Then God sent Vassily Lambiris, a lawyer. A moment's kefi swept him and his fiancée's dowry into the movie business. He did not regret it. *Stella* was a success. He never went back to law. He's still in the film business. *Stella* was made on a shoestring, even by Greek standards. The total cost was $22,000.

Cacoyannis went on to become a director of international repute. His *Electra* with Irene Pappas won universal acclaim. His *Zorba the Greek* from Nikos Kazantzakis' great novel, and with Mikis Theodorakis' music was a smash hit. We developed other gifted directors. There was Nikos Koundouros, maker of *Magic City, The Dragon,* and *The Little Aphrodites,* which won the first prize at the Berlin Film Festival. A whole group of young talent was beginning to emerge when the junta's censors choked the Greek cinema to death.

I promised Helmis I would play Lady Macbeth, and play her I did—badly. I have always contended that Lady Macbeth is a false good part, that she is unplayable. Well, I proved my point. I was God-awful. It didn't help any that during rehearsals I was sleeping only three hours a day. The film was three weeks late on account of card tables. But theatre schedules don't wait. I had to begin rehearsals. For three weeks I played in the film at night and rehearsed in the theatre during the day. I came off the set at six in the morning, slept for three hours, and was at the theatre by ten o'clock. But I do not blame my debacle as Lady Macbeth on exhaustion. I just couldn't cope with the Scottish bitch. The play had a very short life. We knew we were a flop even before we opened. The day after the first performance, we began to rehearse a new play during the day. It was *La Dame de Trèfle* by Gabriel Arout. That was a hit, but it took time and all the perfumes of Arabia to expunge the memory of Lady Macbeth.

Exciting news in this spring of 1955. *Stella* was accepted in the Cannes Film Festival. We couldn't be more pleased. The Cannes Film Festival was at the height of its prestige. Marcel Pagnol was president of the jury. There were hundreds of press correspondents. True, the festival had some aspects of a fair, but it brought together the elite of the world cinema for a cultural exchange. It brought producers looking for talent, distributors to buy films. Some people look down their noses at these festivals. I do not, if for no other reason than that they bring attention to films that are made in small countries whose cinema is just beginning to develop. When we heard the film was enthusiastically received, that it got a fine press, we were thrilled. I was heartsick not to be there, but I was firmly ensconced in *La Dame de Trèfle*.

Then two telephone calls from Cannes. One from Cacoyannis, the other from Marcel Achard, who was vice-president of the jury. Cacoyannis says: "Melina, come to Cannes. I am sure you will win the first actress prize." Achard, sworn to secrecy as a jury member, is more discreet. He just says: "Melina I think you should be in Cannes." The best actress award in Cannes! In Greece that was equivalent to winning the Oscar.

It wasn't necessary for me to ask Helmis to let me go. He was under barrage from everyone. The first time that a Greek film was a triumph in Cannes! It was a national victory! It was as if Greece was sure to win a gold medal in the Olympics and Helmis stood in the way of the victor being crowned. It was all a little absurd, yet touching. Helmis had to yield.

He announced that the theatre would be closed for three days because "our Melina is going to Cannes." It was as if he were saying: "Marlborough s'en va-t-en guerre!" Rena, George Foundas, and I were on the airplane that same evening.

Dialogue between Rena and me on the night flight to Nice:

RENA The festival people are sending a limousine from Cannes to meet us at the airport.
ME I know.
RENA Excited?
ME I guess so.
RENA Don't "guess so" me. You're thrilled.
ME (*A giggle*)
RENA Do you think you'll win the prize?
ME Never.
RENA So why are we in this airplane?
ME Because I'm a bobby-soxer. I want to see the film stars.
RENA Don't say that as if it weren't true because it is true. I want to see the movie stars too.
ME (*A giggle*)
RENA I think you'll win.
ME Rena! Swear.
RENA Are you marvelous in the film? Yes. If Cacoyannis called you to come, doesn't that mean he knows? Yes. Would he let them close the theatre for three days? No. Did Marcel Achard tell you to come? Yes. Is he the vice-president of the jury? Yes. Is Marcel Pagnol president of the jury? Yes. Do presidents talk to vice-presidents? Yes. (*Pause*) You will win.

ME And if I don't?

RENA Don't say that.

ME If I don't, I'll die.

Cannes at Festival time. The first impression—automobiles. Thousands of slow-moving automobiles. You can't see the palm trees for the cars. When you do get a glimpse of a tree, it is hung with a movie poster. Half a mile of movie posters. The walks are crowded with people. They too move slowly, except for two or three runners who push and elbow in a panicky rush to get somewhere. Nobody minds being pushed. They seem to expect it. And all, men and women, are dressed in flowered designs. Flowered shirts, flowered skirts, flowered pants. Two jury members strolling on the Croisette and chatting, followed by a dozen eavesdroppers who walk as if they weren't there. Snatches of conversation:

"—can't win."

"—sure to win."

"—I've got to get to Valauris, there's"

"—I know, Picasso. Pots."

"—will make a fortune."

"—needs tighter cutting."

"—will never play in Spain."

"—get me an invitation or you're fired."

"—no use. The American audiences don't understand the English accent."

A sudden eruption of photographers, ten, twenty. They run, cameras in hand, others hung around their necks, clanking against their chests. Traffic stops. Motorists gape toward the beach. A film star? No. A very young girl, in her eyes dreams of stardom and fright. She strips off her blouse to reveal her bosom. The photographers click-click. Nearby the girl's mother nods her head in satisfaction.

The autograph hunters travel in packs. When our limousine pulled up at the entrance of the Carlton Hotel, they bowled over the doorman as they swooped down on the car. Is it possible they've all seen *Stella*? I compose myself. I get out of the car with smiling nonchalance. They look at me blankly. One of them asks "Who is she?" Another pushes out his lips and shrugs. They retreat in disappointment. Rena swears in Greek. "Just wait, you . . ."

The first evening we were invited to see a French film, but before that there was a reception given by the Russian delegation. Everyone who was anyone was there. I gawked at the celebrities. I nodded demurely to the members of the jury. Achard and Cacoyannis were unable to say much, but they communicated certain victory. I floated in *bonheur*. I partook of the vodka that flowed. In little time I lost what inhibitions I had and kind of became the life of the party. People were getting high. (Oh, those Russian toasts!) Every year the Cannes festival has at least one scandal. That party was the scandal of 1955. What it amounted to was that too many jury members had too much vodka. During the projection of the film, some of the jury were not in condition to judge anything. Two of that distinguished body fell asleep.

The next morning the newspapers had a ball. The fires were fed by a justly indignant director. He had submitted his film to the intense competition of a festival. He had every right to expect that his judges be clear-eyed and alert. His film had to pierce an alcoholic veil. I agreed with him, and yet—why, oh why is there something about me that is provocative to the French press? The newspapers implied, implied, my eye—they practically said that I was largely responsible for the scandal. It was I who had created the atmosphere that led everyone to drink. I wept: "Finished the prize. Everyone is against me. I'm an enemy, hired to sabotage the French film industry."

And Rena finds to say: "You are not an enemy agent. You are a catalytic agent, an enzyme."

"What?"

Hands flat at her sides, in a nasal schoolgirl chant: "An enzyme is an organic substance in animal and plant cells, that causes change in other substances by catalytic action."

"Rena, what are you talking about?"

"I don't know."

We laughed. Then we cried a little more. Then Rena tapped at her wrist watch. We rushed out of the hotel.

One of the constant wrangles in Cannes concerns the hour of the screenings before public and jury. Because of the large number of entries, some films have to be shown in the afternoon. Inevitably the producer's attitude is that his film has been degraded. *Stella* was shown in the afternoon. Michael was unhappy about that, but the enthusiastic press reports restored his spirits. People who had missed the film, and others who wanted to see it again, asked for another screening. Michael set it up in a small theatre in the Rue d'Antibes. He asked me and George Foundas to be present. I watched the film with interest. I was able to achieve a certain perspective. Three things struck me: Michael's imagination that triumphed over our limited means, Manos' music, and the performance of George Foundas, my co-star. I thought it was better than mine.

When the film ended, there was warm applause. People came up the aisles to congratulate us. But one man came jumping over the seats, leapfrogging the backs like a mountain goat. Michael said: "May I present you."

His eyes were very blue.

"Melina Mercouri, George Foundas, this is Jules Dassin."

Chapter Eleven

I remembered reading about Jules Dassin in 1948. In a review of a film he directed called *Naked City,* he was referred to as the father of neo-realism in American cinema. Perhaps it was the word father—in any case, smiling, agile, young, was not the way I had pictured him. Knowing that he was on the Hollywood blacklist, I'd have expected to find a man sad and bitter, with the mark and bearing of a victim. Nothing of the kind. This man who had been blocked in every effort to work for five years, was a gay, optimistic, dancing spirit. I shall never forget how much I laughed at an improvisation of his, in which he half played, half danced the manner in which Americans from different regions of the country paid court to a lady, each in his manner. It was hilariously funny. Yet what struck me most was the obvious affection he had for the American people. That this man should be branded an un-American was grotesque.

When we in Europe first heard of McCarthyism, we considered it a minor and temporary irritation, like a skin rash on the American body. We thought it would quickly and automatically dissolve, just as any normal healthy body rejects a petty virus. But by 1955 McCarthyism had become a malicious illness of epidemic proportions. It was incredible that this philistine, this obvious demagogue, could manage to intimidate an entire country, to create such an atmosphere of fear and, it must be said, to reduce so many men to cowardice. His technique was unvaried to the point of boredom—just to hurl the word "Communist" and to repeat it again, louder and louder. He attacked the universities, the government services, the trade unions, even the army. He smeared General George Marshall, even President Eisenhower. Europeans everywhere were embarrassed and revolted at the spectacle of an America gripped in fear by this vulgar Tartufe. The most frightened of the lot was Hollywood. When, in 1947, Hollywood was attacked as a Communist center, and the House Un-American Activities Committee decided that their films contained red propaganda, it got a belly laugh in Europe. But we didn't laugh very long. The American cinema groveled and collapsed. The studio heads, shamefully aided by the film trade unions, rushed to draw up a blacklist. Hundreds were purged, among them some of the most gifted men in American movies. The all-time low was reached when a genius, one of the men most responsible for the development of cinema into an art form, Charlie Chaplin, was blacklisted.

After three years of unemployment, Dassin was engaged by the French to make a film with their great comic star, Fernandel. But the blacklist arm was long enough to reach across the Atlantic. The French producers were told that a film directed by Dassin would never be released in the United States. The threat worked. Two days before shooting was to begin, Dassin was removed from the film. It caused a minor scandal in France. French film makers set up a howl of rage. "L'Affaire Dassin" was kept alive in the press for a long time. He was voted an honorary member of the French cinema unions. But he remained steadily unemployed. Then, in 1954, a producer turned up who refused to be intimidated and engaged him to write and direct a film. If the producer was courageous, he was also exceedingly prudent. The budget for the film was so low, it was almost invisible. But Dassin turned it into a great success. It was a film called *Rififi*. It was chosen to represent France at Cannes and Dassin was the *enfant chéri* of the festival.

He liked *Stella*. He said flattering things and invited us for drinks. We went to a sidewalk café. When photographers gathered around, a famous American screen star left so abruptly, he spilled his orange juice on the table. The photographers laughed. Dassin did too, but not out of enjoyment. The photographers told us that this had happened all through the festival. The Hollywood people were so intimidated, they were afraid to appear in a photograph with Dassin.

He made us a few more compliments and then got to the point. He was at work on a screenplay based on the Kazantzakis novel *Christ Recrucified* and thought that there would be parts for me and Foundas. Of course I didn't believe him. He said he would come to Greece as soon as he arranged for travel papers. I didn't quite understand that. I learned later that the Americans had taken away his passport. I gave him my hand and said that if ever he came to Greece, I would be his guide. He held onto my hand.

"Promise?"

"Promise."

On this we parted. Rena said: "That man is in love with you."

I told her she was ridiculous. She told me to wait and see. The encounter with the blue-eyed man was pleasant, but I had something else on my mind—my prize.

When the evening came for the awards, I realized that I had one serious rival, Betsy Blair, who gave a glowing performance in *Marty*. We met. She was a charming girl, frank and gay. She was one of the few Americans who were not afraid to be seen with Dassin. Also, I liked her for not hiding that she would hate me if I won the prize.

I did not win. Neither did Betsy.

No one understood why the jury, that year, decided to make no award for the best actress. To anyone's knowledge, that had never happened before. Perhaps it's my "French complex," but to this day, I think it had something to do with me. Rena said: "They are cowards. That jury knows you deserved the prize, but they don't want to give it to you, so they find the solution —no prize."

I tearfully told her to shut up, but deep down I felt there was something in what she said.

In Cannes, the ceremony of the awards is followed by a big midnight supper and ball. Present are all the celebrities, holders of political office down from Paris for the occasion, the jury, those who have won prizes and those who have lost. It's tough for the losers to attend the ball, but not to attend was to show bad grace. Betsy managed a smiling appearance, but I knew how she felt. I couldn't smile. I hid in a corner so no one would see my tears.

"Does the prize mean that much?"

It was the man with the blue eyes. I hated him. He could talk. He got his prize for the best direction. Who the hell was he to talk down at me?

"Does it really?"

I bawled. I bawled like a donkey.

"You're worth much more than that."

He kissed my cheek and went away.

The return flight was silent. In Athens a sad crowd waited outside the theatre, mourning my defeat as if I were the national football team defeated by foul play in a foreign country. The theatre season ended in June. I didn't have the heart for the usual summer tour. Pyros was stationed in Gibraltar. Before he left we had quarreled. This depressed me. I was still very much attached to Pyros. I was tired. Kind friends invited me to a month's cruise of the islands. The sun shone. The sea was blue. It was a lazy, healing time.

When I got back to Athens, I found two letters waiting for me, with French postmarks. I knew at once they were from Dassin. Indeed they were . . . both very short. The Kazantzakis project was making progress. He was considering me for the part of Katerina, the Mary Magdelena character in the novel. For the first time I took it seriously. Still it was too much to hope that he would give me the part. Then another letter. Was Foundas studying French, as he had promised, and if ever I came to Paris, would I let him know. They were strictly business letters, but warm. Rena repeated: "Wait and see."

As it happened, I was going to Paris, but only a stopover on the way to London. I had decided once and for all to learn English and to live in London for a while. I sent Dassin a telegram.

Rena and I checked into the Prince de Galles and without unpacking our bags, went to see a movie. When we returned to the hotel there was a message. Mr. Jules Dassin had telephoned. Why the hell was I so excited? Surely the hope of getting the part, no more. But there was Rena giving me what I called her sphinx look.

The next morning he telephoned again and arranged to come to the hotel at noon. At exactly twelve o'clock he was there. (Dassin is the most exasperatingly punctual man in the world.)

He didn't walk into the room. He danced in. He was wearing a worn duffle coat and scuffed shoes. He said hello to Rena with a pirouette, very Chaplin, very Chagall. For a while we talked about the film. Rena made an eclipse that was so gentle, we only realized it long after she'd gone. I am rather notorious for my appetite, but I forgot about lunch. So did he. We talked for hours. There were no polite preliminaries. The condition just simply existed that we had to make ourselves known to each other. I talked about my grandfather, Pyros, and other men. I tried to explain Pan. I talked about

Greece. And he talked to me about his friends, his boyhood in Harlem, about his wife and children.

At the door, he turned back: "Do you like to walk?"

I never walk if I can help it, but cheerfully: "I love to walk."

"Do you get up early, or late?"

I generally go to bed at five in the morning and wake up at noon, but: "Very early."

"Tomorrow morning?"

"Tomorrow morning."

Rena came back in a little while. "How did it go?"

At first I didn't answer.

"Melina, how did it go?"

"Rena, I'm in terrible trouble. That man is the man of my life."

When Dassin says morning, he means morning. At eight o'clock, more or less the middle of the night for me, the telephone: "Mr. Dassin is waiting in the lobby."

Somehow, I got myself awake and was downstairs in record time. When Dassin says walk, he means a forced march. I never had so much exercise in my life. There was surcease when he suggested a cup of coffee. I was never so happy to sit down. He was offering the sugar. He stopped, sugar bowl in mid air. His tone was apprehensive: "On what day were you born?"

"The eighteenth. The eighteenth of October."

He turned pale. "I knew it, I knew it!"

We added up the coincidences to a frightening total. Dassin was born on the eighteenth of December. His wife, the eighteenth of June. My grandfather was born on the eighteenth of October. The day before Dassin told me of another woman he loved—she was born on the eighteenth of October. His father was born on the eighteenth of December. We met in Cannes on May eighteenth. And many more eighteens.

At the entrance of the hotel, he bade me good-by. I was

leaving for London that evening. He took my hand. He looked at me and smiled. Then he said: "I'm hooked."

He said it in English. I didn't understand what it meant. In the airplane that night, I asked the English steward:

"What does it mean, I'm hooked?"

He explained it.

I didn't hear from him for months. But I drove Rena crazy by dragging her to a cinema on Curzon Street every night. By chance *Rififi* was showing there. Dassin played a small role in the film. I knew every shot in that picture, every word of dialogue by heart. Then he telephoned. He was ready to go to Greece and do research for the Kazantzakis film. He still had no passport. I had told him that when the time came, my father might help him get entry papers for Greece. My father was a deputy in the Greek parliament. He was also the country's delegate to the Council of Europe, in Strasbourg. I flew to Paris and arranged a meeting between Dassin and my father. They liked each other at once. Before the meeting was over, they were addressing each other as Stamatis and Julie. Stamatis agreed to help. We had a moment alone. We were both mute, then: "See you in Greece."

"In Greece."

My father arranged the travel papers. Dassin came with his art director, Alexander Trauner. They were there to find a village that could be adapted to be a village in Anatolia. I had promised to be the guide, and guide I was. It has always given me pleasure to show Greece to people who come for the first time. It is as if you too see it for the first time, but there's no greater joy than to show Greece to the man you love—especially when he falls in love with Greece. He and Trauner went out of their minds. They yelled, they danced, they shouted, and many times they went speechless. Julie—it was Julie now—from the moment he put foot in Greece, was in a constant state of emotion and excitement. He went wild over the bouzouki music, the Greek people, the Greek colors, the

110

Greek museums, the Greek blankets, the Greek donkeys. It would have been perfect except for the deep sadness that came when we saw the poverty in many of our Greek villages. On his first trip to Greece, this American acted as if the Greek people were his people. He has been constant in his devotion to the Greek people ever since. The time came for him to return to Paris, but not before I took him to Delphi. If I live to be a thousand, I'll never forget Delphi with Jules.

A letter from Paris. Problems had developed with the financing of the film. The producer was the same man for whom Julie made *Rififi*, but he had sudden misgivings about the commercial value of the Kazantzakis project. Not to worry, said Julie, he'd fight the whole movie industry to get the film made. Then seven long, unhappy months. I wanted to join him in Paris. He would not permit it. I told Pyros everything. He didn't quite believe me, but when I said that I would leave Greece if I could live anywhere else with Julie, Pyros understood.

Julie too was having a bad time. He was more hopeful about the film, but I had created a crisis in his life. He could not find the resolve to separate from his family. For seven months I didn't see him. There was occasional word about the film, no more. Then a telegram. The film was going to be made. Would I meet him in Antibes to visit Kazantzakis? Would I!

Nikos Kazantzakis vacillated among three influences: Buddha, Christ, and Lenin; and all three permeate his writing. He was a prodigious talent. He created a new language. He translated into this modern Greek, Dante, Goethe, and Nietzsche. I consider his epic poem *The Odyssey* one of the major works of our century. He lived in Antibes because he preferred living in exile to the ugliness of the political condition in Greece. For a time he tried to improve it. After the Nazi occupation he accepted the post of Minister without Portfolio. He earned enemies when he opposed the wave of arrests during the white terror. Finally, when he saw how the Greek army

111

was handed over to the control of the English commander, General Scobie, he resigned in disgust and left the country. His wife Helen writes in her book *The Dissident* that after that it became dangerous in Greece to pronounce her husband's name, that his editor was given a rough time by the Security Police because he published a play of his. In his writing and his being, Nikos Kazantzakis was a profoundly religious man. When I think that he was excommunicated by our Church, I don't know whether to laugh or cry.

Decidedly, Julie had an affinity for the Greeks. On the way to Antibes, I told him that I had caught up on all his old films during my seven-month quarantine. Why hadn't he told me that in two of his films, the protagonists were Greeks. Why hadn't he told me that in a third film, one of our most famous songs was heard?

"Mavri inai i nichta sta vouna."

For an answer, he sang the rest of the song to me. The taxi stopped at the modest little house of Nikos Kazantzakis. Just as we got out, a doctor was leaving the house. By chance Julie happened to know him; he was a doctor from Paris.

"What are you doing in Antibes, Doctor?"

"I return the question. You're visiting a dead man. I've never seen anyone in such an advanced state of leukemia stay on his feet. He tells me he has no time to die. He's got too much work to finish, and he swears he will not quit this world before he has seen China."

Almost coquettishly, Kazantzakis kept a handkerchief to his lips, otherwise he gave no sign of being ill. He was lean, fierce, hawklike. He exuded energy. I had looked forward to the meeting of these two men. I was sure it would make for an interesting exchange—but for the first five minutes there was embarrassing silence, punctuated by a few banalities. His wife served tea. I was surprised to find the men so timid with each other. Then Kazantzakis said: "This won't do."

He proceeded to tell a ribald anecdote that broke the ice.

From then on, they didn't stop talking. Books, poetry, religion, politics. In little time, he decided to adopt Julie as a Cretan. Most Cretan names end in a-k-i. From then on, all through a relationship that lasted for years, it was Dassinaki.

"It was you, Dassinaki, who wanted to make a film from my novel *Zorba the Greek*.

I hadn't known this either. I looked at Julie in surprise. Yes, he wanted very much to make the film, but he wanted the Russian actor Cherkassov to play Zorba. The money people said no.

"Melina, Dassinaki, shall we take a walk?"

The man who was supposed to be so ill was a walker equal to Dassin. I strained to keep up with them. They walked the entire circumference of the ramparts of Antibes. Kazantzakis talked about Greece with love and passion. I realized how difficult must be his exile, but he could not tolerate the Greeks who turned over their country to foreign control, to foreign money and who were developing foreign mannerisms. His speech was filled with imagery. Very poetic, and very Cretan. Cretans are all a bit larger than life. They challenge the Gods and stride mountain tops. Kazantzakis was aware of this, and warned Dassin that it would be a problem in the screen adaptation of *Christ Recrucified*. Then they talked at length about Dassin's approach to the screenplay.

Finally we got back to the house. I ached in all my limbs. Helen Kazantzakis had prepared a charming lunch. Nikos ate sparingly. Before we left, Julie said that we meant to shoot the film in Greece. Kazantzakis shook his head. The authorities would not permit a work of his to be shot in Greece. Julie insisted that he would fight it through.

"In that case, Dassinaki, you must try Crete. Perhaps they will not interfere with you there."

That was a masterpiece of understatement. Crete adored Kazantzakis. Just to speak his name was a passport into people's houses and hearts.

"You will come to Crete when we shoot."

"No, Dassinaki. I'll never go to Greece again."

"You must see Crete again."

I could see that Julie was thinking of what the doctor said.

"We'll see, Dassinaki. We'll see."

Nikos Kazantzakis died a few years later. But not before writing a number of towering works, and not before he had gone to China; but he never saw Greece again.

I signed my contract to play Katerina in *He Who Must Die*, the film title of *Christ Recrucified*. Julie said he would come to Athens shortly, and that from there we would go to Crete to look for locations. He told me he was going to bring his wife and children. I was sure he'd tell me that. But when he came to Athens, it was without his wife. She didn't come. Such hazards or decisions make the patterns of life. Julie and I have been together ever since. I had one thing left to do. I wrote a long letter to Pyros.

The producer was now worried about shooting in Greece. Also, the Yugoslavs had offered interesting conditions. They reached a compromise. Julie would scout locations in Yugoslavia and if there were problems in Greece, he would have them to fall back on. I went with him, determined to sabotage. I could not accept that Kazantzakis should be made elsewhere. Also, I believed that once a foreign company made a film in Greece, other productions would follow. Even Sabina agreed with me. Said she: "Honest cultural exchange, that is all right, and after all it's a work by Kazantzakis."

I've got to admit that Julie and Trauner found marvelous locations in Yugoslavia. Way up in the heights of Montenegro, they even found the remains of a Turkish village, which could be adapted to the needs of the story. But my subversion continued: "Yes, the locations are beautiful—but the faces. Where are the Greek faces?"

Julie grinned. He pointed.

"There, there, and there."

1. Melina and her grandfather Spiro, mayor of Athens for thirty
years.

2. A childhood portrait.

3. At the age of twelve.

4. With her first boy friend at the Acropolis, 1943.

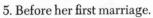
5. Before her first marriage.

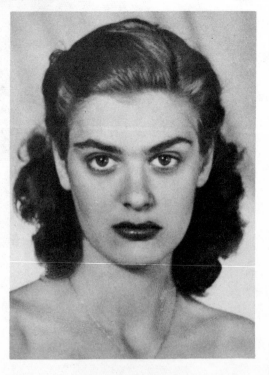

6. Melina at sixteen, the year of her marriage.

7. With her first husband, Pan Characopos.

8. Melina on the Paris stage in the '50s. (Courtesy of George Henri)

9. At the Cannes Film Festival, 1955: a hopeful candidate for the best actress award for her role in *Stella*. *(Courtesy of Pierre Mancet)*

10. With her present husband, Jules Dassin, on Crete.

11. Jules Dassin, Helen Kazantzakis, and Melina at the premier of *He Who Must Die* in Athens.

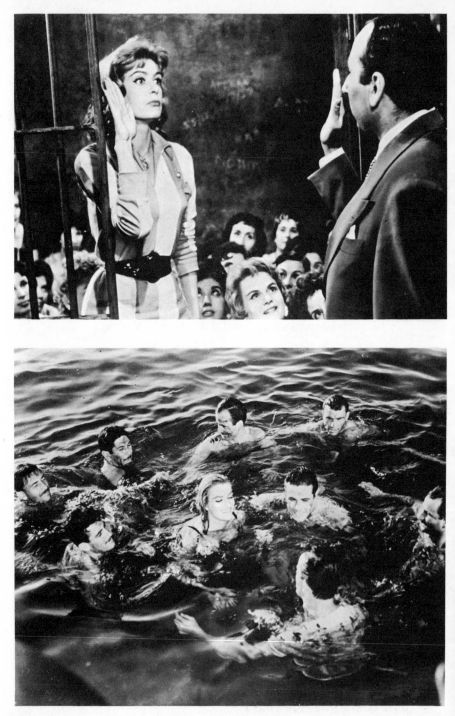

12.
13. } Scenes from *Never on Sunday* (*United Artists.*)

14. From *La Loi. (Courtesy of Roger Corbeau)*

15. Tony Perkins and Melina on Hydra for the filming of *Phaedra. (Courtesy of Constantine Manos)*

16. "Breaking up" with Anthony Perkins.
(Courtesy of Constantine Manos)

17. A scene from *Topkapi. (United Artists.)*

18. Melina with King Constantine before the coup.

19. The picture that caused a scandal: Melina sits while King Constantine stands.

20. Greeted by Queen Elizabeth after a command performance
of *The Victors*. (*London News Agency Photograph Ltd.*)

21. Enjoying Greek island life.

22. With Salvador Dali and James Mason.

20. Greeted by Queen Elizabeth after a command performance of *The Victors*. (*London News Agency Photograph Ltd.*)

21. Enjoying Greek island life.

22. With Salvador Dali and James Mason.

23. Melina with the children of Crete. *(Gian Colombo News Photo)*

24. August 26, 1967: awaiting King Constantine's arrival at the U.N. (The New York *Times*.)

25. September 11, 1967: Melina joins demonstrators near the White House while King Constantine lunches with President Johnson. (*Wide World Photos*.)

"They are not Greek faces. They are Yugoslav."

"True? Then why do you all take the position that Macedonia should not belong to Yugoslavia because the people there are really Greek?"

I shut up.

"But I'm on your side. Let's go to Crete."

We needed more than the physical setting. We needed a village where most of the people would act in the film. Not only extras; small parts as well. Each village insisted that theirs was where the film should be made. No one ever talked about the money that could be earned. It was a question of honor. Kazantzakis was truly idolized. We went from Heraklion to Chania. At each village a reception committee awaited us. Timetables were one thing, but to refuse coffee and refreshments in the mayor's office was an insult. Our schedules collapsed. Julie, in making his daily plan, now allotted two hours each day for coffee and speeches of greeting.

There was a village so small we decided not to stop there. No such thing. A mile outside the village, a reception committee was waiting to escort us into town—about twenty of them. We had only one car. It held the driver, me, Trauner, Julie, and a Cretan painter, Phanourakis, who had offered his help. There was no other way but for the car to crawl toward the village with the committee walking beside the car.

The village consisted of a few houses and a tiny white-walled café, but there was no escape. They had prepared lunch for us. They were exceedingly poor. There was bread, cheese, some nuts, and a bottle of wine. It was a luncheon not easily forgotten. There was a moment when we almost lost Dassin. Only men were present. Out of deference, they insisted on standing. The only man who sat with us was the mayor, and this because he was ninety years old. The village was inhabited by less than a hundred souls, but they had their mayor and they were very proud of him. We soon learned why. At first there were only formalities. I was studying the mayor. He was shabbily dressed, but he wore a jaunty checkered cap and an extraordinary pair of colored glasses. They were very fancy. The frames curved up into the shape of batwings, the kind of glasses worn in Miami Beach. I was busy wondering about how those glasses got to this village, when the mayor addressed Julie. He may have been ninety, but his voice was hearty and downright aggressive. "You're English."

"No. I am an American."

"It's the same thing."

This was said with a belittling tone. I should remind you that in 1956, the Cyprus issue had reached a boiling point. The Cretans had a special resentment toward the English. During the war, they risked and, in some cases, gave their lives to protect and hide English air force people sought by the Nazis. And now the British opposed the Cretan dream of reuniting all Greece. The Americans supported the English position. The mayor glared at Julie through his batwinged colored glasses. "Give us back Cyprus."

He pointed at Julie as if Cyprus were in his pocket. And Julie, thinking it was an amusing game, said: "No. I think I'll hold onto Cyprus."

No one else found it amusing. All smiles and good humor instantly disappeared. A heavy silence fell upon the room. Phanourakis kicked Julie's leg under the table.

"Don't fool around with that," he muttered, "give them back Cyprus."

The mayor leaned forward, challengingly, provokingly. Julie did not like being provoked. He shook his head. And the men began to close in around the table. Now I was really frightened.

"Don't be an idiot," I whispered to Julie in French. "Give them Cyprus."

Perhaps Julie would have conceded, but the mayor said: "You'll give it back, because Americans are cowards."

That did it. It now became a question of honor. Julie rose to his feet. He put on a face like John Foster Dulles. "I need Cyprus for military bases."

The mayor got to his feet. "We want Cyprus."

The men came closer. There was violence in the air. Julie was now a little pale, but he said: "There's only one way you can get Cyprus." He looked around the room. "Take it."

A long, long, tense pause. Phanourakis and Trauner prepared to leap to Julie's defense. All eyes turned to the mayor. Then, in a glorious moment, his face opened with laughter. He took Julie in his arms and kissed him. After that, all was beautiful. When we left, they covered us with flowers.

Built on a mountain slope above the plain of eastern Crete is the village of Kritsa. There we worked and lived for four happy months. It was a very poor village, but the people were kind and generous. They were proud that we had chosen their Kritsa. They took us to their hearts and we, cast, crew, technicians, became one with the people of the village. We were all suddenly richer by hundreds of friends. They all knew of Kazantzakis, but many of them couldn't read. Julie felt that they must be told the story and in detail. He wanted them to understand everything we were doing. It took us three nights, three nights that were so beautiful that every time Julie and I talk about it, we weep.

All day long the people of Kritsa worked in their fields and olive groves. In the evenings they gathered in the schoolyard and I told them the story from beginning to end. I have stood before many audiences, but none so rapt, none so intent on every word, none so completely giving. In the fading light of day, those marvelous faces. They laughed. They cried. They groaned in horror. They applauded the good priest in the story, they jeered at the evil priest. They cursed the Turkish Agha. They clapped with delight when he was outwitted. And after each evening session, discussions of the characters on the steps of the café. They'd have stayed all night and gone directly to their fields, had Julie permitted it.

Casting was not so easy. In the story there were the poor and the rich. The rich refused to give refuge in their village to the poor whose homes were destroyed by the Turks. The people of Kritsa didn't want to play the parts of the rich. They were evil; the devil take them. I explained to them that those who played the rich peasants had much more work in the film. They would earn more money. This moved them not at all. It was only when Julie told them that those parts had to be cast in order to bring the Kazantzakis book to life that they unhappily yielded. But when it came to playing the Turks, there was nothing doing. There they were obdurate, stone. The only way that Julie could fill the roles of the Turkish cavalrymen, was to go to an American military base, eighty miles from Kritsa, recruit young Texas cowboys on their week-end leave, and hide them behind massive Turkish mustaches.

Another problem. The clerical authorities, who found it wiser not to oppose the making of the film, expressed their hostility to Kazantzakis when we asked for permission to shoot in the village church. Their no was categorical. Julie, already pressed with budget problems, had to have a church set built. A last-minute complication had kept Trauner from working on the film. Max Douy, a very talented man, replaced him. His church was built in record time. The set was so true, so impressive, that the village people crossed themselves each time they passed by. They would come to Jean Servais, who played the good pope, and kiss his hand. The film was so real to them that they also kissed the hand of Fernand Ledoux, who played the evil pope, but grudgingly.

In the screenplay, the refugees set up camp on a mountain top named Sarakina. One early morning we went to fix the location of the camp site. We walked along the slope until Julie said wait a minute. He climbed the rocks with easy grace and soon was out of sight. We waited about a half hour. Then

118

he appeared, leaping down like a mountain goat, yelling with glee. He reached us, a little scratched, a little winded. He pointed up high. "That is Sarakina."

I reminded him that not all of us were acrobats and even if he could get the actors up there, what about the heavy movie equipment? One of the village people who was with us held up his hands to me, palms flat, and said: "Shh! Shh!"

It meant, that's our business. Four days later, the road to Sarakina was finished.

Every day's shooting was a joy. My role was not really large. I had comparatively few shooting days. But even when I didn't shoot, I rose at dawn with Julie and went with him. I refused to miss a single day. It was hard but happy work. Only two things happened to slow the shooting. The day we shot the largest crowd scene, there was the menace of a strike. Economically, the film was a windfall for Kritsa. It is sad but true that working only a few weeks for the film, they literally earned more than they normally made in a year. But there was a seventeen-year-old girl in the film who was more sophisticated than the others. When we arrived, she was explaining to all that this film would be shown the world over, that it was a commercial enterprise and that they should be paid more. The producer threatened to take the film elsewhere. There was a storm of protest and outcry, most of it directed against the young girl. She tried to answer. They shouted her down. Then Julie took up a microphone and got silence. He told the people that the girl had a right to be heard. He handed the girl the microphone. Her arguments were persuasive. She won them over. The producer had to unloosen the purse strings a bit. If that gentleman looked at Julie askance, the girl became a devoted friend.

And then there was the day the men of Kritsa decided to kill an actor whom I will call Otto X. Otto was a nice fellow but not as bright as one would wish, and he had a weakness for publicity. He was the kind of actor who carried photographs of himself in his pocket, ready to distribute to any oncomer. He had the notion to write an article on the shooting at Kritsa, and sent it to a newspaper abroad. And he pictured himself as a martyr to his art. The food was inedible, there was a shortage of water, the people were illiterate and savage.

Well, the newspaper story found its way back to Kritsa. A group of men appeared before Julie. They had the air of a vigilante posse.

"We want Otto."

"Why?"

"We want to kill him."

"Why?"

They explained. And dead serious: "Don't you think we have a right to kill him?"

Julie hesitated only a moment. "Of course. But I must ask you to wait until the film is finished."

"Do you promise to turn him over then?"

"Yes."

In the last days of the picture, we had to smuggle Otto out of Crete. Only because they loved Julie were they able to forgive him.

We have so many rich memories of *He Who Must Die*. Let me mention two of them. There was a beautiful little man we affectionately called Garbo. He was one of the oldest men in Kritsa, but exquisite in form and feature. In the film he played a small but important part. He was one of the refugees. He carries a sack on his shoulder. A little boy was to ask him: "What do you have in your sack, grandfather?"

And the old man was to answer: "The bones of my ancestors. On these bones we'll build our new village."

I taught him to speak the words in French, and brought him to Julie for rehearsal. Julie said: "Let me hear you say your lines in French."

The old man was not content to just speak the lines. He acted them. "The bones of my ancestors." His tone was proud

120

but cheerful. And with such warmth and optimism: "On these bones we'll build our new village."

It was a lesson in acting and a deeper insight into the Cretan character.

Later on in the film, the new village is being built. That same old man places the bones in a grave, then he refuses to come out of the grave and says: "Let me stay here. I'm too old to work. I'm too old to procreate. Let me stay here."

We were all grouped around the camera, watching the old man as he played the scene. It was extraordinary. He seemed to be embracing death. Shivers went up and down my back. Many of the crew wept. Julie took the old man in his arms and they held onto each other, laughing and crying.

I saw a miracle, and by incredible coincidence it was related to the need of a miracle in the film script. The protagonist in the novel is a young shepherd called Manolios. At one time the face and body of Manolios is covered with sores, and in a miraculous moment they disappear. In his discussions with Kazantzakis, Julie told him that this would need a photographic trickery that he preferred to avoid, and that he was looking for another way to dramatize the miracle. He told Kazantzakis a story about the time he was directing plays in a summer camp where workers came for their vacations. The camp could not pay professional actors, so Julie cast the plays with the people who worked in the camp: dining-room and kitchen workers, the office staff, and sometimes the guests of the camp. For one play, he went to a young waiter and asked him to accept a part. The young man turned red. It took time for him to say it was impossible because he spoke with a painful stutter. But Julie could find no one else to play the part. He came back to the young man. "You will play the part and you will not stutter."

Unknown to the young man, Julie had separate rehearsals with the rest of the cast. They were prepared to cover the young man if his stutter kept him from going on, or slowed him too much. The evening of the performance, everyone was terribly nervous. Before the curtain rose, Julie again said to the young man: "You will not stutter."

And Julie told Kazantzakis that the young man played the part well and not once did he stutter. Kazantzakis said: "Use it in the film."

And so the scene was written. Manolios, a shepherd, had to appear before a gathering of the entire village. This was the village from which a group of refugees were banished by the council on the pretext that they were diseased with cholera. Manolios learned that this was a lie. The village had to be told. The presence of all the people and the impediment, since birth, of a cruel stutter, made it impossible for him to speak. But his determination was so strong, the need so great, that finally he found speech and in a powerful, joyous cry, called out: "God has freed my tongue."

Pierre Vaneck played the scene beautifully. Yet Julie was concerned about whether the scene would be believed—until the day we saw the miracle.

We were shooting a sequence in which women were lamenting their men, killed by the Turks. The women of the village, dressed in black, were placed before the camera. Julie told them that there was no fixed text, that they could improvise in Greek. He took time and pains to create the atmosphere for the scene. The women responded. Softly they began to lament. Julie stepped away from them. He was about to wave the cameraman to begin shooting, when he saw, standing apart, a woman whose face was like a noble, tragic mask. He went to her and led her into the scene. The people of Kritsa tried to stop him. They explained that she couldn't speak, that she had been struck dumb thirty years ago by the death of her son. But Julie wanted that beautiful face in the scene, even if she didn't make a sound. He nodded to the cameraman. The women felt the scene. Their bodies began to rock, and slowly, a dirge arose. It was terribly impressive. Then suddenly the women began to scream. Some of them rushed away from the camera in fright. And we realized that the dumb woman was speaking, in great sorrow and in beautiful verse. She had regained her speech. She was lamenting her son, dead thirty years.

The film was finished. It was time to leave. Every single being in Kritsa came to see us off. The men. The women. The great-great-grandmothers and the newborn babies. They brought everyone gifts. Some olives in a handkerchief, a fig, a little honey, a small cheese, a flower. The actors, the French crew, were so moved there wasn't a dry eye among them. Then the Cretan gesture, the bigger than life adieu. The men gathered around our car, lifted it high above the ground, and singing, carried it to the road. Everyone followed, singing, waving good-by.

It became a shrine to Kazantzakis. People from all over Crete came to see it. It remained standing for years until finally it was worn away by the wind and the rain.

Chapter Twelve

Before Julie and I returned to Paris, we had three lovely days in Mykonos. On the boat back to the mainland, the radio announced the Anglo-French strike at Suez and the participation of Israeli forces. Julie was in a dreadful state. I asked him to talk to me about Israel. He was in deep conflict with himself. He was angry and unhappy about the conditions of the Arab refugees from Palestine. On the other hand, after the entire world permitted the Hitler genocide, he felt no one could deny the Jewish need for a state of its own. He told me some of the history of the Jewish people. I was embarrassed at my ignorance. I realized that if I were to stay with this man, I had to do a lot of studying. Julie helped me. He suggested books I should read. But *Das Kapital* was my own idea. When he saw me with it, Julie roared with laughter. I soon learned why. I never got through the first chapter.

In the spring of 1957 we were again in Cannes. *He Who Must Die* represented France in the festival. Once more I figured in a scandal, but this time even the most prejudiced had to admit that I was innocent. Jean Cocteau was president of the jury. As always the jury members were admonished not to express any opinions until the day of the awards. When the lights went up in the theatre after the screening of *He Who Must Die*, there was very generous applause. The photographers gathered around our box and were clicking away when Cocteau rushed up to us. He embraced me and Julie. The festival officials were shocked and the next day the press went to town. I did not pretend to be unhappy about this incident. Nor was I unhappy when, in apologizing, Cocteau explained that the emotion of the spectator overcame the discipline of the jury member. The happiest moment of the festival was our reunion with Kazantzakis. He seemed strong and was in very good spirits. We were delighted that he and Helen approved the film.

He Who Must Die won a slew of international prizes, almost unanimous praise from the world press, but was a commercial failure. The next few years were lean. We had very little money. Many days I was alone. Those were the days that Julie spent with his children. He has a son and two daughters. Joe was the eldest and more able to understand. He had been in Crete with us. He worked as assistant to Julie and played a small part in the film. If he was not openly antagonistic, he nevertheless kept me at arm's length. The two girls refused to meet me. It was not easy for me, but I agreed with Julie that it was a matter of time. I was very anxious to see them, and I used to spy on them from a taxi when they met Julie somewhere. Anna decided I needed looking after and came from Athens to take care of me. I told her that we had little money and might not be able to pay her regularly. She insulted me à la grecque. Rena was now living in London and came to see me when she could.

We were living in a small hotel. One day Rena came to take me to visit a Greek friend. But something went wrong and we returned to the hotel in about an hour. Julie gasped when he saw us. He had invited his youngest daughter to tea, assuring her that he would be alone. He didn't want her to think she was being trapped into meeting me. We rushed to leave—too

125

late. Little Julie (her name is Julie too) was knocking at the door. We didn't know what to do. I pointed to a clothes closet and in we went, Rena and I.

We heard big Julie say that they would go out for tea, but little Julie asked him to fix a nail in her shoe. Now Rena and I both suffer from claustrophobia. Getting into an airplane is a problem. We prefer to walk up ten flights of stairs rather than get into an elevator. The closet could barely hold the two of us. In a few minutes we were in trouble. I cursed Julie for tarrying. After a few more minutes, I had to choose between meeting little Julie and suffocation. I chose little Julie. We burst out of the closet, bathed in sweat and gasping for breath. Big Julie quickly explained the situation to his daughter and said: "This is Melina."

Little Julie was then about eleven years old. She stood up very straight and held out her hand. She walked toward me with the bearing of a princess. "How do you do."

I've been in love with her ever since.

The money problem was becoming aggravating. We were looking about for an even smaller hotel, when another American film director came to the rescue. He too was an exile.

A loving letter to Joseph Losey:

Dear Joe,

We were scraping the bottom of the barrel when you gave me the job in "The Gypsy and the Gentleman." Even before I came to England, I was disposed to like you. Julie told me all about you. I knew how you stood up to the Philistines and that they accorded you a distinguished place on their blacklist. I knew that you kept your head above water by making those low budget pictures in England and in Italy. I saw them. I saw how, out of spit and buttons, you made films of quality and personality. Now that all these years have passed, tell me, Joe, didn't I see regret in your eyes the moment I arrived in London? Weren't you sorry you had cast me? You told me that you believed in

"The Gypsy and the Gentleman." Did you really, Joe? Wasn't it true rather, that we were both making the film for the same reason? The need of a job? I knew I was giving a poor performance, but you never stopped trying. You taught me a great deal. I've worked with many directors since, but very few who had your gift for reaching and helping the actor. But I just couldn't make it. I couldn't connect with the character. And, poor Joe, it had to happen to you, that was the first time I worked in English. I had a mouth full of marbles. Well, that's all in the past, and we did fool some of the critics, didn't we? In any event, I've been a Losey fan ever since. You've done such good things. I particularly go for the films you made with Pinter. May your collaboration long continue.

Love,
Melina

Things were looking up. We were going to do a film in Italy. It was called *The Law*. It was based on a novel by Roger Vailland. I was so delighted with Julie's script that I didn't care that my role was small in comparison with the character of a fifteen-year-old girl. She was the leading character, and that was the way it had to be. I was happy. So was everyone else. We all felt we were going to make a wonderful film.

But five days before shooting began, Julie had a terrible row with the producer. The entire cast was in Rome, ready to go south on location. Julie had assembled a crack crew—and still not one contract had been signed. He was furious. All those people had gathered in Rome because he had assured them that all was in order, that he had verified that the financing was secured, and yet there they were, at that late date, without contracts. The producer said that all would be settled the following morning. Well, the following morning the producer told Julie that the money wasn't there any more and that everyone was to be sent away. That was the first time I realized that I was living with a man who could become very violent. The producer straightened his tie and brushed off his clothes. He said: "I'll have the money in one hour if you cast Gina Lollobrigida."

"In what part?"

"The fifteen-year-old."

"Gina Lollobrigida is at least twice fifteen."

"Rewrite the part."

"That means rewriting the script."

"Rewrite the script."

"In four days?"

"In four days."

"I promised the part to the new girl I found, Claudia Cardinale."

"Then there's no money."

We talked for hours that night. Julie felt that the thing to do was to chuck everything and go back to Paris. Yet he could not bring himself to tell all those people that there was no film, no jobs.

He rewrote the script in four days. We tried to persuade ourselves that the project was still valid.

In the tiny village of Rodi Garganico in southern Italy, I met Miss Lollobrigida. She disliked me on sight. I disliked her. I tried to be philosophical about the whole thing. Perhaps I'd been too lucky all my life. Perhaps it was too much to hope that the affection I felt for my fellow actors, and their friendship to me, was a condition that could go on forever. We disliked each other so intensely that we both considered it useless to make any pretense and did what we could to stay out of each other's way. It was not a happy time for Julie.

When the film was finished, we looked at the rough cut in the projection room. It bothered me that I found Lollobrigida's performance better than I thought it would be, and that I didn't like myself at all. But what was immediately clear was that it was not the picture Julie had set out to make.

First screenings of a film are always painful. It is a time that I call "judgment in the ice box" time. There is such a need to believe in the film. So much work and heartbreak goes into the making of a film, even a bad one, that its makers, professional as they are, judge it poorly. Julie did agree that it was not the film he had set out to make, but clutching at the needed straw, he said that perhaps this other film could work.

It didn't. Yet when I reflect on that period, I think about it with a good deal of warmth, because little Julie and her sister Ricky came to stay with us. Joe was there too. He played a small role in the film, and also acted as one of Julie's assistants. It was lovely to have the company of those three kids. They were bright, they were interesting, we laughed a good deal. And when Julie and Ricky came, they had this to say: "Since we decided to come and stay with you, we decided to love you."

Our hearts were made lighter by an interesting development. The United States Supreme Court ruled that it was illegal to deprive American citizens of their passports. Finally Julie could get from one country to another without rigmarole and acrobatics. Then a call from New York. United Artists, the young booming film company, asked Julie to come over and discuss a contract.

It should be said that a little earlier *He Who Must Die* had opened in New York. The press reviews were superlative and business was great—one of the few cities in the world where the film made impressive profits. And before that, *Rififi* had earned a fortune in the States. Yet Julie was hesitant. The major American companies had refused to distribute *He Who Must Die* in the States. It was true that they offered to distribute *Rififi*, but on one of two conditions. One, that Julie sign a declaration repenting of youthful indiscretions and stating he was duped into subversive associations. Failing this, to agree that his name be removed from the film as writer and director. Julie refused to play these ridiculous games, so both films were released by small distributors who did not belong to the association of the majors, which had unofficially, but effectively maintained the blacklist. Yet here was the call from United Artists.

"No catch?"

"No catch."

"No declarations of repentance?"

"None."

I was worried about Julie's going to the States. I was afraid that somehow he would stay there, far away from Greece. We were now living in Lausanne. When we worked, we operated from Paris. That permitted us to go to Greece quite often. But from the States? Yet I encouraged him to go. I pointed out to him that if he worked again for the Americans, it would be the beginning of the end of the blacklist.

New York. At first I hated it because it made men so small, but in little time I saw its beauty and its poetry. It was a homecoming for Julie. He had been away a long time. He introduced me to friends and family. There were happy and emotional reunions. I liked the theatre people. They were bright and aware—and so talented. We went to the theatre every night. I didn't see one bad performance. The New York theatre had fought off the blacklist; they refused to bow down to any pressures. This was not true of radio or television. They were terrified of McCarthy even though he was dead. He died the day of the showing of *He Who Must Die* in Cannes, but McCarthyism was still very much alive. As a matter of fact, when the United Artists people summoned us to California, it was not to Hollywood. It was decided that it would be more prudent to have the meeting in Palm Springs. They preferred that our presence be unknown until a deal was made and presented as a *fait accompli*.

I had never seen a desert before. The way to Palm Springs in California was breathtakingly beautiful. Even the enormous posters advertising beer and toothpaste could not conceal the wonder of it. We were set up in a luxurious villa, swimming pool and all. We were alone for five days. Sometimes we did our own cooking. It was great fun. I've got to admit that I adored the giant supermarket with miles of everything in colored packages. We pushed little carts that we filled to overflowing. I developed a passion for American corn on the cob. It was a lovely vacation.

My image of the Hollywood producer was somewhat shaken when I met the United Artists people. I found them extremely bright and progressive. The deal was made quickly. Julie was to write and direct four films. They even gave us some money to bind the deal. It couldn't have happened at a better time. But what pleased me most was that the films could be made in Europe. Julie was to submit whatever project he liked. If they agreed to the project, Julie would have complete freedom in its making, and he could shoot them wherever he pleased.

Now that the deal was made, we could visit Hollywood if we liked. Of course I was curious to see that place of legend, but also there was a screening of *He Who Must Die* for Hollywood celebrities, and the distributor asked us to please be present. When we reached Hollywood, Julie expressed some surprise that invitations to see his film were accepted. He was right. The morning of the screening, a few people phoned to say that they were struck by a flu bug. By evening it had reached epidemic proportions. Three Hollywood people did come: Richard Brooks, Gene Kelly, and Walter Wanger. They had no fear of flu bugs—or anything else.

The United Artists people gave Julie an office in Paris. We could now rent a pleasant furnished flat, and another Greek was added to the household. Anna was having pains in her legs. She needed help. Enter Angeliki. Greek, able, tiny but tough. Like Anna, she picked up languages with astonishing speed. There was an unspoken arrangement—Anna was to take care of me, Angeliki belonged to Julie. She has been with us ever since, to love us, to take care of us and to become the benevolent dictator of the house. We liked our flat, money

131

problems seemed behind us, the children visited often. Things were looking up, until someone sent us a copy of *Variety*. *Variety* is the most important trade newspaper of American cinema and theater. It is called the "bible of show business." The issue we received headlined American Legion displeasure at United Artists because they had been in discussion with Jules Dassin and—who else?—Charlie Chaplin. They again threatened that any films made by these un-American elements would be met with massive picket lines.

It may be unfair to say that these threats influenced United Artists' judgment of the projects Julie submitted. Yet we had to face the fact that one after another was being rejected. When they turned down suggestions to make *Sundays and Cybèle* and *The Longest Day* (both were made later with enormous success), Julie stopped submitting things.

Offers from French producers were scarce. Some only wanted Julie to make a rehash of *Rififi*. Others didn't like me. My "French complex" was again raising its ugly head. Julie said that was all in my imagination, and I replied that that was why I called it a complex. The complex remained even though, by this time, I had worked in French films, with other directors. In this matter, I had the better of a one-sided deal. Julie insisted that I must make films with other directors, but he did not like to make any without me. His point was that no relationship could survive long separations. If I made a film that called for me to go away, the usual work period for an actress was about ten weeks. But a writer-director gives about a year's work to a film. I was pleased to accept this argument, but I also had reasons of my own. I suffered terrible jealousy at the thought of his making a film without me. I don't like his working with other women. Director-actress relationships are by nature too intimate. But the truth is that I would be just as jealous if he were to make a film cast only with men. A director is someone who gives his entire being to a film. He works on it, broods on it, day and night. His heart is there, his mind is there, his love is there. He creates a private world that no one can really enter unless he's working in it. The idea that I could be shut out of Julie's world for a year has always frightened me.

At the moment, that was all academic. Neither of us had work. We outdid each other in pretending to be unworried. But we had time to read, to go to the theatre, and to enjoy the company of new friends. Our favorite was Françoise Sagan.

A friend is a friend is a friend is Françoise. She'll always be there for you. Her life is to give to her friends. She's straight as a die. It is not generally known that her pen can be dipped in acid. She once wrote a series of articles in opposition to the French venture in Algeria that was admirable in its anger. It was a joy to be with her. Françoise is someone with a special, quiet charm. She's bright as hell and very funny. Julie always says: "Françoise, you're the wittiest person on earth, when you can be heard."

For not only did she have a slight imperfection of speech, not only did she speak very quietly, not only did she chain smoke and talk with a cigarette in her mouth—but she also saved her funniest stories for nightclubs. She favored a club called Jimmy's, and in Jimmy's the music was loud. By experience I knew how to shut out the blare of an orchestra and listen to a conversation—not Julie. Nightclubs were not in his ken. He hated them. In a nightclub, this man, amusing, gay by nature, became a dreary, suffering companion. He used to go mad trying to listen to Françoise tell a funny story, her quiet voice filtered through a cigarette and making no concessions to rock music.

And so during this tough time we found solace in our friends, pleasure in the children, and then Mama came to visit. My mother had to rationalize. She liked Julie, but her daughter was living in sin. After all, we were both still married. Julie and Pan had met many times in Athens and in Lausanne.

They got along well as long as they didn't talk politics. Pan, being Pan, did not oppose my living with Julie, but he did ask me not to divorce. Julie's wife was not ready to divorce either.

It took a time for my mother to adjust to a changed Melina. Sin or no sin, there was a suggestion of domestic order in my life. She had never seen me in a frame of quiet evenings at home. She found that my speech habits had changed. I no longer pronounced the word "responsibility" as something boring. The word "honest" no longer inferred hypocrisy. I was careful about the use of a phrase like: "All of Athens says," because my partner in sin would say: "All of Athens—or just your circle of friends?" In short, I had accepted a small measure of discipline. This was new.

My mother was also worried about Julie's reputation as a dyed-in-the-wool Communist, and she would say so. Julie, knowing that my mother was a religious woman, would open his eyes wide with pretended shock: "But, Mamoushka, Communism is a Christian concept."

This would set off a chain of arguments that often left us limp with laughter. Julie developed a sinister technique in these arguments that drove Mamoushka out of her mind. He quoted the Bible. His game was to say something like: "Well then, you're in disagreement with St. John. St. John says . . ."

And Mamoushka would protest: "St. John never said any such thing."

And Julie would leap to open the Bible to chapter and verse. This would reduce her to exasperated silence. She was furious that he knew the Bible better than she did. She created a phrase that became a catch phrase in the house: "With your permission, I would like to think that—"

One Sunday morning at breakfast Mamoushka and Rena told us that they had seen a movie the night before. I asked them if they liked it. Mamoushka pointed at Julie: "Do we have his permission to like it?"

And then Rena said: "Julie, before we met you, we always knew whether we liked a film or not. Now we have to wonder if we are supposed to like it!"

Julie received this in silence. He put his hands to his mouth. Rena began to speak. I waved her to be quiet. I always loved to spy on Julie when he was writing a script. When an idea came, the same thing always happened. His hands would go to his mouth. He would keep them there until his eyes began to bulge. Then the hands would drop slowly and his face would take on a far away and absolutely idiotic expression. His eyes were bulging now. My mother wanted to say something. I cut her off, saying: "Quiet, he's pregnant."

Another few minutes of silence, then: "I have an idea for a movie. It's about a man who tries to make people think as he does."

He paused. I said: "Keep talking."

He continued. "He's a guy who can walk into the happiest environment and by the time he leaves, succeeds in making everyone miserable. He screws everything up. He—he meets a woman."

He looked up at me. "She's Greek."

I said: "And he's American."

Julie nodded. "That's right. He's an American. Wherever he goes, he tries to impose the American way of life. He's not a bad guy. He's just dangerously naïve. He's a boy scout. She . . . She's so happy, he can't stand it. He doesn't think she should be happy. Wait a minute."

I didn't have to wait. I knew we had our next picture and that it would be shot in Greece. We all yelled in delight when he said: "The story takes place in the Port of Piraeus."

Chapter Thirteen

We had no title. We referred to the story as *The Happy Whore*. When the film was finished, it was our dear friend Harry Kurnitz who baptized it *Never on Sunday*.

Julie had a construction: a beginning, a middle and an end, but wanted to write the script in Greece. He put nothing on paper. It had to come to life in Athens, in bouzouki tavernas in Piraeus and on the port. He was raring to go but there was the matter of financing to be resolved. We never considered that could be a problem because so little money was needed to make it. He went from one producer to another. Nothing. Nobody cared about *The Happy Whore*. We plotted. We drew up lists of rich people we knew and called on them. Nothing. We contacted Onassis. He was not interested. We got a nibble from one producer. He liked the idea of the whore but suggested cutting what he called the American crusader. From this Jules deducted that he was not making it clear that it was a comedy. He made the rounds again. Nothing. I went to Greece to look for money there. Julie went to England and Italy. Still nothing.

In Greece I received a phone call from Rena. She said Julie had told her something in confidence, but that she felt obliged to tell me about it. Abby Mann who had written the screen-play for the very successful *Judgment at Nuremberg* had turned producer. He was preparing a film for Ingrid Bergman and Burt Lancaster; he wanted Julie to direct it. He said that Ingrid Bergman was not intimidated by American Legions and that Lancaster, whom Julie had directed in one of his earliest successes, *Brute Force,* was ready to work for him again. Julie did not know whether he had the right to refuse and finally talked to Rena and asked her opinion. She urged me to call Julie and convince him to accept the offer. I thought hard and I did call Julie—but to tell him the contrary. I knew I risked being misunderstood, but I reminded him of his faith in *Never on Sunday,* our excitement when he got the idea; and that we had to see it through, that we had to stay together.

Then Julie thought of United Artists again. He went to see Charles Smadja who was the head of its European organiza-tion. Smadja liked the idea at once. He asked to read the script. Julie shook his head. There was no script. It had to be written in Greece. The conversation went as follows:

"If you have no script, what do you want me to finance?"

"The idea."

"I like the idea, but . . ."

"Why but? I've directed films that made millions. You've had films that lost millions. At the very worst all you can lose here is $120,000. You can't make a film for much less."

"That's true," said Smadja. "That's true. But . . . is there nothing on paper?"

"Nothing."

"What's her name?"

"Whose name?"

"The happy whore."

Julie had no name. In the next office at United Artists was Ilya Lopert. Julie said: "Ilya."

"That's a man's name."

"Illya. Two L's."

"Oh."

Pause.

"Do you know at least how the story begins?"

Julie had an inspiration. He plucked it out of the air. "Men are working on the docks of Piraeus. A girl comes running down a pier. She undresses as she goes. Stark naked, she dives into the water. In a matter of seconds every man on the docks leaps into the water to join her."

Smadja said: "I love it."

A few hours later, I received a telegram in Athens. "God bless Smadja. Clear the decks. We've got to be shooting in a month."

We took a top-floor flat in Dimocritou Street, on the slope of Mount Lycabetos. This was dormitory, restaurant, café, and club. There was a constant traffic of technicians, actors, musicians, accountants, well-wishers and family, all with the same worries and the same hopes. There was endless chatter, joking, the click of backgammon dice and the strumming of bouzoukis. I marveled that Julie could write in all that noise, but it was precisely the atmosphere he wanted. Sometimes he'd put down his pen, we'd dash to see something in Piraeus, then back into the noise, and the writing resumed. The script was finished in ten days. I proposed an evening's celebration. It was then that Julie told me the entire truth of his arrangement with Smadja. The only money we had was in the form of a partial loan. If United Artists liked the script, we'd get the rest. If not, Julie had to return the money with six per cent interest. I felt faint. We had already spent some of the money.

"What if he doesn't like it?"

"I think he will."

He phoned Smadja. He told him that summer was coming to an end. He didn't want to lose days for the script to be mailed and for Smadja to read. It would save precious time if he would come to Athens. The next day, Smadja was in

Athens and Julie was reading him the script. He was kind enough not to keep us in suspense. "Actually, it's for the New York office to decide, but I'll persuade them to give you the money. Go ahead. Do your picture."

Everyone had been toeing the mark. Smadja's go ahead was like the pistol crack that starts a foot race. A lawyer drew up papers in two hours. A businessman friend set up a producing company. My brother Spiros rushed to the ministries for permission to shoot in streets and public places. Julie flew down to Perema to get clearance to shoot in a ship repair yard. Pan got a bank to guarantee the completion of the film. Denny Vachliotti and I dashed to buy materials for costumes. Stephanos, machinist, electrician, driver, one man orchestra, ran to buy, borrow and steal props. My father, by miracle, got us a telephone and Mama brought samples of wallpaper for the sets. We were a family army. We were beautiful amateurs. We worked with love. Vassily Lambiris, the man who put his dowry into Stella, became our production manager. If our flat was home and office, Vassily's car was our sole means of locomotion in this pre-production period. He had an ancient Mercedes. It was a museum piece, but if you put gas in it, it still rolled. There were times it held more people than the famous Marx Brothers' stateroom. That was a valiant car. We named it Rocinante.

If any of this suggests panic, I'm giving a wrong impression. Julie's calm was lovely to behold. He knew exactly what he wanted. His volunteer army complemented American know-how with Greek speed. All of the casting was done in our house. I was delighted that George Foundas was chosen for the romantic lead.

Titos Wandis was an esteemed actor. He played major roles in the Kotopouli theatre and in a company of his own. Julie asked him to join the cast. Titos said he'd love to work in the film, but he had read the script carefully and the character Julie wanted him to play had not a single word to say.

139

Julie assured him that it didn't matter, that the role was important. Titos said: "If you say so, that's good enough for me."

Then Julie called on one of my closest friends, Despo. In almost every presentation of a Greek tragedy, Despo was the leader of the Greek chorus. Julie offered her a comedy part. Despo said: "I think you are making a mistake. I am a tragic actress. I have never played comedy."

"Perhaps I'm making a mistake, but I'd like you to play the part."

"What part?"

"A tart in Piraeus."

"Me?"

"You."

"Melina, he's crazy, your American."

"Like a fox," I answered.

"Should I play it?"

"Play it."

"I am a tart from Piraeus, God help us all."

We were all cast, except for the character of Homer Thrace, the American. We could find no one to play it. When Julie wrote the part, he had an image of a Jack Lemmon or a Henry Fonda. But they were so far beyond our reach, we couldn't even think of it. Julie checked and rechecked our budget. The most we could pay an actor for the role was six thousand dollars. You couldn't get Lemmon or Fonda to work for one day for that kind of money. Julie said: "How can you find an actor to work for nothing?"

I said: "I know someone who will work for nothing."

"Who?"

"You."

"Melina, you're out of your mind. Look at my face." Julie then tried for Van Johnson, but he couldn't pay him either. He heard there were some interesting actors in Rome. He flew there and returned empty-handed. In the end, Julie tremblingly agreed to play the part.

Remembrances take on a color, a quality of light. The souvenir of *Never on Sunday* is diffused in sunlight. Yet we had our share of shadow. To see a man beg for work is a painful experience. We saw it every day, at home, in a restaurant, in the street. By this time, I had found my political identity. I knew where I stood. I found Prime Minister Karamanlis too conservative, too prone to accept American controls. I was on the other side of the fence, but that didn't stop me from looking over the fence longingly and wishing "he was here." Despite the disagreement of friends, I thought he was honestly struggling to improve economic conditions in Greece. But progress was slow. There was the constant heartache of seeing thousands of young people leave Greece each year to look for work abroad.

Being without an office, we had no other place to interview extras but our own flat. Julie had kept the opening he improvised in Smadja's office. He put out a call for strong swimmers. Literally hundreds of men crowded into our living room. The most Julie could engage was twenty.

"There will be more work in other scenes. This scene calls for men to jump into the Bay of Piraeus. Will only the strongest swimmers raise their hands."

Every hand in the room shot up.

Julie pointed to a heavy-set, elderly man.

"Are you a strong swimmer?"

The man didn't deign to answer. He just pursed his lips and moved his hand in circles. In Greek that means: "I'm great."

Julie pointed to a round, jovial man.

"Are you?"

He answered: "Esther Williams."

A small, frail man, wearing glasses, had edged forward to tug at Julie's sleeve. Julie looked at him doubtfully. "The current in the bay is tricky."

The little man laughed. "I grew up in the islands. I swim with the dolphins."

I saw a quick bulge of Julie's eyes. On the spot, he invented the incident that got one of the biggest laughs in the film. "Melina, make a note. He'll take off his glasses, pocket them, jump into the bay, surface, put his glasses on again, and swim out of the shot."

When we came to shoot the scene, the little man was impeccable. He calmly took off his glasses, jumped, with easy timing put the glasses on again, swam a single stroke out of the shot and then proceeded to sink like a stone. He couldn't swim! Thank God, Yorgo was engaged as one of the extras. Yorgo, a man with massive shoulders was a powerful swimmer. He spent most of the day fishing "dolphins" out of the sea. They needed work so badly, they risked drowning in the Bay of Piraeus. Ay! The water was cold that day. When I hit the water, I wanted to cry out with the shock. But I had to be laughing and provocative. And laugh gaily I did, through chattering teeth. The scene didn't call for me to swim so close to Yorgo, but the scene is one thing, drowning is another.

Cast and crew stayed together for dinner that night. We had a marvelous time. We toasted the "Olympic swimmers," we drank rezina wine, we danced the Chasapico, and everybody loved everybody. The director loved the crew; the crew loved him; the actors loved their parts, and we were all crazy about Greece.

And I adored Illya. I loved her independence, her sense of friendship, her intense need for people to be happy. I loved her Sundays at home. We had done some research in Notaras Street, the red-light district of Piraeus. The girls received us graciously and in the most bourgeois manner. There was tea, little cakes, and polite conversation. They liked me. If I had become a symbol for outlaw women because I sang their sorrows in *Stella*, with Illya I became the mascot of the whores of the world. I received letters from everywhere thanking me for portraying their profession with dignity. Some years later we visited the famous Reeperbahn in Hamburg. That's the place where some enterprising genius dreamed up the idea of placing the girls in exhibition windows. One of the girls beckoned to me. She called me by name.

"Melina, I have a present for you."

She ducked out of sight and reappeared to give me a little paper Greek flag, a souvenir left by a Greek sailor. I still have that flag.

All films seem to have the moment when disaster strikes. With *Never on Sunday* there was a curious repetition of what had happened in *Stella*. Shooting came to a full stop after five days. This time it was not a question of funds lost at a gambling table. Yet it was related to a gamble. Julie was playing a scene where he climbed a ladder to reach a dock and came to me hand outstretched. He stopped dead, his arm hanging in the air. Something in his back was dislocated. He got through the scene, but I saw the pain in his eyes. I called a doctor. He was bedded down for three weeks in a mass of weights and pulleys. The crew sent a delegation to say that they would stay together and wait as long as they could without being paid. Julie hesitated a long time before he refused the offer, and I know why. The United Artists people will only find out now, if they read this book, that contrary to all business custom, the film was made without an insurance policy. Julie simply didn't have the money. It was a dangerous gamble, dangerous to our careers. Three weeks of inactivity and the payroll bit deep into our budget. Finally the good Dr. Zaoussis, understanding that despair was more serious than a dislocated back, allowed Julie to resume work, on condition that he wore a neck brace. Of course all of the crew addressed him as Mr. Von Stroheim.

The neck brace didn't stop him from giving me the hardest slap I ever received in my life. He had rescheduled the order of shooting so that his scenes could wait for the brace to be

143

removed. The first thing we did was the scene in which I sang Manos Hadjidakis' great song, *Never on Sunday*. If Julie was locked in by a brace, I was imprisoned by a playback. A playback is the invention of a man without a soul. If you have a song to sing in the movies, it is recorded before it is shot. On the shooting stage it is played back to you and while the camera turns, you sing with the playback. The synchronization must be perfect. When you hear the word love, you must sing the word love, and not be a split second too early or too late. If you are "out of synch" the camera shows your lips moving when they should not move. I had never sung to a playback before. I railed at Julie. I told him it was like working in a strait jacket. With grim patience he tried to make me understand that a playback assured good quality of sound, and did I expect him to put an orchestra on stage, and that without a playback, editing was difficult. All of this made no sense to me. We shot the scene again and again. I hated him every time he said: "Cut. It's out of synch."

"I am a Greek," I cried out. "I have to be free. You chain me to a tempo. You put me in handcuffs. You can take your American playback machine and . . ."

But with Teutonic insistence Von Stroheim ordered me to do it again and again. I was getting slightly hysterical, and to make me even more furious, my beloved Stephanos, our one-man orchestra, was on Julie's side. He called out to me in Greek argot: "He's right. That's the way it should be done." Teeth clenched, I shuddered and tried again.

"Cut. Not only are you out of synch, you're growling." That was it. I stormed out of the set, yelling: "I won't sing another note."

Stephanos moved to block my passage and push me back into the set. I saw red and slapped him hard in the face. The defender of the proletariat, neck brace and all, reached me in one bound. He roared: "Don't you dare," and he gave me such a whack, the whole stage began to swim. With the sound of the slap comes a scream from Anna. She lunged for Julie, nails out like a cat. Lambiris grabbed Anna. Anna kept screaming. Julie kept yelling. I began to wail. I don't know who laughed first, but we didn't stop for ten minutes. Then I kissed Stephanos. Anna kissed Julie. Julie kissed me and led me back into the scene with the playback. This time I got it right.

We looked at the first rough cut of the picture. Julie loved me and hated himself. I thought I was good but that Julie was better, and that the film had charm and point. As a Greek, I agreed only too well with Julie that American foreign policy inevitably led to support of regimes hated by its people. The parallel was made in the film with the relationship between No Face, the Greek super-pimp, and the American, Homer Thrace. Homer wants Illya to quit her way of life because he knows what's best for her. No Face wants her out because her independence might give ideas to the girls who work for him. They become inevitable allies. "Melina, in a week, I'll have the final cut, but the film will really come to life when it's scored."

It's astonishing but true that in today's cinema, it happens often that the composer makes his first contact with a film when he sees a finished product. He has had no part in its making or its planning. Julie had begun to work with Manos while he was writing the script. And what a team they were. It was a honeymoon. They are both improvisers, and it needed just a word or a look to set them off. One day they broke all records of improvisation. We were shooting a scene in a taverna. Julie said: "As background to this scene, I should have had people dancing a Chasapico. It would have made a nice exit for Illya if, for a moment, she joined the dancers."

The assistant director said: "Manos is on the recording stage. He's doing something for another film."

Julie went quickly to find him. "Manos, please take a minute to record something on the piano. Just beat out a rhythm so that I can have people dance. We'll add the music when the film is finished. Do it now. I'll be shooting the scene in an hour."

In an hour Manos came to the set. He brought not a "rhythm track"; he brought a Chasapico beautifully composed and recorded by the orchestra. It was to become a record that sold in the millions.

All the songs had already been done with the infernal playback system. But all the underscoring, the vital background music, was yet to be done.

Came the day of recording. The musicians were gathered and Manos wafted in. He's a man who weighs more than 200 pounds, but he moves lightly as a feather. Julie asked to see the conductor's score. Manos looked at him blankly. There was no conductor's score. Julie turned pale.

"You've had months to prepare."

"But I am prepared." He dug a few scraps of paper from his pocket and a cigarette box on which were scribbled a few notes and went to the piano. He called out to the drummer: "One-two, one-two, one-two-three."

The drummer took up the rhythm. Manos improvised a little motif. He didn't like it. He tried another. Julie was paler than ever. I took him by the arm and led him to a chair.

"Relax, darling, Manos is going to improvise the background score."

"Mon Dieu." That was Roger Dwyre, our cutter. "Imagine if we had a symphony orchestra that was paid to sit and wait while he improvised the score."

Roger was French, of Scottish descent. Both the pragmatist and the Cartesian were aghast. Julie, who was at this point counting pennies, nodded in dumb agreement. I took his hand.

"Julie, these musicians are the best in Greece. Each one is a virtuoso, but none of them can read music. Manos doesn't write for them. He plays for them."

Manos found a theme that pleased him. He turned to Julie. Julie smiled for the first time. Manos played the theme again.

Again. And again. Now the first bouzouki player had it in his ear. He played along. The guitarist kept beating out the rhythm. Then Manos played the harmony for the second bouzouki player. He picked it up at once, and in a matter of minutes the music for an entire scene was formed. Then another. There was such give and take between musicians and composer, such perfect rapport, such excitement was generated, that soon Julie leaped into the fray and it became a glorious day. We were sorry when it came to an end.

Smadja was the first to see the finished picture. We asked Harry Kurnitz and Julie's daughter Ricky to come along. I begged them to laugh out loud wherever they could, even to force things a bit, to influence Smadja. It was an unnecessary precaution. Smadja said: "I am very happy with this picture."

The key screening was for Arnold Picker, United Artists vice president, in from New York. Faithful Smadja came with Ilya Lopert. Also present was Arnold's wife, Ruth Picker. She is an attractive, charming woman, but she has a maddening habit. While watching a film, she knits! They watched the film in stony silence. Not one laugh, not one chuckle. The only sign of life—the clicking of the knitting needles from Ruth Defarge Picker. The film ended. More silence. I was contemplating the different methods of suicide when Arnold approached. He's a very tall man. He looked down at us with the expression of someone offering condolences for a bereavement. "I love it. It will make a lot of money."

Again the Cannes Film Festival. This time a film directed by an American representing Greece. "French complex" or no, I had to admit that everyone was very friendly. There was one man, very handsome, dashing mustaches, who pursued us wherever we went. His name was Eddy Barclay. He was a top music publisher from Paris. He had by some mysterious manner heard the music from the film and was determined to have the publishing rights for France. He was a bulldog in perseverance. Notes, flowers, invitations to dinner. Finally Julie was so impressed by his energy and enthusiasm, he persuaded United Artists to give him the rights. The moment Julie told him this, he said: "You'll hear Melina's song on the radio in a half hour."

Julie replied: "How? I'll have to make magnetic tapes for you."

Barclay said: "I already have them."

Julie said: "Impossible. When? How?"

Barclay grinned. "Never mind how. I'm a good man and I knew I'd get that music or die trying."

In exactly a half hour, we heard the song on the radio, already titled in French "Les Enfants du Pirée." They never stopped thereafter. Barclay, a diabolical organizer, promoted the song into a hit before the film was ever seen.

Of all the countries represented in Cannes, Greece was the only one not to make an official reception. I could find no one to tell us why—not even Helen Vlachos, who was then publishing Greece's leading newspapers and had come to join us in Cannes. The United Artists people were disappointed. These receptions got publicity and photos in the press. Julie asked them if they still believed in the film. They said yes. Then Julie said: "Then give me money. Lots of it. I want to bring a bouzouki orchestra from Athens, dancers, a decorator and six other people. We'll make our own reception. Nothing stiff, nothing formal. We're going to make a party such as Cannes has never seen."

The U.A. people said: "Go."

We telephoned my brother Spiros in Athens. "We want a great bouzouki orchestra, dancers, Mr. Moralis and six of the liveliest Greeks you can find in the tavernas. The screening of the film is in two days. That's all the time you've got."

Spiros said: "In two days, impossible, but they'll be there."

148

The screening went beautifully. There was laughter all through. The audience clapped its hands in rhythm to the music. The applause was so generous that I was caught up in it. I applauded too. Thank God, no one saw me.

And we did give a party. I'll speak modestly about the film, about my acting, about anything, but not about that party. It was fabulous. There were seven hundred people and every one of them went wild. Spiros delivered like a champion. The orchestra was sensational, the dancers without inhibition. Moralis had transformed the cold Ambassador Room into a Greek taverna. The "livelies" whom we named the "kefi makers" encouraged every one to sing and dance. A la grecque, they smashed glasses and plates. The guests took up the cue. The place was littered with broken glass, but it was that bouzouki sound that they had never heard before that made the people crazy. It didn't matter to them that they did not know the Greek dances. It was impossible for them to sit still. Mr. Favre Le-Bret, the organizer of the Cannes festival, stood open-mouthed, watching seven hundred people, black-tied, begowned, celebrities, dignitaries, diplomats, jumping up and down in time to the music on an ocean of broken glass. At daylight, the party was still going strong. The United Artists people were delighted. Stories and photos of that party appeared in the newspapers of the world. The film was launched with a bang.

I was in the bath when Julie told me: "You've won the best actress award."

I tried to dry my tears. I got soap in my eyes and tears in my soap. Dripping wet, I rushed to telephone my mother. Her reaction? "You see. That's the kind of daughter I made." That's my mama.

Chapter Fourteen

We were hot.

In cinema parlance, that meant everybody wanted us. Forgotten were the blacklists. We were darlings. What do you want to do? Here's the money. Anything you want to do—except, be careful, Melina's role should reflect *la joie de vivre*. *Never on Sunday* is a smash hit and has given her a golden image. It's money in the bank. Whatever you do, don't change that image. Melina must be laughing and gay—and, important, not too sophisticated. They didn't ask outright for a sequel to *Never on Sunday* except one man who came with radiant presence from Manhattan. "Kids, you'll make a fortune. I'm giving you the title for your next picture, *Illya Goes to New York*. All I have to do is tell you the opening shot. Get this. New York Harbor. Coming down the gangplank is Illya, carrying a bird cage. She waves. The camera pans over to see a half a dozen whores from Piraeus who follow her down on the gangplank. Get it?"

We got it, but we didn't want it. Light and arrogant, we went to the other extreme. We had made our Greek comedy; now we'll make a Greek tragedy. The idea came from Margarita Liberaki, Greek novelist and playwright. *Phaedra. Phae-*

dra, set in the twentieth century. There was some hesitation. Long discussions on the wisdom of transplanting and modernizing classical tragedy. Shakespeare and the ancient Greeks based their tragedies on kings or gods who came to naught, the theme of the mighty fallen. Who were the gods and kings of the twentieth century? Margarita's position was that a king was someone who had an empire. Today, big money built empires. General Motors, I.B.M. were empires. *Phaedra* could be set in the empires built by Greek shipowners.

Greek shipowners. I know many of them. To begin with, very few live in Greece. If you are a Greek shipowner, you operate out of London, New York, or Paris. Of course you maintain homes or apartments in the important capitals of the world. They are staffed twelve months a year. You can drop out of the sky in your private jet and be sure that your suits are pressed and your shirts laundered. No chic shipowner should be seen with a valise—you are allowed a brief case. Of course you visit Greece from time to time, especially in the summer. You load one of your yachts with dazzling foreign guests and you "do the islands." On these occasions you go all out in your Greekness. You keep the bordeaux and the burgundy for shipboard and drink retsina everywhere else. When you're listening to bouzouki music you snap your fingers louder than anyone can. You take off your jacket whenever you can. It looks democratic as hell. You are to the manner born and you know that the reason you're put on this earth is to amass great fortunes and to pay little or no taxes.

Don't get me wrong. I believe that for the most part, paying taxes is immoral. When you know that most of the money of a national budget goes to the manufacture of deadly weapons, to building and maintaining military bases all over the globe, to paying agents to go muck around in other countries, to prop up unsavory regimes—when you know all this, and help pay for it with your taxes, then you're not being a decent citizen yourself. But let's face it, most of us prefer to sell out our principles rather than go to jail. Periodically, we are pacified by international conferences. Much talk and little results. The quickest way to get disarmament is if John, and Jean, and Ivan refused to pay one penny's tax toward the purchase of bombs and missiles. But that cannot be the excuse of the shipowners. Even gang leader Papadopoulos would have to admit he has not reached the exalted stage of imperialist power. Greece is poor. It is undeveloped. We need schools and hospitals, and Greek billionaires avoid paying taxes by flying convenient flags of Liberia, Panama and Graustark.

But the shipowners have power. The power of kings. I even have to grudgingly concede that they have glamour. And in 1961 I hated them less than I do today. That is not to my credit, but it's true. In any event, for better or worse, we decided to do *Phaedra* and to make her the wife of a Greek shipowner. Now to find our Hippolytus.

The prophet without honor in his own country is a well-known phenomenon. Whereas, some people in the American cinema underestimate Anthony Perkins, in Europe he is adored. The night the script was finished, Julie and I went to the circus. A tall young man on the other side of the ring stood up and blew me a kiss. Julie said: "That's Tony Perkins. Do you know him?"

"No," I replied, "but he likes me."

He was in Paris, filming *Aimez-Vous Brahms*, based on Françoise Sagan's novel. I nudged Françoise to take me to lunch at the studio, and she introduced us. We loved each other at once, what the French called *coup de foudre*. I browbeat him into coming home to dinner. Before we finished soup, Julie decided that Tony would be our Hippolytus. He loved the part. Julie gave him his word as producer-director that he would have fresh milk every day. (Tony loved milk—well no one is perfect.) And shortly after, *Phaedra* began shooting in Hydra. Hydra is one of the most beautiful islands in Greece and we lived and worked in the most beautiful house in Hy-

dra. It's an old house. It was built by the famous Hydra Kape-
tanios. In the garden, there's a tiny chapel and a little family
cemetery where the old pirates are buried.

It is not a large house; perhaps six rooms in all. But everything is white, the ceilings, the walls, the floors are white. It
was simply furnished, but in rich, dark woods. And outside,
three levels of terraces with lovely trees and plants. The terraces are white, white, and below the sunlit sea. We had a
happy time making *Phaedra*. We loved Tony and we were
working in Greece with our old crew.

Before we left Greece, there was an adventure with a flesh
and blood shipowner, a certain Stavros Niarchos. Mr. Niarchos
owns a giant shipyard in Scaramanga near Athens. In *Phaedra*
we had a ship-launching scene. Our production made arrangements with the administration of the shipyard to shoot it there.
Agreements were drawn up and signed. As it happened, there
was a boat that was in repair on a floating dock. It served the
purpose. There were a few gaping holes in the sides, but we
covered them with colored streamers and ribbons.

It is rare that a film goes off without problem or hitch. But
there seems to be a law that when you get into a jam, it's got
to be on the day when you have the most actors, the most
extras, and your costliest set. Accidents just don't happen in
inexpensive scenes. The morning went well. We made a number of shots of brass bands, marches, and our fictive shipowner
going through a crowd of handsomely dressed guests distrib-
uting gifts. Then we went to lunch.

We had risen from the lunch tables and were about to return to work, when the man in charge appeared. Let me, with
justification, call him Mr. Flunkey. He came to our table and
without any preface announced that there would be no more
shooting and that everyone was to leave the premises at once.

"Why?"

"A phone call from Paris. Orders of Mr. Niarchos."

153

Julie turned pale. His voice got very low. "Give me his number. I'll phone him myself."

"I don't know his number."

"That's impossible."

"He can't be reached. He's somewhere at sea."

"You just said Paris."

"I did not."

Julie turned, and in a loud voice: "Everybody back to the boat."

And to the flunkey, quietly: "The production has invested a lot of money in this scene. We have signed agreements."

He took me by the arm. "Let's go."

Mr. Flunkey stopped us. "It's useless. We also have orders to put the boat to sea at once."

Julie laughed. "With holes in it? That would be a neat trick. Now, please, you're in our way."

Mr. Flunkey called after us: "The police will put you out."

Julie grinned in such a way, I fell in love with him all over again. He pointed a finger to Mr. Flunkey. "That will be fun."

Just as we reached the boat, a voice was heard from a loud speaker: "If you don't remove your cameras in a half a minute, they will be submerged with the dock."

The shouts of protest from actors and crew were cut short when Julie sprinted down to the dock and took his place beside the cameras.

"Go ahead."

And believe it or not, the bastards began to float the dock. The water covered Julie's ankles when Nicos, blond giant electrician called out: "Ellate pedia."

In Greek that means, let's go, kids—and they did. The whole crew dashed down to stand beside Julie. Raf Vallone, who was playing the shipowner in the film, got there before they did. Now all the men, actors and crew and extras, were in the water. And that dock kept sinking. The women gathered around me and looked at me questioningly. I looked at my beautiful chiffon costume. The women looked at theirs. We all looked to the dock. The water was knee deep and the men had lifted the cameras to their shoulders. I said: "The hell with the costumes, let's go."

We flew down to the dock and joined the men. Now it became great fun. There was shouting, squealing and singing. If Niarchos' poor ancestors could have heard the Greek invective hurled at them and their progeny, they'd have spun in their graves. I, now budget-conscious, lifted my skirts high and ordered all the women to do the same. We shamelessly held them above our waists. Then Tony Perkins came loping down with a Kodak in his hand. "Make photographs. Get the holes in the boat. It will be proof that they're phonies."

Julie yelled, "That's right. Where's Corbeau? Corbeau!"

Corbeau was our still photographer. And there he was, slowly splashing in the water, looking for his tripod. Julie went to him and shouted in his ear: "Never mind the tripod. Hold the camera in your hand."

And in the midst of that pandemonium, Corbeau, bald head held high in dignity, said: "Mr. Dassin, I am a professional. To make acceptable pictures with all this movement, I need my tripod."

But by the time the whole thing was over, Corbeau and Tony had shot two rolls of film. With those pictures, the shipyard could never use the excuse that the boat had to be put to sea. They stopped submerging the dock shortly after the women entered the fray. Now it began to slowly rise. Precautions or not, our costumes were ruined. We marched out proudly, but we were a pretty bedraggled lot. Julie told everybody to go home, that they would be telephoned. But there was Mr. Flunkey again, to say: "No one will leave the shipyard until we have those photos."

I had anticipated this. Before we left the water, I had taken the two rolls of film from Tony and Corbeau and hidden them.

Don't ask me where. If a woman wants to hide things, she has ways.

"I want those photographs."

"What photographs, Mr. Flunkey?"

"The photographs you're hiding."

And that's when I broke up, because Julie, forgetting he was soaking wet and looking slightly ridiculous, said in the tones of a Victorian John Barrymore: "Sir, I have nothing to hide but my contempt for you."

I couldn't stop laughing, even when Julie lifted his hand to Mr. Flunkey and the police menaced Julie and the crew menaced the police. "I have nothing to hide but my contempt" became a phrase that stuck. We have since used it on hundreds of occasions. If ever Julie and I quarrel and it goes a little too far, one of us remembers to say, "I have nothing to hide," and that ends the quarrel.

More police came. They said we would not be permitted to leave! I asked by what authority we were detained, and we were informed that Mr. Niarchos' shipyard was considered a naval base. That was news to every Greek present. I asked them to declare that we were prisoners of the navy or the government. All they would say was that we would not leave until we had surrendered the photos.

"No sirs," said we.

"Then you stay," said they.

Stalemate. In the hours that passed we made all kinds of speculations. Why was the shooting ordered stopped? Then some of the crew came to tell us that they had talked with shipyard workers. These workers asked them if it were true that our script was such a vicious attack against the Greek royal family! We were speechless. There was no mention of, or reference to the royal family in our script. It was getting dark by now, and I was getting very hungry. I managed to steal off to a small office where I found a telephone. I called my father. A few hours later, he appeared with a lawyer. They went into conference with Mr. Flunkey and associates. When they returned, the police told us we could leave. We left, and the photos went with us.

The following morning, our apartment was crowded with reporters and photographers from local and foreign press. We were not there to receive them. Julie and I had been summoned by the Minister of Commerce. It was with him that we made all arrangements for the filming in Greece. We left word that we would be back shortly. We knew that by the time we returned, the photos would be developed and we would have interesting things to show, and that if the Minister withdrew his support from the film, we would have interesting things to say.

The Minister, in our presence, spoke into the telephone. "You can tell everyone in Scaramanga that I will side with Mr. Dassin." He hung up. "You will go back to the shipyard and finish your shooting, but . . ." He hesitated: ". . . there is the question of the photos."

Julie said: "I will not give them up."

The Minister smiled. "I didn't think you would, but if you give me your word they won't be published, that would be good enough."

"Is that the condition to going back to Scaramanga?"

"No. I began by telling you you'd go back to shoot. But if you publish the photos, there'd be a little war. It would take time to win. Do you have much more filming in Greece?"

"Not very much. We begin to shoot interiors in Paris next week."

"Would a delay be costly?"

"Very. We're already paying the studio. A crew has been engaged."

"Well, you're the producer. It's for you to decide."

Julie was grinding his teeth. The citizen in him was in conflict with the producer. I understood his conflict, and sympathized, but when he opened his mouth and shut it again, and his head began to bob up and down, I felt a laugh rising in me. He felt it too and gave me such a dirty look, it stopped dead in its tracks. Then with self-hatred, he said: "We've got to get to Paris."

Two days later, we finished shooting in Scaramanga. The same boat was there, of course. The workers at Scaramanga treated Julie as if he were a hero, but he was ashamed. He had sold out to the producer.

Phaedra had a strange career. It did well in the Catholic countries and poorly in the Protestant countries. Why Catholics are more tolerant of the idea that a woman can go crazy with desire for her son-in-law, I have not been able to analyze. Our judgment of the film was that we had failed. It was an honest attempt, but finally it became more a bourgeois drama than a tragedy.

United Artists tried hard to make the film a success. They spent a great deal of money to send me on a publicity tour through the United States and Europe. They dressed me in splendid clothes and hats. I was elegant as all get out. It impressed no one. On the contrary, they didn't like me that way at all. At one stop in Sweden, I pulled off my Dior hat and my hair fell in disorder over my face. The audience applauded. I got the message. They wanted the *Never on Sunday* girl. It depressed me to think that the man who proposed *Illya Goes to New York* was not quite such a fool after all.

The tour was exhausting. I dreamed of a long stay in Lausanne. To rest, to read, to go to the movies, to take an occasional stroll in the lovely streets of the old city. But first there was a commitment to Carl Foreman to act in *The Victors*. I couldn't understand my listlessness and depression. I was losing weight. For the first time in my life, I was without energy. I'm afraid I gave Carl Foreman a bad time. I knew what he wanted from me. He was very articulate, but I couldn't function.

I understood why, when friend and doctor, Lester Lipsitch frowned at an X-ray of my lungs. He ordered me to bed for three months. It didn't matter to me that Dr. Lipsitch swore by all that was holy that it was trivial. It didn't console me that Rena and my mother came to stay with us and never left my side. I had never been ill a day in my life. Bed was a prison; illness a defeat. It embarrassed me, it humiliated me. I was perfectly hateful in my behavior with everyone around me. God forgive me for the way I taxed Julie's patience.

It was after the second month, when I felt myself getting stronger, that I stopped behaving like a hyena. I played cards with Rena and Anna. I began to read. I began to reflect. Who was it who said it would be good for a man if, from time to time, he would break his leg, that it would give him time to think?

I thought a great deal of Pyros. My beloved Pyros had died a few years before. He had succumbed to a heart attack. My grief was the grief I felt when my grandfather died. I was inconsolable. The only relief I could find was remembering that Julie and Pyros had become friends. It was Julie who told me that Pyros was dead. He had received a phone call from Athens. We were in Paris at the time. I was in bed, resting. Julie and Anna came into the room. I saw that they were shaken. Julie gave me a sedative. It was strange. I took it without questioning. I knew he had terrible news. I just put myself in his hands. Then he told me. At first I didn't cry. My first instinct was to get dressed. Julie told me that the last scheduled flight for Athens had already left. He was trying to find a charter plane but the weather was bad. Pyros was truly one of Athens' most adored people. Countless thousands followed him to his grave. When our plane finally arrived, the funeral was over. I went to the cemetery with Julie and my brother Spiros.

I also found myself thinking a good deal of my father, and how odd it was that our relationship had really become strong since I'd been with Julie. He was still D'Artagnan, so strikingly handsome, so young in body, so seemingly insouciant and yet all his time, all his effort given to making Greece a better place. I thought of Nea, his wife. What a good marriage they had, what good friends they were. And for the first time, I really thought of marriage with Julie. He was going to be free; his wife had finally agreed to a divorce. Julie and I had been together for seven years and even if we didn't marry, it was time to ask Pan for a divorce. There was now a firm friendship between me and Julie's children. I loved each one of them and was happy in their company. They knew I was not thinking of having a child with Julie. I had told them this a long time ago when they might have thought that if I gave Julie a child, it would change their positions. So I believed they were absolutely sincere when they said: "You are so good together—why risk making it different by getting married?"

But most of the time I thought about Greece. I tried to analyze what was at the heart of my love for that country. My being born there? Its beauty? My childhood? My grandfather? My friends? I was being called a "professional Greek" and didn't mind it at all. I had, by this time, accepted work as a sort of unofficial ambassador for the Greek tourist bureau. I was quite simply a salesman going from country to country, telling people they hadn't lived until they saw Greece. It was work, a chore, but I was happy to do it. The film *Never on Sunday* was an international success, it gave me a name, it was nominated for five Oscars, but the deepest satisfaction was that it stimulated hundreds of thousands of people to visit Greece. What is this thing called love of country? Normally, words like patriot, patriotism, national flag, national anthem make me uncomfortable. They are concepts I do not trust. Yet all things Greek move me. I am thrilled by the Greek flag and the national anthem can make me cry.

Julie was working on a project of a film whose protagonist was to be Socrates. We read a great deal on the Age of Pericles. It did not take long for me to see that Pericles was far from the perfect democrat. There could be no doubt of the contributions he made, but the film would also show the aspects of a ruthless imperialist. I wondered if Greece would allow such a film to be made. Julie laughed and said such censorship would be contrary to the concept of Periclean democracy, that Pericles could sack and burn foreign villages but still permit Aristophanes. Poor Greece, it created the idea of democracy and never got to live it. Was it always doomed to fail, or can we say of democracy what Bernard Shaw said of Christianity when he suggested that nobody could say Christianity was a failure because it had never been tried?

Oh, I had lighter thoughts too, on that bed of convalescence: career, parts I would like to play, dresses I would buy, but always I would return to thinking of Greece. What I did learn was that I could be thrilled by the Greek flag, because for so many centuries we lived under foreign flags, and that I could cry on hearing our national anthem because it sings of *elefteria*–freedom.

Julie, as a film maker, is slightly schizophrenic. He believes that films are valid when they teach, when they uplift, when they protest. At the same time, he loves to hear an audience laugh. He enjoys making films whose sole purpose is to entertain, but then later gets embarrassed about it. This doesn't sit well with me at all. We've even had sharp words about it, and I made long speeches about entertainment being a social contribution. Nevertheless, this was his attitude when we went to Constantinople (all right, Istanbul) to make a film called *Topkapi*. I let him think that I believed he was doing it to earn some money. (United Artists were not too eager to do *Phaedra*, so we agreed to do it for little money. If it were to succeed, then we'd have a share of the profits. Alas, the profits were small.) But poverty was not at our door. Once the film

161

began, I told Julie what I really thought—that he was doing it because it amused him. He stubbornly denied it and still does today, despite the fact that the film was successful. The truth was that it was I who for the first time did not enjoy making a film. Despite the doctor's declaration that I was completely healed, I was nervous and not too enamored of the role I was playing. It got me the Donatello prize in Italy later. I've always wondered why. But I was fascinated by Istanbul-Constantinople, and once again learned the basic emptiness of national enmities. From our early youth we Greeks are taught that the enemy is the Bulgarian and the Turk. What dangerous nonsense. In Istanbul I saw Greeks and Turks live together well. I saw that they could be friends. I saw the same thing in Cyprus. I was in Nicosia when the city was divided, when there were barriers and check points. Julie and I ignored the barriers. We went from one side to another. On numerous occasions, Greeks gave us messages for Turkish friends or a little gift to deliver, and the same thing happened on the Turkish side. Greeks and Turks would live together in peace if politicians didn't find it useful to keep animosities alive.

I was crazy about making movies. I loved it as an art form and I loved the atmosphere of a studio stage or an exterior location. By 1966 I had made a respectable number of films. I had worked with a variety of fine directors, among them Losey, De Sica, Claude Autant-Lara, Bardem, and Ronald Neame. But I had started late and during my illness I realized that time was running out. The cinema wants young people. I didn't see myself clinging to the cinema till the last possible moment. I wanted a graceful exit. I felt that ever since I played Alexandra Del Lago in Mario Ploritis' brilliant adaptation of Tennessee Williams' *Sweet Bird of Youth*. Alexandra Del Lago was an aging movie star who becomes terrified of the camera and for whom a close-up becomes a nightmare. I didn't want to reach that stage and I was happy in the idea that in six or seven years, I would bid adieu to the cinema and build a theatre of my own in Athens.

I had kept a foot in the theatre. It had given me satisfaction to do a play in Paris, directed by Julie, and to receive unqualified praise from the French critics; and it was a joy to do *Sweet Bird of Youth* with Koun in Athens. I have an affinity with the women written by Tennessee Williams. The play had a tremendous success. Any bitterness that might have remained, when I remembered the cruel reception of my début in Athens, was erased when an entire delegation of young people came to see me backstage.

"Don't leave us, Melina. You belong to Greece."

And I was amused, yet touched, by a story that my uncle Pyros Lappas told me. He was an admiral in the navy. He was host to a group of American naval officers who had come to Athens for the first time.

"I guess the first thing you'll want to see is the Acropolis."

"We want to see the Acropolis, but first, we want to see the house of Illya in Piraeus."

And I was happy that Greece had adopted Julie. Even the ministries and the businessmen appreciated him because he had pioneered the way for foreign companies to make many films in Greece and spend many millions of dollars in our country. And the leap forward in tourism began with *Never on Sunday*. But what really warmed my heart was that he was loved by the Greek people. Wherever we went, he was greeted by his first name. Greeks find it difficult to pronounce the name Jules, so taxi drivers, waiters, passers by in the streets called out: "Hello, Zyl." Once, at a football game, thousands of people in the stadium waved to him and chanted his name Zyl–Zyl.

There were times when the affection of the people became a little trying. We were leaving the Hilton Hotel one day, when we saw thousands of people marching toward the British embassy to demonstrate for the independence of Cyprus. The leaders of the march saw us and the cry of "Melina–Zyl" went up. They crossed the street and came toward us, and the whole parade followed. Julie is one of those idiotic people who has no physical fear, but the one thing that frightens him is large crowds. I remembered the time we had gone to the dressing rooms of a stadium to congratulate a victorious Piraeus football team. When we came out, people came running toward me to ask for autographs. Julie shouted to me, telling me to refuse, that if I stopped, a crowd would gather around us, but I didn't obey and began to sign autographs. In a matter of seconds I couldn't breathe. The crowd became bigger and bigger, all pushing toward us. I became panicky. I truly thought we'd be crushed to death. Julie understood my panic when I began to laugh hysterically. He began flailing with his fists to open a passage. Those who were closest to us realized what was happening. They formed a protective wedge; then they pushed their way forward by inches. It seemed an eternity before we were free.

And so, when Julie saw those marchers coming toward us, he took my hand and we raced toward a taxi. They were quicker than we were, only this time they didn't close around us. Before we knew what was happening, or could do anything about it, we were lifted onto shoulders and the chant began: "Free Cyprus—Melina and Zyl are with us." The British embassy is just across the road from the Hilton Hotel, and with Melina and Zyl on their shoulders, they continued on their way. This time my laughter was not hysterical. I'll never forget Julie, in that surging mass, trying to pull down my skirts which had gone awry.

Much had changed in Greece. The Karamanlis regime, weakened by the Lambrakis assassination and conflicts with the royal family, was no longer in power. Karamanlis had chosen self-exile in France. He was succeeded by George Papandreou, whose centrist party now had the clear majority. Greece was moving toward reform and liberalization, but

Papandreou made many compromises. He had accepted as members of his cabinet people whose first allegiance was to the royal family. This was to lead to his undoing. The rich and the American embassy might have worked out a *modus vivendi* with George Papandreou, but they were rabidly hostile to his son, Andreas.

Andreas Papandreou had achieved reputation and prestige as a leading American economist. He was a young man when Metaxas, not to be outdone by Hitler and Mussolini, became the dictator of Greece. Europe was becoming less and less attractive. Andreas worked in the underground resistance movement until he reached the point where he could no longer stomach life under a dictatorship and managed to get to the United States. It is likely that a savage beating by Metaxas toughs influenced his decision. The night they dragged him to a prison cell and broke his jaw must have made the idea of America more appealing to him. In time, he became an American citizen, and by 1956 he was head of the economics department of one of America's largest universities, the University of California at Berkeley. He published a number of major economic works and was one of the fair haired young men of American academic life, but chucked it all to go back to live and work in Greece.

There exists a false impression that Andreas Papandreou returned to Greece when his father came to power. The fact is that he returned in 1961 when Karamanlis was Prime Minister. Karamanlis welcomed his talents and his formation of the Center of Economic Research. Andreas was even appointed to be counselor of the Bank of Greece. However, there was no doubt, when his father appointed him to be Minister to the Prime Minister, that everyone considered him the likely successor to his father. This was dimly viewed by the politicians of the right and the Americans hated his guts. There was a whole list of crimes. He forbade Voice of America broadcasts in Greece that he considered hostile to the interests of Cyprus.

He decided that money given by the American CIA to the Greek intelligence service, KYP, should pass through the control of the Chairman of the Greek Council. He prohibited KYP from communicating with the CIA intelligence of military matters concerning Cyprus. The cardinal sin was to express some reservations about the allegiance to NATO and to say that the Greek army had a tendency to be more loyal to NATO than to Greece itself.

It was the army issue that brought down George Papandreou. He expressed the naïve idea that the army should be controlled by the elected Greek government, not by the palace, or anyone else. Soon all of Greece was informed that the Papandreous, with Andreas as flag bearer, had created a secret organization in the army called Aspida, whose nefarious design was to bolshevize the Greek army. At first the people considered it a huge joke, but they stopped laughing when they woke up one morning to find out that George Papandreou was no longer Prime Minister. He had demanded of King Constantine that the Minister of Defense be removed. This was a gentleman called Garoufalias, whom Papandreou himself had appointed in concession to the palace. He soon learned that Garoufalias did nothing without approval by the palace. He now insisted that Garoufalias be dismissed, and that he himself take over his office. Constantine refused. Papandreou left, threatening to resign. That suited Constantine fine. He acted as if the threat were fact and announced to the country that Papandreou was an ex-Prime Minister.

It caused an uproar. The King asked for the creation of a caretaker government. It fell—no popular support. Another. It fell. Another, headed by Prime Minister Stephanopoulos whose one claim to fame was an expression so enigmatic it earned him the nickname "the Buddha." The Buddha's government had the splendid majority of one single vote. The huge demonstrations that took place all over Greece made it clear that new elections could not be avoided, and it was obvious to everyone, including the American embassy, that George Papandreou would be re-elected.

It was in this atmosphere that at a social function I was introduced to a man at an adjoining table. "Melina, say hello to Mr. Nikos Farmakis."

I knew that name well. Nikos Farmakis was a notorious right-wing extremist. I turned my back on him, saying: "I don't care to say hello to a bloody fascist."

"I'm not ashamed to be a fascist, Melina. It's the fashionable thing. Why not join us? Tomorrow we'll be in the driver's seat."

I shrugged him off as an idiot. I was the idiot. I realized it the following April in New York. The telephone rang in the middle of the night. It was the voice of Manos Hadjidakis. "Melina, there's been a putsch. The army has taken over Greece."

Chapter Fifteen

In my wildest dreams, I could never have imagined that I would play in a musical comedy in New York—but I did. It came about because Julie wanted to get rid of me for about a year. Well, not exactly rid of me—just out of his way. For a long time, he wanted to do a film that had no room for me. I had the wrong complexion. Like many Americans, he considered the situation of the black people in the United States an outrage. He wanted to make a film on the subject, with an all-black cast. His problem was what to do with me. He found a solution—not of the best—but a solution. Since the opening of the film *Never on Sunday,* a New York producer had wanted us to adapt it into a musical comedy for the Broadway stage. He asked me to play in it, and Julie to direct it. We said no. For years the project lay dormant. Now Julie hypocritically told me how excited Manos Hadjidakis was to write new songs and that Joe Darion, fresh from his success of *Man of La Mancha,* was eager to do the lyrics. I told Julie he wasn't fooling me for a minute, but that if his conscience could handle keeping me away from Greece for more than a year—I'd go do his musical comedy.

I am writing this in 1970. It is more than four and a half

years that I have seen a Greek summer, but God granted that it was a beautiful summer in Spetsai. We lived in a marvelous house on the edge of the sea. It was there that we prepared the musical comedy. Manos came, as did Joe Darion. We worked hard, but there was time to swim, to boat and to ride muleback through the pines.

My mother came to stay with us, and later on my father visited with his wife, Nea. She was ever beautiful. She was tall and elegant. Her face had noblesse. It was she who should have played Phaedra. The first time I saw her was in Spetsai, when I was a child. She came up the road that led from the sea, wearing a white dress and an immense straw hat. The sun filtered through the brim and gave her face a golden diffusion. "Do you see that woman?" my mother whispered to me. "That is the beautiful Madame Nea." Perhaps she would have been less generous had she known that the beautiful Madame Nea would one day be my father's wife.

And my father? D'Artagnan *toujours*. He was born elegant. Even in an old pair of shorts and a cotton shirt, he was a joy to behold. His body was young and lean. His carriage was splendid—ever the cavalry officer sitting his horse straight and proud. The young girls ogled and flirted. It pleased him no end. It also pleased Nea and me. He and Julie had become close friends, even though it humiliated him that this American would constantly beat him at the Greek game of tavli.

Politically, my father had moved to the left. He was a deputy to parliament who had taken his place with EDA, a progressive coalition, and I thought it good. Of course, the rightist press referred to him as a Communist, which he never was. They went as far as to scold the hosts of a reception made for King Constantine because the daughter of the Communist Stamatis Mercouri, the notorious actress Melina Mercouri, had been invited. Indeed I was invited to the reception. Kolograd was being much kinder to me. Especially after I made a one-hour documentary for American television produced by a group that had made Elizabeth Taylor's London, Sophia Loren's Rome, and who asked me to do "Melina's Greece." I accepted with joy. We shot in Athens, in Corinth, in Delphi, and in the islands. The film had beautiful music by a new composing talent, Stavros Xarchacos. He was very young, and slight in stature. He was being mentioned along with Theodorakis and Hadjidakis. They were called the tall, the wide, and the small. The documentary got lots of publicity and the tourist bureau adored me. Maybe that's why I was invited. In any event, it tickled me to go.

I decided to be beautiful. I went to the hairdresser. The place was overflowing with *la crème de la société*. They sat in a long line under the hair dryers, and there was not one of them who was not married to a banker or a shipowner. A short circuit in the electricity would have made widowers of half of the millionaires of Greece. They all smiled at me with cat's teeth. One of them, with great sweetness, gave me gentle hints on how to behave in royal company. There was no doubt that I needed such instruction. I have little talent for courtly behavior. When Constantine was still crown prince, he came backstage to visit after a theatre performance. The next morning the newspaper photos showed the actress sitting down and the future king on his feet. I couldn't believe the number of letters I received, critical of my shocking manners. At another occasion, a command performance of *The Victors* in London, I covered myself with glory. There was a long line of film stars, and Queen Elizabeth went from one to another, greeting them graciously and with charm. I found her very sympathetic, but I knew that I would have a bad time if I tried to curtsy. I took courage when I noticed that some of the people just bowed to take the queen's proffered hand. That, I could manage. But when Her Royal Majesty reached me, something went wrong with my reflexes. My right hand remained glued to my side and my left hand went up, and

God knows why, way up. It was a matter of inches and divine intervention that I didn't stick my finger in her royal eye.

At the reception I behaved. I was suave and ladylike, a model of discretion. No one could find fault with me, but all the cats' teeth became fixed in fanged smiles when the king invited me to dance. Photographers made a rush, flash lights went off like mad. Someone in the retinue gave orders for the photos to be destroyed, but some of the photographers were nimble-footed and got out. The photos received favored space in the next day's press, as did our parting exchange. As he was leaving, Constantine called out: "Good luck, Melina."

I answered: "And good luck to you, Your Majesty."

That's all I said, but many present swore that I added: "You'll need it." If it's not true that I said it, it is true that I thought it. In the theatre we are trained to speak the text, but to play the sub-text. Perhaps my reading was not too subtle.

Spetsai that year was the site of an international conference on biochemistry. The rich of Spetsai were all aflutter with the presence of a number of Nobel prize winners. The competition to get them to their dinner tables was bloody. The most sought after was the American, Jim Watson, who won the Nobel award for a breakthrough in genetics. The ladies were chagrined that he preferred the company of us theatre people. Jim and I quickly became friends. He's a fascinating man, a strange mixture of wildness and timidity. He had all the qualities that I find attractive in Americans. He was inquisitive, restless, angry, progressive, and had that wonderful boyish charm that some Americans have even when they're eighty. Jim talked to me for hours about his work. He was so passionate about it that I had neither the courage nor the decency to tell him that he might just as well have talked to me in Chinese. Of all the things I don't know, science heads the list. I know that H_2O is water. My scientific education stops there, but I didn't know how to slip that into the conversation. I listened with such intensity that he didn't realize the totality of my ignorance. I paid dearly for my cowardice. One morning, he knocked at our door with a manuscript in his hands. He had just finished his book *The Double Helix*. He wanted me to be the first to read it. I was delighted and flattered. I threw myself into it with enthusiasm, but it was like rushing a stone wall. I couldn't understand it! There were long passages of scientific hieroglyphics that paralyzed my brain and defied comprehension. Julie was submerged in work with Manos and Joe Darion. There would be no help from that quarter. Vassily Vassilikos was visiting with his American wife, Mimi. I begged her to read it for me. She did. She isolated parts of the book that could enter into my head. Thus armed, I faced Jim and tried to talk easily but in very little time he understood my plight. I'll always love him for the infinite grace with which he let me off the hook and began to talk of other things.

Vassily Vassilikos had also just finished a book. This was one I understood. It was about the murder of Lambrakis. He had decided to entitle his book Z. How could he have known that in one year he would be exiled and that in his exile his book would become a tremendous film success? Vassilikos was the fair-haired boy among the new, young writers emerging in Greece. He won immediate success and attention with his first book, *The Plant*. The hostesses of Spetsai wanted him at their tables too. He accepted these invitations because he was a master of the Greek game "placa." It's a terrible game, a mixture of wit and cruelty. The object of the game is to get a rise out of people, to make them believe anything; the more outrageous the better. When your opponent has completely lost his composure, the game is won. The champion of this game is my brother Spiros. Vassily ran him a close second. He would begin by calling his hosts political fossils. When they were sufficiently heated up, he would evoke the day that was coming when the Spetsai donkeys would be dragging them in tumbrils to face the people's wrath. With a perfectly straight face, he would draw lurid pictures of homemade guillotines and juries of fishermen's widows who would glare at them through slits of black masks. When his auditors were completely discountenanced, he would break into snatches of revolutionary song. "Placa" is played well only when it is clearly established that the game is on. Yet it's extraordinary how soon one forgets that it is a game. The thing that was interesting that summer in Spetsai was that the theme of the placa was almost always politics. The ferment, the agitation of the political conflicts in Greece dominated all else.

But politics, Nobel prize winners, and brilliant young authors were all forgotten when a caïque sailed into Spetsai carrying Greta Garbo. I've loved her all my life. I've been in love with her all my life. She is the supreme beauty, the supreme artist, the supreme magician, the world's greatest actress. The physical love of woman for woman is something I can understand, intellectually—Sappho was one of our islanders. I'm ready to accept that it can be beautiful but it's something that I have not known or felt—except for Garbo. But I also know that she is beyond any one sex, and that it is perfectly in order for man, woman and child to react erotically toward Garbo. She is the essence and the ultimate of all sex.

The caïque belonged to a good friend, Cécile de Rothschild. She invited us to come aboard to meet Garbo. I felt a shock of excitement and fright. I was reminded of the time that Julie took me and his daughters, Ricky and Julie, to visit Charlie Chaplin. Both Ricky and I were so tense that when our car entered the driveway, we asked Julie to turn back, to find an excuse, that we'd come another day. Of course he kept on going, but he understood the state of our nerves, when at the sound of the doorbell, both Ricky and I wet our pants.

She received us with that Garbo smile. That smile that confounds you by its beauty and that gossamer suggestion of sadness which gives a smile its most precious meaning. I heard Julie say: "I command you to remember me."

He had met her many years ago and had told me marvelous stories about her, which I made him repeat hundreds of times. Julie went out of his mind because she refused to indicate whether she remembered him or not, and I swear that he was jealous because Garbo paid more attention to me. She was wearing dark glasses. Somewhere I found the courage to ask her to let me see her eyes. In a film she once made, called *The Painted Veil* there was a moment when she sat before a mirror and with infinite grace, unwound a turban from her head. It is an image that never left me. And with that same loveliness of movement, she put her hands to her glasses and slowly raised them and those beautiful eyes smiled at me. Another vision came to mind. In Corsica there is a small bay in a seaside town called Porto. It is framed by formations of red rock that rise out of the sea. About six miles above Porto there is a village called Ota. And every evening I witnessed an extraordinary ceremony. Hundreds of people came down from Ota to sit on stones or small folding chairs to watch the sunset. As the sun dropped into the sea, the rock formations took on tones of flaming red, and then the reds were touched with gold. And as the sun descended, the reds and golds descended with it as they followed the sun into the sea. And at that moment, the people of Ota burst into applause. It was as if they were applauding God. It had the sense of spectacle and religiosity that was at the heart of our ancient Greek theatre. Then, as night fell, they took the winding road back to Ota. When Garbo made that simple gesture of raising her dark glasses, that vision came back to me. If all of this sounds a bit delirious, I can't help it. I did refrain from applauding, but only because I lacked the courage.

The next night, we gave Garbo a party in a garden taverna. Bouzouki music never sounded better. Julie was completely restored when a few times she whispered in his ear. Everybody had kefi that night. Everybody let go. In little time the floor was littered with broken glasses and plates. The fishermen of Spetsai danced for her and she was delighted.

She asked me to dance for her. I did, not caring at all that I was barefooted. The climax came when the kefi and the music reached her and she smashed her first glass. That did it. From every table plates and glasses flew. Julie dashed through the hail of it, into the kitchen, to return with a stack of twenty plates. She smashed every one of them. This time I applauded, as did everyone else.

Before she returned to the caïque, we sang her Greek songs. They went right to her heart. When we sang Kaimos, one of the great songs by Mikis Theodorakis, she wept. She asked us to sing it again. And still once more, so that she could hear it as the boat took her away from us to the caïque.

I don't know when I'll see Greece again. I don't know how long I can hold out. As time goes by, I feel growing in me a germ of capitulation. Perhaps only Greeks will understand what I mean when I say that exile is especially tough when the moon is full. That's when I break down. There's nothing anywhere like Athens, Delphi, or any village or any island in Greece when the moon is full. That's when I want to wail with all the other demon lovers, only my cry is: "I want to go home."

And I want to take the first plane to Athens and tell anyone who would listen that I apologize for everything I ever said or did against the junta, that I cannot take banishment any longer, that I'd accept humiliation, prison if need be, if only they'd please let me into Greece. Then I tell myself that of course they'd let me in, that they'd do nothing to me, that they'd use me to show their magnanimity, and I grit my teeth and find relief in inventing new obscenities for the colonels. There are other daydreams: a clandestine re-entry, working with the underground resistance, heroic acts. Then I think of my height, that I'm too big to hide among other Greek women, that I'd stick out like a sore thumb, that my face is known and that anyway, I'd be scared to death. And the longer I'm away from Greece, the more I try to hold onto the memory of that last beautiful summer in Spetsai. Sometimes it sustains me; sometimes it makes me weep with longing.

Before we went to New York, Pan finally gave me a divorce and Julie and I were married in Lausanne. We felt a little embarrassed about it after living together for ten years and were willing to pretend that it was due to a determined campaign led by my mother, and that many American hotels still gave people cold receptions if they didn't sign the register as Mr. and Mrs.

There was no need to sign a hotel register. Kermit Bloomgarden, our producer, had arranged a lovely surprise—a handsome flat that looked over Central Park, with an exciting view of the Fifty-ninth Street skyline. I had prepared a martyr face to show to Julie, but he gave me no time to be homesick. He cast as many Greek-Americans for the musical as he could find. He brought Despo from Athens and Titos Wandis, and a fine young Greek actor, Nikos Kourkoulos. Nikos brought his wife. His wife brought their newborn baby. Of course there was Angeliki, soon followed by Anna. Theoni Aldredge, our costume designer, was born in Athens. Our Greek colony stood around the piano to hear Manos Hadjidakis play his new songs. He looked up and asked: "Am I in Manhattan or Piraeus?"

A reception was given in our honor by the Greek consul in New York, another in Washington by the Greek ambassador, Mr. Alexandre Matsas. Of course, there were many Americans invited, but many Greeks as well. I had little opportunity to practice my English. At the Washington reception, we had fun. There were hundreds of people invited and we had to be introduced to each one of them. Julie remembered a game that William Faulkner taught us in Athens. Mrs. Q., a notorious celebrity hunter, had captured the great writer for one of her parties. She planted him in a fireplace and brought her guests to him to be introduced. This went on for hours. To fight off

176

boredom Faulkner drank lots of whiskey and demonstrated his theory that very few people listened to introductions. He said anything that came into his head, just barely slurring his diction. "How do you do, Mrs. Goatherd." "Happy to Ague-cheek, Mr. Talleyrand." And I swear it: "Up your urinal tract, Liza."

And each time there would be a smiling bow and a murmured "How do you do" in return.

Julie decided to play the game at the reception. The arriving guest would be greeted by the ambassador and his wife, then he would be introduced to me. I would introduce him to Julie, who was on my left on the receiving line, and Julie would introduce him to Manos Hadjidakis, who was on his left. Here's the way it went. The ambassador said, "How do you do, Mr. Smith? Mr. Smith, this is Melina Mercouri." Then I'd say: "Mr. Smith, this is Mr. Dassin," and Julie would say: "Sir, this is Mr. Vivaldi," "Madam, this is Mr. Donizetti," "Sir, this is Mr. Verdi." Manos kept kicking Julie in the shins, but he wouldn't stop. "Mr. Brown, this is Mr. Brahms." He had it coming to him when he said: "Sir, this is Mr. Debussy," and the gentleman presented said loudly, "That's funny. My name is Debussy too." Like many Europeans, I carried a number of prejudices with me when I came to the capital of the United States. At Mr. Matsas' reception, some of these prejudices were knocked down. I was particularly impressed by a group of university people who were called on by the government for advice, for special projects and commissions. They were keen young men, cultured, aware of the imperfections of the system and much more to the left than I'd have dreamed.

Onna White was engaged to do the choreography for the musical, which, for some Broadway reason, had been baptized *Illya Darling*. I had already met Onna in Spetsai during the summer. She had come to Greece to do some research on Greek dances. She told me then that she was going to give me a rough time. That was an understatement. She put me into training as if I were a prize fighter. I, who had spent a lifetime avoiding physical exercise of any kind, was now flung into a bruising program of calisthenics, athletics, acrobatics, and other sundry tortures. I howled in protest, but she was relentless. She warned me that a musical comedy was a rigorous business, that I would need toughness of body if I were to dance in eight shows a week. At first, I was so stiff and sore, I walked like a crab. I cursed Julie; I cursed Onna. Later, I was grateful to her indeed. One afternoon, after a grueling session with Onna, the telephone rang. I crawled to the telephone.

"This is Rex Reed."

"Ah, so you are Rex Reed. Let us make an appointment."

The last film we had made was called *10:30 on a Summer's Evening*. It was to open soon in New York. Rex Reed was a critic. I had been told that he hated the film, but wanted to interview me. He had a reputation as a tough, mean critic, and so I was amazed to meet a slender youth, eyes more beautiful than Elizabeth Taylor's, eyelashes most women would kill to have and a dazzling white American smile.

"So this is the tough critic. I will eat him alive."

My eye. He was made of steel. He wouldn't yield an inch. He hated the film and would tell it to the world. It took only ten minutes for me to realize that he was much brighter than I was, that he knew infinitely more about movies and was abreast of everything going on in the world theatre. Decidedly, I had underestimated the Americans.

Except for about three people in the whole world, everybody agreed with Rex Reed: *10:30 on a Summer's Evening* was a disaster. This hurt on a number of scores, but the most painful was that we had failed Marguerite Duras, on whose novel the film was based. Marguerite Duras, aside from being an important talent, is one of the kindest, most generous people I know. And she's tough. She's a fighter. Anyone who is in trouble has a champion in Marguerite. Any injustice, she will

178

fight with pen, on the radio and television, and on picket lines. This diminutive, soft-eyed charmer can write polemics that cut like a razor and at the same time create prose images of exquisite delicacy and nuance. We were miserable to have let her down.

On top of that, the work on *Illya Darling* was not going too well. The truth was that Julie was working badly. To begin with, he was frustrated by the little time he had for rehearsal with his actors. They were always needed by the music director to be integrated into the chorus, by the choreographer for dance rehearsals, by the composer for solo rehearsals, by the costume designer for fittings. He could rarely get the entire ensemble together on the stage. But more important was the fact that he was not a very good collaborator. The director, in a straight play or a movie, is used to being supreme boss, but in a musical he has to co-ordinate the work of a number of collaborators whose work is as important as his own. If he fails to impart the same tone, the same spirit and style to set designer, choreographer, composer, lyricist, and costumer, then he's in for a bad time, for a goulash. Well, Julie failed—but it was the most successful failure I've ever seen.

We opened in Philadelphia. Cheers from the audience. Praise from the critics. Word flew to New York that we were a hit. The management from New York phoned the next day to say tickets were selling there like hot cakes. Were we satisfied? Oh no. There's an axiom in the theatre: "Don't muck around with success." But who were we to be bound by axioms? We mucked and mucked and the show got worse and worse. Julie kept writing new scenes, new dialogue. He dogged Manos for new songs and Joe for new lyrics. He drove everyone crazy by saying the show was not Greek enough, that it was too heavy, that the characters were too thin. He disapproved of some of the orchestrations, the arranger was brilliant but he wasn't Greek. Julie fought for Manos to redo these orchestrations. That led to a mess. Julie was everywhere but on stage working with his actors, where he belonged. We worked like slaves. We would rehearse a new scene and put it into the show the same night. This used to drive me mad, because on stage I kept remembering the old scene. We continued the same frenzied routine in Toronto and Detroit.

No one knew better than Julie that he was not working well. He even looked for another director to replace him. By this time I had made six films with Julie; I had worked with him on the Paris stage. There was always an atmosphere of good humor. I trusted him completely and admired his authority. I never knew him to flounder for a moment or to be in conflict with his collaborators. But here, the show got away from him. He couldn't make it his own. It broke my heart to see him so unhappy. In Detroit he fell ill for a few days. His blood pressure went down so low we were alarmed. *Illya Darling* was no picnic. Yet wherever we went, business was terrific. And wherever we went, Greeks came to greet us. They'd fall on our necks, bring us flowers and Greek dishes and insist that we come to their homes for a late supper after the show. It was like touring the Greek provinces.

When we reached New York, there was an enormous advance sale of tickets—something near two million dollars. Despo and I took pencil and paper. We calculated that to earn such a sum at the box office in the Koun theatre in Athens, we would need capacity audiences seven days a week for fourteen years! Of course this gave courage to the entire troupe. Optimism took over. The consensus was that if we got fair notices we could run forever. The show was really no better, but everyone began to talk as if we had a hit. Not Julie. He thought we would have a bad press, and in New York that meant instant death.

Even in Greece we had heard of the power of the New York critics, but we thought there were many of them. We were amazed to find that there were only three daily newspapers and moreover only one of them, the New York *Times,* had a decisive influence. That made its critic, Walter Kerr, the man, the single man, who decided whether a play would live or die. Even George Bernard Shaw, the greatest theatre critic who ever lived, never had such power. Naturally then, Walter Kerr was much feared and there were some who hated him. For my part, I found him a most erudite gentleman, totally honest, and a man who truly loved the theatre. I expressed this opinion once at a luncheon with a producer and a playwright. They were so upset with me, they stopped eating.

There is a tradition in New York which still lives. After a premiere, the troupe goes to a restaurant called Sardi's. Many glamorous first nighters are there too and actors from other companies. Dinner is served, but there is only a pretense of eating. Everyone is waiting for the New York *Times* review, which appears only a few hours after midnight. This custom has always struck me as shocking. The critic begins writing his review minutes after the final curtain. He has no time to think about it or to reflect. It's barbaric. As a matter of fact, if you go to an opening night in New York, you will see a hallucinating spectacle. The final curtain has not quite touched the stage floor and men rush out of the theatre as if they are pursued by the furies. Thank God I had been warned about it. I'd have thought the theatre was on fire. These men charging up the aisles are critics, speeding to write their reviews against a deadline. Imagine. A man sometimes gives years of his life to write a play. The play can represent his dream, his purpose, his citizenship. Actors and technicians go through a collective agony to make the play live, and all of that need, all of that effort is judged in a matter of moments. What would have happened to Sophocles if a Periclean Walter Kerr had seen *Oedipus Rex* with a baleful eye because he was hastily writing his review while suffering from gastritis or a troubled liver? As it turned out, Walter Kerr resigned from his job soon after reviewing *Illya*. People who knew him said it was because he himself thought the responsibility was too heavy to bear.

But that night in Sardi's, he was still on the job. We picked at our food and awaited his verdict. I was struck by the good will and the good wishes of the other actors present. American actors are the most generous of all. We Europeans do not take with such pleasure the success of others. Finally, Jim Proctor, press agent for the show, and dear friend, burst in with the New York *Times* review. It was not good. Nor were the others that followed. They had kind things to say about me. The dignified Mr. Kerr wrote:

> Melina is a creature you would be happy to take home to mother, if mother was out.

There was a news commentator on the television whom I had come to respect. His name was Edwin Newman. He was an honest outspoken reporter. He spoke in a rather dour fashion, but he never minced words. You always knew what he thought and felt about the issues of the day. He also reviewed plays for the television audience. Well, if I liked him, he did not like me. I don't remember his exact words, but they were something like this:

> *Illya Darling* is dedicated to the principle that Melina Mercouri is irresistible—well, not to me.

The date was April 10. That left me eleven days in which to enjoy letters, gifts and press clippings which flattered my actress ego. Most everyone, even those most severe in their judgment of the production, had a little bouquet for me. The resumé was that the play was so-so but that Melina had a personal success. In Greece it was presented as a personal triumph. There, the press was exuberant. It spoke of a small noble band of Greeks that conquered New York. "The children of Piraeus were on Broadway and were adored." I did nothing to correct these exaggerations. Like all Greeks, what I really cared about was the golden opinion of my home town and if the Greek press chose to color things a bit, I was not girl scout enough to make the exact truth known. But it did embarrass boy scout Jules Dassin. It only added to a bout of melancholy that lasted until he threw himself into his film project.

Illya Darling was to run for almost a year—neither hit nor flop. We were, as the French say, half fig, half grape. We were now installed in a hotel in Greenwich Village which I adored. We began to have the visits of black writers who came to discuss Julie's film. These men were impressive. They were talented and articulate, but what filled the room in form so palpable you could touch it like Macbeth's dagger, was a profound, unyielding anger, and it frightened me that some of that anger seemed to be directed at Julie. These were men who knew him. They knew what side he was on. Some of them were old friends. Yet there was something unbridgeable that finally came down to the difference in the color of their skins. Not only did they say: "No white man can really understand what a black man feels," they seemed to preclude that this comprehension could ever be attained. It was interesting that this attitude did not exist toward me. I was Greek. It was something reserved for the Americans.

I met other writers. John Steinbeck intimidated me. Tennessee Williams charmed me. My favorite was Edward Albee. He fascinated me, not only because of his genius, but also because of his good looks. No one that talented had a right to be so handsome. We became good friends. Julie and I loved to have dinner at his house. There were always interesting people and the cuisine and wines at the Albee house were fabulous. And I came to understand and love New York and the New Yorker. He was friendly. He made me laugh. He has a quickness of mind and a wit that is unique. And the show that the skyscrapers put on every night was irresistible. Those huge canyons of steel and glass, all lit up in fantastic light patterns, took my breath away. Yet many times it would give me pause. There are still villages in Greece that have little or no electricity. We were trained to use electricity sparingly. I still have the reflex of putting lights out when I leave a room —it happens that I do so in other people's houses. And here, these enormous buildings with all lights left on—and no one in them.

Life was good. I liked the actors in the theatre. The backstage technicians played affectionate practical jokes and I was in love with every boy and girl dancer who, in the New York theatre, were called "gypsies." Jim Watson invited us to Harvard where he taught. I met twenty of his students, each one so brilliant that they reduced me to awed silence. I went to see a Yale-Harvard football game. American football, that is something else again. For a Greek it is a weird experience. You find yourself in an enormous stadium. Everyone is frozen by the cold, yet pretty girls, practically naked, prance about and lead the people to cheer twenty-two colossal men on a stripe-painted field whose one purpose seems to be to break each other's skulls. After each effort, they form a circle to have a little meeting, then rush out of the meeting to break more skulls. Jules and Jim told me I would understand the game better if I kept my eyes on the ball. I found that impossible because the players did the utmost to hide the ball from the spectators. Anyway, I stopped believing Julie about sports when he tried to overcome my boredom at a baseball game by telling me that the big star's name was not really Mickey Mantle, but Michael Mantolopoulos.

All my fears that I would be unhappy in New York were gone. I had my work. I had new friends. I had my Greeks, whose ranks were swelled by the arrival of my mother and my brother Spiros. On the evening of April 21, I saw the year ahead as pleasant and productive—but in the middle of the night, Manos Hadjidakis called to tell us that freedom was strangled in Greece.

Chapter Sixteen

"There are no communications with Greece."

All night long, we received the same answer. We phoned the Greek embassy in Washington. Ambassador Matsas was ill and hospitalized and all we could get from members of his staff: "There are no communications with Greece."

The consul in New York, George Gavas: "No communications with Greece."

Each time we heard it, it sounded more ominous. Every few minutes we called the wire services. They confirmed that there was a military coup but had little more information. We got through to a journalist friend in Paris. He was as much in the dark as we were. We tried to reach my father, who was in London. No answer.

All through the night, friends gathered in our hotel room. We made feeble attempts to make light of it. A dictatorship in Greece? It couldn't last forty-eight hours. The people would not permit it. The Americans would not accept it. All of Europe would isolate it. But each time we tried the telephone and failed, there would be a long, wakelike silence, and in these silences we grappled with the fears that we refused to speak aloud.

There had been talk of a dictatorship in the making since

George Papandreou was removed from office as Prime Minister in 1965. In 1966 there was open speculation in the Greek and world press. In Spetsai we talked about it every day. Talk of a coup had died down a bit when Papandreou made a deal with the rightist parties and the palace. This caused a split between him and his son Andreas. This was not enough for those who wanted Andreas' head. The charges that he had plotted to corrupt the army were renewed with vigor. It was revealed that people had been offered huge bribes to testify against him. A general of the army named Tsolakas declared at the Aspida trial that the whole business was a frame-up. The general was simply kicked out of the army and the clamor continued. The sponsors of the "get Andreas" slogan went so far as to demand his own father to help destroy him.

Andreas himself had not been brought to trial because, as a deputy, the constitution granted him immunity. But this immunity would no longer be in effect forty-five days before election. This was the time when the pack meant to close in. George Papandreou's Center Union party pressed for an amendment to the electoral law which would extend immunity through the pre-election period. The palace and the right, who had smelled blood, howled with rage. This maneuver would let their game slip away. They put all kinds of pressure on the old man to withdraw the amendment. That was asking too much. On this he would not yield, and talk of a coup came back stronger than ever.

Less than two months before the coup, Andreas addressed the Foreign Press Association in Athens. He came out swinging. He attacked all the sordid aspects of the establishment's political maneuverings. He protested the King's collusion with the military in the Aspida affair. He said that if Greece had chosen to be a member of the Western alliance, this in no way compromised its right to chart its own international political course or its independence as a nation. He protested the interference of the CIA in Greek affairs. Two men from the American embassy stalked out during the speech, à la Gromyko. All of this raised hell, and the cries for Andreas' blood became more shrill than ever.

The refusal of the old man to sacrifice his son was construed by the right to be more than a paternal attitude. It meant that he could not be trusted to play their game, that he might turn his back on the deal made with them. George Papandreou, all his life, in word and deed, had been violently anti-Communist. Yet wild charges were made that he would tie in with them and this made it necessary for the military to be vigilant. Mr. Cyrus Sulzberger, known to be close to the palace, had written an article for the New York *Times* saying that if Constantine felt that the "extreme left" would change the regime in Greece, then he would "use all means to save the nation from disaster."

To most Greeks this was pure baloney. We knew, just as I believe Mr. Sulzberger knew, that it was ridiculous, that the extreme left had no such power. The effect of this piece and other hogwash written by Mr. Sulzberger, was to justify the need for a strongman government. The Greek people were alarmed. They saw which way the wind was blowing. On numbers of occasions, hundreds of thousands of people took to the streets to manifest their support of democratic government and free elections.

We reviewed all of this as we sat in the hotel room. My brother Spiros took a clipping from the New York *Times* from his pocket. It was dated April 17, just four days before.

It is the King, however, who has wedged himself into a corner, where the only option to the return of a Papandreou government may be an army-backed dictatorship.

Spiros had just finished reading when the phone rang. We leaped toward it. The call came from England. It was my

187

father. He was the only deputy who happened to be outside of Greece on April 21. He had been very ill, and was under medical care in London. He told us that there were tanks in the Athens streets, that there had been wholesale arrests, and there were responsible reports that all civil rights guaranteed by the constitution were suspended. He was particularly concerned that the article forbidding physical torture was also suspended. We asked him what the people were doing to resist.

"Nothing."

George Papandreou had warned that if anyone tried a coup, all the church bells of Greece would summon the people to the streets and that hundreds of thousands of people had sworn to stop dictatorship with their bodies.

"There are no church bells. There are no people. Anyone capable of organising a resistance is either in jail or in hiding."

His voice, despite the anger, seemed very tired. I asked about his health. He said he was well. He had just called a press conference to condemn the military take-over. His was the first act of public resistance.

It took more than thirty-six hours to piece together what had happened. At first, there had been slogans broadcast on the radio that were calculated to confuse and mislead. "Greece is resurrected. The true freedom of the people has come."

Then nothing but military march music. Finally, a communiqué which proclaimed "the dangers that menace the public order and the security of our country" and the suspension of civil rights. It was signed by Constantine, King of the Greeks, the Council of Ministers, the Presidency, its members. Then a second communiqué, unsigned:

People and vehicles to be kept off the streets.

Anyone in the street after sunset would be shot.

Any attempt to stock food would be considered as sabotage and offenders would be court-martialed.

It is prohibited to withdraw money from banks.
All schools closed.

Then the proclamation of a state of seige:

Arrests and detention are authorized without due process. Length
of detention unlimited.
Any gathering, public or private, is forbidden and will be dis-
persed by force.
Entry and search of public buildings and private homes are authorized, day and night, without restrictions.
All correspondence is liable to censorship.

The theme and the language was like that of the Nazis during the occupation. We were reliving a nightmare.

During the night, 10,000 people were arrested. Of course
Andreas Papandreou was among the first. He was brutally
dragged out of his house and carted off. Thousands were
shaken out of their sleep to face army rifles and were pulled
into waiting cars and trucks in a state of undress: trade-
unionists, public administrators, members of youth organizations, professors, lawyers, journalists, actors. This was the
natural behavior of fascists, but confusion set in when we
learned of the arrests of dozens of deputies and most of the
ministers of the legal government. These were ministers of the
rightist parties! Then came the startling announcement that
Panayotis Cannelopoulos, the Conservative Prime Minister,
had been arrested! It made no sense. Why would Constantine
permit the arrest of an ERE Prime Minister? Cannelopoulos
was the outspoken opponent of Papandreou. Once again we
phoned the wire services. Were they sure that the communiqués were signed by Constantine? They were sure. Had the
arrest of Cannelopoulos been confirmed? It had been confirmed. When the news came that Makis Arnaoutis, the King's
close adviser and personal secretary, was arrested, we were
completely lost.

We had a right to be puzzled. Soon we learned that we were witnessing a tragic farce. The King's signature was a fraud! Three unknown colonels, Papadopoulos, Pattakos and Makarezos had hijacked the coup that was prepared by the generals, and proceeded to attach the King's name to their communiqué without even a by-your-leave.

Perhaps this explained why the coup caught everyone with their pants down. It was generally assumed that if a coup were to come, it would take place after the elections, if Papandreou refused to play footsie with the right and the palace. A plan, worked out by NATO, called the Prometheus Plan, would go into operation. It was a blueprint for the capture and paralysis of a state. Well, it was bloody efficient and it worked, except for the small detail that the colonels double-crossed the generals and swiped the plans for themselves.

It is one thing to capture a state—another to hold onto it. The question of popular opposition was dealt with, at least temporarily, by the lightning imprisonment of the people's leaders and the seizure of all communications. And the bastards used the radio not only to frighten, but to confuse.

"Who are we? We do not belong to any political party. We belong to the class of toil. We shall stand by the side of our Greek brothers."

There remained two risks—calculated risks. If the King opposed them, they would fall. If the United States opposed them, they would fall. The colonels judged Constantine well. He caved in like a wilted marshmallow. The heads of the navy and the air force were ready to counterattack. The admiral of the navy had already ordered the fleet to sea and beseeched Constantine to give the order to move against the junta. The King refused. He said he wanted to avoid bloodshed. Yes, the colonels had judged their man well. Evil tongues claimed that they judged his mother well, too. The man whom the junta designated as Prime Minister was Constantine Kollias. He was the notorious prosecutor general of the supreme court who turned many Greek stomachs by his cover-up tactics over the Lambrakis assassination. He was Queen Frederika's friend and collaborator. So the reports that Constantine was trying to hold out against the colonels gave only faint hopes and they died when the world was treated to the official photo of the junta chiefs. Smack in the middle of the photo, stood forlorn King Constantine. *Der Spiegel,* the mass circulation magazine in Germany, printed a story that has never been denied. It concerned the moment when the King had to affix his signature to the document which would give sanction to the colonels' regime. His refusal could have still brought on their downfall. *Der Spiegel* story has it that when Constantine had a moment's hesitation, that the Queen Mother ordered him to: "Shut up and sign."

As I say, the story has never been denied. In any case, he signed.

As for the American government, it rose up like an angry giant in defense of democracy and morality. It brought down all its weight to give the junta a slap on the wrist and to express the hope that there would be an early return to a parliamentary system. Yes sir, that was telling them. Many Americans, in political life and in the press, expressed their shame. The more moderate of the critics were embarrassed by U.S. sanction of the junta. The most outspoken made charges of collusion. Those of us who had been watching the power play from close view, were ready to bet that there was quiet, but joyful celebration in the inner sanctums of the State Department. The Papandreou dybbuks were exorcised. It was a job well done. Of course, the colonels were a little vulgar, a bit low-class. The generals would have been less embarrassing, but one can't have everything.

The days that followed were hell. More and more stories of junta brutality, arrests, and deportations. It quickly became clear that no political party, not one, supported the colonels. The continued arrests of politicians from the right proved their complete isolation and it became equally clear that to survive, the junta had to purge the army. They went at this with a will. In little time, more than two thousand officers were to be purged. The press was completely muzzled. Censorship was total. There were no signs of active opposition. Greece lived in fear. Then came that insane statement from Papadopoulos that left me trembling with horror. He declared that Greece was ill, that it had to be strapped to a table and to be operated on. He was the surgeon who would cut out the sickness. I saw that my country was in the hands of a mad butcher.

It was Easter. I think it was the first Easter in fifteen years that I had been away from Greece. It is our most beautiful holiday. It is a time of brotherhood and love. It is a time for celebration. When Greeks greet each other with "Christ is Risen" it is not a religious ritual. His resurrection is a reality and a time for rejoicing. The Greek Orthodox church in New York was filled to overflowing. We stood outside in the rain and wept. In Athens, the new masters, the assassins, were photographed celebrating Easter. Their resurrection smelled of death.

The chains that held Greece were drawn tighter and tighter. It was agony for me to be cut off, to be so far away, to feel so helpless, and it was sheer torment to go on playing *Illya Darling*. Here I was, acting in a play that showed a Greece that was free and gay. I had to sing and dance to symbolize the joy of Greek life, when Greece was ruled by court-martial and torture. And it drove me mad that pictures of me were prominent in the junta newspapers with stories celebrating my success in New York—"Our Melina"—I was being used as a publicity agent for the colonels' regime.

Our nights were sleepless. I told Julie that I had to speak out. I had to denounce them. I had to do what I could to hurt them. Julie said I had no other choice, but he warned me that

I would have to see the fight through to the end; that these were killers who meant to stay; that they were lying when they announced that their purpose was to clean up the country and then retire, their noble mission accomplished; that they would only leave when they were overthrown. He talked to me of Picasso and Casals who had attacked Franco and had not returned to Spain for thirty years. He explained to me what it meant to be without a passport. Yes, I must speak out, but with the certainty that the junta would react, with the knowledge that I might not see Greece for a long time, if ever.

I told my mother and Spiros that I had decided to talk to Kermit Bloomgarden, the producer of *Illya Darling*. I knew that the fate of a hundred people depended on my staying with the show, that I was bound to a contract, but it was torture to continue. I was going to ask him to let me make a curtain speech, telling the audience that this free Greece seen in our play did not exist any more. Spiros thought I was extremely naïve, but that there was no harm in asking. My mother begged me not to do anything until she had returned to Greece. We in turn pleaded with her not to go back. She was adamant. She would leave in two weeks. Her husband was there and she reminded Spiros that his wife and children were there. Spiros said that he would return with my mother, get his wife and children out, and as soon as they were safe, we would go into action. Then we became afraid that if Spiros went to Greece, they would not let him out again. My father had declared himself an enemy to the regime and they would not look kindly on his son if he tried to leave with his family.

It was at this point that Julie announced that he had to interrupt the work on his film project and go to Lausanne for a few days, and once there, go on to London to see my father, to ask his advice. He thought it best for me to keep my silence until he returned in about a week. This made sense to us all. Before he left, Julie asked Manos Hadjidakis to write a song whose theme was freedom and could be used against the colonels. Manos agreed, and we arranged for me to appear on a national television show in ten days time, where I would present the song. The last thing Julie asked me before his plane left, was to keep after Manos and see that the song and the orchestration be ready in a week.

The censorship of the Greek newspapers, the inevitable front-page photos of the various colonels, made reading them a nauseating chore, but we rushed to buy them as soon as they arrived. We read each page, always fearing that the name of a friend would appear. Six days after he left, I saw a photograph of Julie at the Athens airport. He was in Athens! I was speechless with shock. The telephone to Athens was working erratically. It took five hours to get through to a friend. I asked her to find Julie and have him call me. The phone rang just as I was leaving for the theatre. Julie didn't give me a chance to howl my anger and fear. He explained to me in language that only we could understand, that he had gone to see what could be done to get Spiros' wife and children out, and at the same time, find out what friends were in trouble and needed help. I felt more than silly talking in code, but I knew that overseas calls were being tapped. I conveyed to him that I was frightened; that he was known to be a man of the left. He laughed and said that he had known I would think that way and that was why he didn't tell me he was going to Greece; but not to be ridiculous, he was an American citizen and they would be idiotic to do anything. I asked him, did he know that the press announced he was there to prepare a new film. He was so furious at this, I couldn't keep from laughing. When I asked him to tell me something about the children, he said he would ring me from London in a day or so.

Three days later, he was back in New York. He had much to tell. Athens was a city of silence and fear. Even friends of long date were afraid to be seen with him. When they did see him, they preferred to make it look like a chance meeting in a public park. They warned him not to talk in restaurants or in taxicabs, that vast numbers of waiters and taxi drivers were being paid to report anti-junta statements from foreigners as well as Greeks. Many people close to us were in prison or in hiding. Everyone was talking of torture of political prisoners. There were countless families who were destitute. Men were deported to prison islands and their wives and children left without any means of sustenance. I asked about my friend Sabina. Had she been arrested? No. He had seen her. She was hidden in the home of a famous artist. This was illuminating and encouraging, because the artist in question was known to be a very timorous man who had always refused to get involved in anything political. If he was ready to risk court-martial, then we could hope for the quick formation of a broad resistance movement. Here Julie shook his head. By what he could gather, that would take years. Spiros' children? Again he shook his head. To get the children out, Spiros had to sign a formal request and submit it for consideration—but he would have to go to Athens to make the request. If Spiros went to Athens, would he be permitted to leave again? Julie expressed doubt. He thought the best thing was for his wife, Alexia, who was English, to enlist the help of the Foreign Office. (The struggle to get the children out was finally won, but it took a year and a half to win it.)

Julie talked with emotion of his visit to my father in London. He was very ill, very tired, but he drove himself with his remaining strength to combat the junta. He traveled all over Europe, creating committees, organizing public meetings, seeking help from the democratic parties, pleading before the Council of Europe. My father was to die a few months later. Till the very end, he continued his struggle against the junta. Today, his body still lies in a small chapel in London. Nea, Spiros, and I have kept him there because we know that, could he speak to us, he would tell us not to bring him back to Greece before Greece is free.

It is bitter when an old friendship comes to an end. I don't know when Manos lost his courage. None of us felt more degraded and angry when the dictatorship seized our country. I remember how passionately he urged Julie to visit Karamanlis in Paris and beg him to make a public statement blasting the junta. Now, when Julie asked him if the song was ready, he became angry with us. He stopped coming to see us. Some time later, I was dumfounded to see an interview that Manos gave to a newspaper, criticizing my anti-junta activities. Shortly after, he returned to Greece. When I saw a photo of Manos with Colonel Makarezos, I thought my heart would break. I haven't seen him since. Manos is now out of Greece. Deep down, I'm sure he hates the junta. Perhaps one day he will join the fight against it. I know that I miss him, that despite everything, I'll always love him—but he knows there's only one way in which we can become friends again.

Who were they? This unholy trinity of cheap Hitlers? Before April 21, 1967, like most Greeks, I had never heard their names. Research told us what breed they were but little more.

George Papadopoulos: colonel in the artillery and liaison officer between the Greek secret service, KYP, and the American CIA; a record of treatment for nervous disorders; during the Karamanlis regime, a member of a "secret committee in the fight against communism." In 1964 he was stationed near the Turkish border. He reported a Communist plot of sabotage. Sugar had been poured into the gas tanks of army trucks. The charge was investigated and boomeranged. It was revealed that Papadopoulos himself was responsible for staging this bit of comedy. He was reprimanded and transferred to a lesser post. In 1966, he turns up again in the post of director of psychological operations(!) and propaganda to the chiefs of staff of the infantry. This was the spot from which he organized the coup.

Stylianos Patakos, the Mrs. Malaprop of the junta: tank commander of the Athens area; member of the Congregation "Zoe" whose aim was the reorganization of the church and society into a puritan pattern. It was then consequent that, the moment the junta came to power, he banished miniskirts and beards. When he became a laughingstock, he made a complete turnabout and authorized an international miniskirt contest in Greece. Speaking of the political prisoners, he said: "If they have to be executed, they will be executed."

Yet Mr. Cyrus Sulzberger wrote: "He is a courageous, respectable and devout man."

This devout man later proclaimed that the slogan for the "national revolution" was: "Stop, or I'll shoot."

Nikolas Makarezos. There was little known about him, except that he too worked for KYP. Athenians would have it that he was made supervisor of the economy "because he was the only one of the trio who could add and subtract."

The day came for my mother's return to Athens. A few hours before we were to take her to the airport, I had accepted to do a routine radio interview, to talk about theatre, movies, and such. I regretted that the interview had not been set for the following day, when my mother would be back in Greece. It would have been a good opportunity to speak out against the junta, but I had assured my mother I would do nothing until she had arrived safely. The tape recorder was set up in our hotel room. My mother and Julie were present. The interview was going smoothly. We talked about theatre, acting techniques, roles I had played, uses of rehearsal, etcetera. I began to feel miserable when all his questions were directed to *Illya Darling*. I railed at myself for being an idiot. Obviously, I should have expected that the interview would be concentrated on the show. It was like twisting a knife in my ribs. The questions came faster. The audience reaction? The character? Did I enjoy playing her?

"I hate playing Illya. I hate it." I did not know I was going to say it. But it had to be said. The interviewer was a clever man. He knew what would come next.

"Tell me why?"

My mother looked at me pleadingly.

"Because it's a lie. There is no happiness in Greece today. It's a country in chains."

"Are you making a statement against the colonels?"

My mother cried out: "No."

I said: "Yes."

"May I begin with a question about American tourists. Should they go to Greece this summer?"

I looked at Julie. He smiled at me.

"If you can sail the Greek islands, knowing that some of them are prisons where people are tortured, then go to Greece."

My mother begged me to stop.

"If you want your dollars to support a fascist regime, then go to Greece."

The interviewer cut off the tape recorder. He said he would like to come back in a few hours with a television crew and camera. He would like an interview on this theme. It would be put on a national hookup that went across the country. I said yes.

When the lights were on me and the camera was set up, I had more difficulty in answering the question. While they were out looking for the crew, I thought of how hard I had worked to bring tourists to Greece. I thought of all the tours I had made, of all the foreign artists I had persuaded to come and work in Greece. I thought of the time the Minister of Tourism had sent me to Stockholm and as a result of my visit, thousands of Swedish tourists were enrolled. When I came to New York, the tourist office in New York printed little posters that appeared everywhere: MELINA IS HERE. And a picture of me—and the Acropolis. At a government reception before the coup, I had been introduced as the "unofficial ambassadress at large."

The voice came from behind the camera. The same question: "Should American tourists go to Greece this summer?"

I knew the answer I would give would keep me away from Greece for a long time. Tears came to my eyes. And strangely, I felt ashamed to tell people to stay away from my country as if it were a plague. But it was a weakness that lasted only a moment. I said everything that was on my heart.

My mother wept a good deal before she got on the plane. She was afraid for us, afraid for herself. Spiros told her nothing would happen to her. Her brother, who was the admiral of the navy, still had great influence. Of course we were worried, but there was no turning back. I embraced my war against the colonels. My silence had been suffocating me.

The interview was included in the NBC news program. It was repeated a number of times during the same evening. Immediately after the first broadcast, our phone began to ring. It didn't stop until I left for the theatre. Friends and people unknown to me were hailing me with "bravos" and "well dones." One said, "Melina, you've raised the banner of resistance." So, feeling like a Greek Betsy Ross, I made my way to the theatre. A number of the troupe were waiting at the backstage entry to receive me with applause. By now, I was feeling like La Passionaria. The doorman stood, with telephone receiver in hand, pointing at me. I prepared my modest thank you as I moved to the phone. Everyone around me could hear the voice that bellowed: "You son of a bitch, shut up or we'll shut you up."

When I came off the stage for the entr'acte, there were literally hundreds of telegrams waiting for me. Most of them were hostile and almost all were signed: "a Greek American" or "a loyal Greek American." The telephone, a rasping voice, in Greek:

"You whore, you communist whore. The colonels stopped an invasion of 50,000 communist troops from Yugoslavia and Bulgaria. Do you think there will be any problem stopping you?"

The enormities that were swallowed, the idiocy of what was believed, lay somewhere between tragedy and burlesque. The new spokesman appointed by the junta, declared to the press that the military took over in the nick of time, because two days later, George Papandreou was to lead a revolution in Salonika. I should mention the new spokesman's name. It was Nicholas Farmakis, the man who told me: "I'm proud to be a fascist. Soon we'll be in the driver's seat."

The next days, many letters. Some were beautiful. Some were like little poems of love. But for each of these, there were others, filled with hate and vicious threats. It was revelatory that the most threatening were replete with images of sexual torture and perversion. These were the defenders of the junta. If these letters were frightening and revolting, the reaction of one official in New York was heartening. He was among the first to call. He spoke with emotion: "Bravo Melina. Thank you. Please keep it up."

I've known this man since I was a child. His father owned the hotel, at whose inauguration my grandfather tried to impose my acceptance of his fair-skinned Nana. I had talked with him every day since April 21. His attitude toward the colonels was hostile and contemptuous. I thought he should announce his resignation, and told him so. I could not understand that he represent a regime that he detested. He almost wept. He said he was ashamed but that he was a man without means, or, as he put it "a poor employee." After this phone call, I thought that perhaps it was wise for him to stay on. I had visions, à la James Bond, that he could use his office to work against the regime. I sadly underestimated the powers of corruption. Not much later, this same man was to charge that "the actress Melina Mercouri and her Jew husband were being financially supported by the American Communist party." (!) Alas, he was not to be the last of the turncoats. Dictatorships breed rabbits and lambs and toads.

After that first broadcast, there was no respite. There were requests in incredible number to appear on radio, and television, to give interviews to newspapers and national magazines. Everything seemed so out of proportion. What had happened? I was an actress who said what she thought of the gangster colonels and asked the help of the American people to help restore democracy in Greece, and it made headlines the world over. I'm not quite a fool. I knew that for the most part, the news media were calling on me because I was a curiosity, the *Never on Sunday* girl who took on the colonels. It made "a good story." That was all right with me. I was willing to pay the price to be heard, but as the weeks went by, that novelty wore off and I had to grapple with the fact that for some time at least, I had become a spokesman for all the Greeks who were unable to speak. The responsibility became a heavy one. It helped that most people who interviewed me were themselves sincere in their loathing of the dictatorship that forced itself on my country. I learned what people meant when they said there were two Americas. There is the Pentagon-State Department America that bolsters the Ky's in Vietnam and the Papadopouloses in Greece, and there are the vast number of Americans whom these policies anger and embarrass.

People would come up to me in the street and ask what they could do to help. I'll always love that beautiful burly cab driver who brought his taxi to a squealing halt, paid no attention to the klaxons protesting the holding up of traffic, and ran across the street to take my hand and say: "Give 'em hell, Melina."

I began to receive letters of a different kind. They came from every state of the Union. There was always the question: "What can I do to help?" and sometimes in the letter, a dollar bill or a five-dollar bill. "Please see that this gets to the families of the prisoners."

I accepted speaking engagements at universities and high schools. These were perhaps the most thrilling experiences

I've had in my struggle against the colonels. The brightness of the young people in America was dazzling. There was no monkey business about them. They wanted clear, direct answers. Humbug or temporizing was unacceptable. They wanted the heart of the matter. They were remarkably well informed. When I hear people tolling the bells for the imminent downfall of the American civilization, I laugh. If I have faith in the future of a bright new world, it's because I got to meet and know the young people of the United States.

I never dared appear before them without doing lots of homework. The same thing was true of appearances on television. The power of this medium is formidable. People still repeat to me a phrase I might have said on television years ago. I sincerely believe if the good or evil spirits of a country could take command of the television chains for two weeks, they could change the face of the nation. As a technician and a theatre person, television was an exciting discovery. I sparked to the speed and intimacy of this medium. My English, at best, was halting, but there is something in television that made me think faster, that keyed up my reflexes. But sometimes I didn't have the answers. I railed against opportunities lost to strike at the gangster colonels because of lack of knowledge and political education. I understood the dilemma of Rosemary Brown.

Rosemary Brown is an English lady who insisted that the spirits of Liszt, Beethoven, and Bach communicated to her. They told her that there were works of theirs that had not been published and that she was chosen to note them down. Liszt, she said, gave her permission to play these works, but Bach and Beethoven forbid her to do so because she had insufficient talent as a pianist. She was charged only to receive and deliver the message that these works existed. Rosemary Brown admits that she's not a very good pianist, that she was frustrated not to be able to play this music, but that she ac-

cepted the responsibility to deliver the message. I sat with a
group of friends, listening to Rosemary Brown tell all of this
in a radio interview. They all smiled as they listened. Not me.
I knew what she was talking about.

Chapter Seventeen

There were two men I leaned on heavily. One was Julie. The other was Jim Proctor. Jim was a press agent and much more. He's a beautiful man and any progressive cause has his help. Jim arranged a schedule of speaking engagements; he advised me; he criticized me, and made himself available twenty-four hours a day. Julie organized a team of speech writers for me and others. He helped the creation of committees from New York to California in defense of Greek democracy. He took a crash course in modern Greek history and became a sort of research department that anyone could call upon. Then suddenly I lost Julie's help and presence.

Greece was getting to be yesterday's news. The Middle East crisis was claiming the headlines. The Egyptians announced the closing of the Gulf of Aqaba to Israeli shipping, and U Thant ordered the withdrawal of the UN peace-keeping forces from the Egyptian-Israeli borders. There were reports of troop movements on both sides. Canada called an emergency session of the Security Council of the United Nations. These meetings were broadcast on television. We sat watching the debate on television for hours each afternoon. Despite calls for restraint, it was obvious that the situation was deteriorating.

Julie said: "If there is war, I will go to Israel."

I said: "Don't be silly. You're too old to carry a gun."

He replied: "I'm not too old to carry a camera."

I knew what he was feeling. It was something many Jews felt, particularly Jewish Americans. Since the Hitler genocide, they carry a guilt, a guilt of being alive, of having survived, when six million of their people were destroyed. And they could never understand the mystery of why so many went unresisting to their deaths. They resolved this would not happen again. Those days, I often passed the Israeli consulate on my way to the theatre. I saw thousands of men, not all, but mostly Jewish, who came to volunteer for military service in the event of war. Once there was such a crowd, my car could not pass. A man, not very young, recognized me and came to greet me. I asked him if he saw no justice on the Arab side. He answered: "I don't know. Maybe. What I do know is that if Jews are killed again, this time I will be with them."

Yet I could not believe that Julie would leave me alone in New York. He knew how much I needed him. He knew that we needed his help for the Greek resistance, and whereas many were ready to go to the aid of Israel, there were few actively working for Greece.

We had taken a house in Long Island for the summer. I was preparing to leave for a matinee performance when a call came for Julie from Paris. He spoke very briefly. I heard him say something about sound equipment. He hung up and walked me to the car.

"Who called you from Paris?"

"Oh, just a television crew asking for some advice."

"The truth?"

"The truth." And he kissed me.

The traffic into New York was heavy. It took a long time to reach the theatre. All the way in, I worried about that call from

Paris. As far as I knew, Julie had never lied to me before. Was he lying to me now? When I arrived at the theatre, there was an urgent message to call Angeliki.

"Melina, he hit me when I tried to stop him. He's on the way to the airport. He's going to Israel."

For a moment, I couldn't move. I felt a terrible cold in my back. Anna got me back to the dressing room. I wept with pain and anger. He knew I'd be lost and desperate. I love Julie. I don't think I can ever stop loving him, but I'll never be able to forgive him for leaving without telling me, for lying to me. I sent my understudy in a fast car to the airport. I instructed her to tell Julie that if he left, I wouldn't play that night, I'd close the show. Julie said: "She's a professional. She'll go on."

And he boarded the plane for Paris on the way to Israel. When my understudy returned to tell me this, I sent for the producer. I knew I wasn't making any sense. I could not be reasoned with. "Bring him back or this will be my last performance."

They reached him early the next morning in Paris. A few hours later he was on a return plane to New York. He gave me no time to feel satisfaction. "Melina, I knew you would try to stop me, so I left without telling you. I came back only to apologize. Now I tell you, I'm going to Israel." And then he went away. For the third time in thirty-six hours, he crossed the Atlantic.

Despo came to stay with me at the house, as did Julie's daughter Ricky. Jim Proctor watched over me like a brooding hen. The entire company at the theatre was at my *petits soins*. Yet I never felt such an intense solitude. I had neither heart nor energy, but I did not miss a performance of *Illya Darling*. I went on making speeches against the colonels.

I have no powers of premonition, but ever since Manos called to tell us the tragic news of Greece, I have become sensitized to the ringing of a telephone. I know that pragmatists will tell me that the sound of a telephone bell is unvaried, that it's always the same. It may be a fact, but it's not true. I know, I just know, by the sound of the telephone ringing, when the caller has bad news to announce.

It was just before curtain time at the theatre. The call came from London. Again I felt a cold in my back. It was Rena. She found the words to tell me that I would never see Stamatis again. Stamatis, my friend, my father, D'Artagnan.

My father was dead and I had no time to cry.

I got through the performance. Everyone knew it was best not to talk to me. No one was to tell me how sorry they were. Anna allowed no one into my dressing room after the show, except Orianna Fallaci, Italian journalist and friend. She brought a lovely plant. "It's your father's soul."

After the performance, I was scheduled to talk and sing at a meeting for Greece. I went but I could not sing. In the name of my father, I asked them to renew the combat.

Julie was somewhere in the Sinai Desert. It took more than a day before he received the message to call me. There was a helicopter going to Tel Aviv. He phoned me from there. I told him my father was dead. He got to London in time for the funeral. The services were conducted in a Greek Orthodox church in London. Spiros was there, and Nea, and Rena. I was in New York, singing and dancing in *Illya Darling*.

Three days after his death, I received my father's last letter. "My dearest, I wish you were here beside me."

It was a time of nightmare, but little sleep, a time when the sun was cold, when I saw sinister shadows everywhere. For the first time in my life, I welcomed my enemy, solitude. I sat alone in my dressing room reading and rereading a resolution passed by the newly "reformed" actor's union of Greece. Because of my "anti-Greek activities," I had been expelled from the union. I knew that on the first day of their existence, the junta had dissolved all trade unions and the present one was a fake. Yet those who voted were actors. It was likely that I had acted on the same stage with some of them, perhaps some were former friends. I could understand the pressure that was brought upon them, but it hurt. It was their defeat, their surrender, that hurt most. The colonels were corrupting Greece; they were corrupting my friends. I thought of all of this with a detachment that was strange to me. Why do some people resist? Why do others yield? Perhaps it has to do with the riddle: "What's life all about?" When I ponder cosmic questions that are beyond me, things lose a sense of reality. Things change physically. I feel neither gravity nor my own weight. This was my condition when Anna opened the door to tell me there was a priest to see me.

"A priest?"

He seemed to be all black. His clothes were black, his hands, his face. "I am a Trappist monk. I have prayed for you for seven years. Tomorrow, I am leaving for a leper colony in Africa. I will soon die of cancer. When I am dead, my brother will bring you a message."

It was too much for my strained nerves. I screamed in panic. People burst in and took him away.

Another visit—this one from Mr. Vranopoulos of the Greek embassy in Washington. We used to be friends. The last time I saw him was in his house after a reception given for us. We danced the Chasapico till early in the morning. That was before April 21. He too was horrified by the coming of the junta. In the days that followed, we talked often on the telephone. I asked him why he didn't resign. He said there was time, that we must be clever and patient until they revealed their true colors. I pointed out that they had revealed their true colors from the first moment. His attitude remained: be patient, wait and see. The phone calls became less frequent. When we did talk, his tone became more and more cool. And soon he was announcing that the regime was moving toward a new, enlightened democracy.

Shortly before his visit, the syndicate of Greek Tourist Agencies had declared me a traitor to my country. His manner was sympathetic. It was as a friend that he came to ask me to be silent. I was making life difficult for everybody and myself. I showed him a newspaper clipping. Dora Stratou had been arrested. Dora Stratou! No one had worked harder to preserve the culture of the Greek people.

"If you drop your campaign, we will let her go."

"What about all the other prisoners?"

Vranopoulos flew into a rage. "You asked for it. You force us to be nasty."

Early in the morning on July 12, 1967, the telephone. That sound. It was a newspaperman calling from England: "Madame Mercouri, Mr. Patakos, the Greek Minister of the Interior, has declared you an enemy of the people. He says you have damaged the country morally and economically. Your property will be confiscated and you are deprived of your Greek citizenship."

For a moment, I couldn't speak.

"Do you have any comment?"

I tried to find my voice.

"Madame Mercouri, Mr. Patakos has declared you a non-Greek. Do you have any comment?"

The words came. "I was born Greek, I shall die Greek. Mr. Patakos was born a fascist. He will die a fascist."

It took hours before my anger subsided. I vowed to fight them until I died. Then I was overtaken by fear. I thought of the body of Mandilaras, washed up on a lonely beach soon after the junta took power. Mandilaras was Andreas Papandreou's lawyer, who had done so much to expose the fraudulence of the Aspida trials. He paid for it with his life. What if they decided to kill me? What country would care? I was on no one's record now. What was my identity? I was alone in a foreign country, without a passport. Could the State Department send me away? When I conquered those crazy fears, I felt nothing but sadness. The solitude was too much to bear. I had lost Manos. Spiros and Rena were in London. My mother was in Greece. My father had died, and Julie was somewhere in Israel.

Despo was a bulwark. She didn't leave my side. Despo and Ricky. I think I'd have lost my mind if they had not been there. And suddenly it became clear that the colonels had made a blunder. They were attacked and ridiculed from all sides. My comment "I was born Greek and I shall die Greek" was quoted everywhere. Two days later, shops in New York were selling lapel buttons with the slogan MELINA IS A GREEK. Orianna Fallaci did a long article about me and our fight for Greece in *Look* magazine. It was read into the Congressional Record. It was only then that I realized we could get congressmen and senators to create a committee for Greek democracy. Irene Pappas, our beautiful tragic actress was in Rome. She called a press conference to protest the theft of my nationality. Telegrams and letters came in huge canvas bags, urging me to continue the fight against the junta. From Europe, South America, Australia, and Japan. From everywhere. Mr. Patakos had provided me with arms against him. There was a beautiful letter from Michael Cacoyannis. Cacoyannis was a man who shunned politics, but he was a democrat and a friend. Later on, he telephoned from Europe; we wept together. He told me he would see me soon. He was coming to New York to direct *Iphigenia in Aulis* with Irene Pappas. When *Iphigenia in Aulis* was produced with great success, it was hailed not only for its artistry, but also as an expression of a free Greece.

Ten days after my nationality was taken from me, Julie was back in New York. He had been away for only six weeks, but I had gone through too much without him. I hoped he would not talk about any of it too soon. He did not. Nor did he treat me too tenderly. That was good too. For the first few days I asked little about Israel. We respected each other's regrets. We knew that there was a bridge to cross and we gave each other time. Soon we were together again.

A secret service background makes the ear a sensitive organ.

If the colonels have small mind and no heart, they have big ears. Of course, their favorite sound is that of tanks clattering through city streets. They understand its effect. They also know what sounds most effectively drown the cries of tortured prisoners. Many who testified before the Human Rights Commission of the Council of Europe, told of the use of motorcycle motors, charged in full blast to cover the screams of those being tortured on the infamous terrace of the Security building. And the junta ear was sensitive to the music of Mikis Theodorakis. Sensitive in the medical sense: allergic. They forbade the Greek people to buy, play, or listen to anything composed by Mikis. Offenders would be arrested. One would have to be Greek or to have lived in Greece to fully realize what this interdiction meant. I don't remember a single day in Greece when I did not hear Mikis' music, be it on the radio, in the theatre, in a cinema, in a taverna, on a record heard from someone's open window or a boy whistling in the streets. His music was part of our daily life. The colonels' allergy was understandable. Mikis' music for *Zorba the Greek* goes right to the bone of the Kazantzakis' character. Zorba is above all a free soul. The pursuit of happiness and freedom is his way of life. Freedom and happiness have no place in a fascist state. The vibrant music for Ritsos' magnificent poem "Greekness" must make the colonels particularly uncomfortable. It is a pledge that tyrants will not long endure on Greek soil. So Mikis was outlawed, along with Ritsos and Kazantzakis. When Julie went to Athens, one of the first people he inquired about was Mikis. None of our friends knew where he was. There were rumors that he was hidden in a house "above suspicion" but everyone feared that the junta agents would not rest until he was behind bars.

The people at the theatre were concerned about the threatening letters I received, and orders were given not to permit any strangers backstage. One evening late in August, the doorman came to tell me that there was a stranger who would not give his name. He spoke with an accent and refused to leave. Julie was in my dressing room and went out to investigate. He came back to say: "Someone with a message from Athens."

He was very young, slight of stature, with features as delicate as a girl's. From time to time, during the last few years, this young man has come to me in different parts of the world to give me a message and to leave almost immediately. I still don't know his name. That first night, his message was: "Mikis is all right. This is from him."

Wrapped in an airmail envelope there was a small band of magnetic tape. We heard the theatre orchestra begin the overture. I embraced the boy. He left. It seemed the performance would never end. I rushed back to the hotel without removing my make-up.

We listened to Mikis' voice on the tape. It was recorded in almost a whisper. One immediately felt the atmosphere of a hiding place, doors and windows closed and this giant of a man bending to speak quietly into a microphone. It was a thrilling and eloquent call to resistance. It was followed by a song. There was no musical accompaniment, just the sound of Mikis' fingers drumming out the rhythm and Mikis' voice:

"The front calls the Greeks to combat
On our flag is written liberty or death."

We listened to the tape again and again, until I stopped trembling, until I had no more tears. In the years that followed, I was to sing that song countless times for audiences all over America and Europe.

Sometimes destiny, or whatever it is that monitors the movement of men and time, is cruelly capricious. The very same night we received the tape, the radio announced the capture and imprisonment of Mikis Theodorakis in Athens.

When Andreas Papandreou was arrested, there was a flood

of petitions and telegrams demanding that no harm come to him. I am convinced that this quick action saved his life. We spent all of the next day telephoning artists and composers in Europe and America asking them to organize a similar campaign for Mikis. We learned that Simone Signoret in Paris and Betsy Blair in London were making the same calls. I talked with Kermit Bloomgarden, our producer. He and Julie had had differences, but I shall always be grateful to him. When I asked him to let me make a curtain speech that night in behalf of Mikis, he did not hesitate for a moment. His permission was wholehearted. The audience applauded when I asked them to wire the State Department and urge its intervention. When I sang "Zorba the Greek," they all rose in tribute to the man locked in a junta prison.

There were others who looked on all of this with a jaundiced eye. So-called friends came to warn me "that an artist who meddled in politics would finish by destroying his career." I took recourse to the first dirty word I learned in English: "Bullshit." The narrowness and inhumanity of the notion that fighting for your freedom and the freedom of others is "meddling in politics" makes me furious. I suggested that they brush up their history and etymology. History would tell them what role the artist has always played in the fight for justice and freedom, and demo(s) in the Greek word democracy, means people. Artists are people too.

Thank God many artists refuse to accept the role of court jester, or sequestration in ivory towers. In Italy, the brilliant writer, Albert Moravia, was presiding the jury of the Venice film festival. He wrote a petition that was signed by all the members of the jury and the film people attending the festival. It was addressed to Mr. Fanfani, who was then the Italian Minister of Foreign Affairs. The petition requested that he use his offices to have a Red Cross inspector go to Athens and investigate the conditions under which Theodorakis was detained. From France, came a petition bearing, among other signatures, Jean-Luc Godard, Juliette Gréco, Michel Magne, Yves Montand, Marie-José Nat, Michel Piccoli, Simone Signoret, and Jean-Louis Trintignant. In the United States, Arthur Miller forbade the performance of any of his plays in Greece. Edward Albee had already drawn up a petition enjoining artists not to participate in the Athens festival. It was signed by Lindsay Anderson, Peggy Ashcroft, Leonard Bernstein, Betsy Blair, Sir Maurice Bowra, Bill Gaskill, John Knowles, John Le Carré, Edna O'Brien, Irene Pappas, Vanessa Redgrave, Karel Reisz, John Schlesinger, and Kenneth Tynan.

And there is another superb artist who has never ceased working for a free Greece. He is the American political cartoonist whose signature is Herblock. He has a sharpness of wit and a sense of caricature that can be devastating and at the same time one feels enormous compassion and goodness. Greece owes him much. In the American press, Clayton Fritchey, Pete Hamill, Murray Kempton, Drew Pearson, Max Lerner, Harriet Van Horne, Evans and Novak can be counted on to give a truthful image of what goes on in Greece. There must be others, but these are the names I got to know in the New York press. In general, the press attitudes break down into three groups: those who are apologists for the junta, those who are against them, and those who pretend to be against them. The last group is the hardest to take. They all, more or less, use the same technique: the creation and perpetuation of a myth. It goes something like this:

> Of course no one likes a dictatorship. Yet one must admit that before the colonels took over, Greece was in a mess. It was inefficient, bureaucratic, the political atmosphere was Byzantine, the economy was disintegrating and the Center Union was moving into the red embrace.

An expert at this kind of writing is Cyrus L. Sulzberger, correspondent for the New York *Times*. He's damned clever at it. For instance, you can scan each word of all the columns he's written on Andreas Papandreou and you'll never find it said that he was a Communist, but somehow the sum total of the column is that Andreas Papandreou is a Communist. Sulzberger will tell you that the colonels are not very nice, but somehow make you feel that Greece had no other solution. He will remind you that if Democracy is a Greek word, so is Anarchy. Oh, he's a beauty. He leaves you with the impression that Greece was floundering and unable to help itself.

Yet it cannot be said that Sulzberger represents the attitude of the New York *Times*. Some of the editorials most critical of the junta appeared in that newspaper. To tell the complete truth, I am obliged to tell tales out of school. It is disagreeable to reveal confidences, but what the hell, this is a war. I can vouch that there are people, highly placed in the New York *Times* who are embarrassed by Sulzberger's reporting on the Greek situation, and that they were pleased by a debunking piece written by Paul A. Samuelson for *Newsweek* one month after the colonels' coup.

Mr. Samuelson exploded the myth of a Greece in chaos and economic stagnation. He came up with statistics to prove that in the sixties, the Greek output grew faster than that of any other European country, and that the Greek price index had been one of the steadiest during the period. In 1966, the year before the coup "the real gross product grew 8.2 per cent." (Faster than that of the United States and the U.S.S.R.!) Mr. Samuelson states flatly that the Center Union party of George and Andreas Papandreou was no threat to the economic prosperity. As for Mr. Sulzberger's reliability as a correspondent, quote:

> For a score of years, American economists have known the younger Papandreou, his numerous books, articles and lectures. Careful reading of them shows no trace of Marxist or totalitarian leanings. The many dispatches of C. L. Sulzberger in the

New York Times appear to be as misleading on Andreas Papandreou as were the disastrously inaccurate appraisals of Fidel Castro by Times reporter, Herbert Matthews.

Unquote. (Mr. Samuelson is no slouch, either as editorialist or economist. He's a Nobel prize winner in economics. He knows whereof he speaks.)

It is not easy for me, this anger I feel toward Mr. Sulzberger. His wife, Marina, and I were close friends. I was fond of her. I still am. But I have to deal with my conviction that those reports in a newspaper as widely respected as the New York *Times*, have done extreme harm to my country. I even think that in this recent period, Mr. Sulzberger has compromised his friendship to the royal family. That brings me to August 25, 1967 and King Constantine.

From the time Constantine got his picture taken with the colonels, very little was heard from him. One had to imagine that in the four months that followed, he was doing something, because all those thousands of dismissals of officers from the royal army needed to be signed by him to go into effect. Of course, it's possible that the colonels just kept on forging his signature. They had already proved that they were capable of such practices, but I'm afraid that is a charitable view, a hangover from my childhood royalist partisanship. Naturally there were rumors in Athens. Some said Constantine was unhappy and that his mama was having second thoughts about the junta. Other rumors went further. They had it that Constantine now opposed the colonels and was kept a virtual prisoner. Whatever his feelings were, he had maintained a majestic silence.

On the morning of August 25, we received word that Constantine was on his way to the United States! We phoned the newspapers and press services. They had no such information. We got accentless people to phone the Greek consulate and the embassy in Washington. They said there was no truth to the matter. This was puzzling. Our source was reliable. We kept on making calls. Finally, a wire service confirmed his arrival and a luncheon that very day at the United Nations. Just for fun we called the consulate and the embassy again to see if they would persist in the denial. They did.

As sensitive Greeks, we deemed it unthinkable that our King should sneak into the country. He had to have a reception. We got busy to make him one. Everyone phoned everyone else to phone everyone else. In an hour's time, with the help of the American Committee for Democracy and Freedom in Greece, we had a respectable demonstration organized and on the way to the United Nations building, and Jim Proctor had the press alerted. During that hour, we drew up a petition to be handed to the King. It was in the form of thirteen questions. I would like to put them down here, because even though some are rhetorical, others are still pertinent today. Here they are, just for the record.

Your Majesty, why was your coming to the United States kept a secret until the last minute?

Why did the Greek Embassy in Washington and the Consulate in New York refuse, up until a few hours ago, any information to the press about your arrival here?

Royal visits are usually announced with fanfare. Why this silence?

A proud representative of a country does not slip into another country in silence. Are you not proud of the regime that rules Greece today?

Are you afraid of questions?

Are you afraid of embarrassment by the American press?

Your apologists say that you were not free to speak in Greece. Here, you are free to speak. You have never made a statement explaining your attitude to the military junta. Will you make one now?

Are you using your offices to free the thousands of political prisoners now in Greek prisons?

Are you using your offices to restore a free press?

Are you using your offices to restore constitutional government in Greece?

This military regime took power in Greece by force. They said they acted in your name. Did you give them your name?

Do you give them your name today?

Will you break your silence?

I once saw a film in which there was a marvelous fight. It was John Ford's *The Quiet Man*. The fight scene was delicious —dead serious, but very funny. The Irish call it a donnybrook. We too were dead serious, but it turned out to be great fun as well. It developed into a comic contest between the demonstrators and the King for the attention of the reporters, photographers, and television cameras present. It was raining outside the United Nations building. Some of our group were allowed into the lobby. We planned to wait there for the King's arrival and then go out again and try to hand him the letter. I sat down near the Marc Chagall window. I heard a loud voice: "There's Melina."

The reporters and photographers who were outside, awaiting the King's arrival, dashed into the building; on their heels, men carting lights and pushing television cameras. Jim Proctor suggested an impromptu press conference. Lights went on, the cameras turned and I read our letter to Constantine. Then came a series of questions from reporters. My answers were being noted and filmed when shouts were heard outside.

"The King."

Half of the reporters and photographers left me flat and rushed outside again to meet the arriving, police-guarded limousine. The television cameras trundled after them. Our demonstrators outside in the rain made themselves heard, and the King was whisked into the building. He disappeared into an elevator before we could get to him. The guards now moved us into the auditorium of the Dag Hammarskjöld Library. Again a voice: "She's still here."

Once more a movement of men and cameras. The lights went on again. The cameramen took their positions. Before they could start shooting, the sound of motorcycles. A man who had been pushing the cameras back and forth let out a low groan: "Oh no."

The automobile carrying Queen Anne-Marie was just arriving. Wearily, the men began to gather up their equipment, then gave up. They decided the Queen was too far away.

The New York *Times* reported the next day that Queen Anne-Marie did not seem slighted. Their story reflected the spirit of the whole affair. I was declared the winner. The headline said: MELINA UPSTAGES GREEK KING AT U.N.

Constantine didn't get our letter at the UN. It was against protocol. Before we left, I asked a guard if he could get it delivered. He said in a glorious Brooklyn accent: "Sister, I ain't no letter carrier, and this ain't no post office."

We had to be satisfied to send the letter to the King's hotel. But we did not consider it a defeat. Our questions were aired on radio and television. Most of the press was sympathetic to the demonstrators. They all agreed that Constantine had come to the United States to solicit increased military aid for Greece and they were against it. Harriet Van Horne, expressing her disapproval of the royal visit in the New York *Post*, said something about me that I would like to repeat. I am not too embarrassed to quote what she said, because I consider that it was addressed to Mr. Patakos, who deprived me of my citizenship.

Melina Mercouri embodies more of the grandeur of Greece than the entire Royal family.

Nor do I blush at the word grandeur. It was Miss Van Horne's way of saying that the Greek people are more grand than all the Glücksbourgs and Wittelsbachs.

The royal family's itinerary included a visit to President Lyndon Johnson in Washington and the Canadian exposition on

Greece's national day. It was difficult to reconcile the King's rumored opposition to the junta, with a request for military aid to the army that the junta controlled, and his representation of Greece at an international exposition. The London *Times* summed it all up nicely:

> The King may say he doesn't like the Junta, but the Junta certainly likes him.

Another demonstration was scheduled the day of the visit to the White House. This matter of arms was a serious business. The American administration, sensing the universal revulsion when the colonels grabbed Greece, gently chastised the junta by a reduction of arms—no jet planes but plenty of guns. We denounced military aid of any kind. We understood that the full resumption would give prestige and strength to the colonels. It was only an hour's flight from New York to Washington. There was easily time to get to the demonstration and be back at the theatre for the evening performance. The demonstration was lively. It took place in a small park that faces the White House. It tickled me to see many people wearing the buttons MELINA IS A GREEK. I had a short speech to make. I was supposed to finish the speech with:

> Greece doesn't need guns. It needs freedom. The choice of either can come from the President of the United States.

I got up to make my speech before a battery of microphones. It must be that Constantine puts a kind of hex on me. Every time I get involved with him, it comes out funny. I was sailing right along in my speech, right to the very end, when I heard myself say, by vocational bias and royal hex:

> "The choice of either can come from the President of United Artists."

There is a God. He ordained that the last words be drowned out by applause, but Julie heard it. I thought he'd have a stroke.

There were high moments and fighting the good fight makes you feel all right in your skin, but I came back from Washington with a heaviness in my heart. I had never believed that the junta could last. It was too evil, too monstrous, too ignorant. But there was something about that demonstration in Washington that dragged at my morale. There we were, Greeks and Americans, sincerely, passionately making our feelings known to the President of the United States. We weren't there on an issue that was doubtful. We weren't a group defending petty interests. We were talking about dictatorships, about tyranny. And there was that great stone symbol, that building so white, so graceful, so deaf. And what emanated from that building and the smiling arrogance of the police protecting it was a benign tolerance and immovability. *Let them demonstrate. Let them blow off steam. Then they'll go home and we'll get on with our business.*

I unburdened myself to Julie. I told him that we were wasting our time and energy, that no one would help, and that if the Greek people wanted the dictators off their backs, they'd have to do it alone. I asked myself a nagging question, a question put to me every day, and that until now I had parried: "What are the Greek people doing? Where is the resistance?"

I had all the right answers. The people's leaders in jail, the constant arrests, the tortures, the junta spy system spread over Greece like a horrible web made organization slow and difficult. And the people were tired; tired of sacrifice, tired of going to jail for ideals that were never realized, tired of shedding their blood. The souvenirs of the civil war were too present, its wounds still open. All these answers were true, but deep down they did not satisfy me. What had happened to all those hundreds of thousands of Greeks who vowed that fascism could pass only over their bodies? What I never said, but felt, was that the Greek people were paralyzed by a profound pessimism. How could you fight the junta when you knew that the immense power of the United States was behind them? Must we too become a Vietnam? All Greeks knew that without American support, the junta could not last forty-eight hours, and what they saw took the heart out of them. They saw big American corporations rushing to take advantage of bargains offered by a craven junta and to exploit the situation to their profit. They saw regular communiqués from the State Department that shammed belief in the dictator promises of an early return to democracy, and they saw huge photographs in the press of junta chiefs being entertained at cordial luncheons on the American flagship of the Sixth Fleet. And all in the name of NATO. What a sick joke! In the campaign to win our affection for NATO, we had been taught that its members undertook to safeguard democracy, individual freedom and law. In that case, how could the membership of a gangster government be justified? More than justified—protected. In a speech I made in Washington, I suggested that either Greece be kicked out of NATO or that the pact be rewritten to admit that democracy was not required of its members. Some people applauded, others were honest enough to laugh. The Scandinavian members, Holland, and Italy did take the position that Greece had no place in NATO. This only caused slight embarrassment to the Americans. The Pentagon skin is thick.

There were those who had looked to the east for help. And here too, they saw only hypocrisy. The Soviet Union and other "people's democracies" at one and the same time denounced the junta and helped them live by increasing trade with them. Yet the Greek is a wise man. He knows how to discount his own discouragement. He knows that the microbes organic to dictatorship will eventually lay it low. And repeatedly, when we were depressed in spirit, something would happen to lift us up. An act of heroism, a clever pamphlet, a defiant speech of a prisoner facing a military court, a bomb well placed, testified that the people's fight continued. The devils are not all on one side. Neither are the angels. Conservative publisher Helen Vlachos shut down her newspapers rather than accept the colonels' censors. Put under house arrest, she made a daring escape to England and kept fighting the good fight from there. Equally conservative former Prime Minister Cannelopoulos has never stopped attacking the junta. Totally censored in Greece, he got through to the foreign correspondents to debunk the red myth. He branded as completely false the claims of the military regime that it acted to save Greece from chaos and Communist takeover. "This is not true," he said, "simply because there was no chaos."

He was in a position to know. He was Prime Minister up until a week before the coup. We had no illusions. We didn't expect people like Vlachos or Cannelopoulos to take to the barricades, but their opposition to the junta was sincere and was respected. I had less respect for Constantine Karamanlis. Like everyone else, I knew he despised the junta, yet, aside from two early noncommittal communiqués, for nine months he had maintained a stony silence. On December 5, we heard that he had finally given an interview to the French newspaper *Le Monde*. We rushed to find a copy at a foreign newsstand. We read it, standing in the street. He said:

The putschists had betrayed their promises to restore democracy and had no intention of leaving power, that they had isolated the country internationally and were vigorously disapproved by the great majority of the people.

So far, so good. But when asked what steps he would take if the junta refused to step down, his answer had all the dynamism of a flat tire.

I have no personal interest in politics and only issue this statement because the people are waiting for an orientation.

What a letdown. What orientation? The Greek people knew their position in relation to all points of the political compass. They knew north from south and east from west, and they also knew the difference between a hawk and a handsaw. For nine months, everyone waited for Karamanlis to speak. Conservative or not, he had kept office for eight years. Much of the country still held him in esteem. The colonels had just capitulated miserably to sell out the Greeks in Cyprus. They were being villified and cursed. A principled fighting statement from Karamanlis might have moved people to action. It didn't come. The whole interview smelled of a politician operating in the worn customary grooves. After nine months of pregnant silence, Mr. Karamanlis gave birth to a titmouse.

On December 12, one week later, we stayed up all night. The young boy with delicate features had brought us more tapes from Mikis; new songs that he had composed and managed to record in captivity. The same atmosphere, the voice recorded low, the fingers tapping out the rhythm—but another dimension in the songs. They were always militant, always strong, but now they were touched with irony and sadness. By what recourses they had been smuggled out, we didn't ask. Nor were any explanations offered. We spent the night preparing a television program built around the songs. It was daylight when we went to bed. Just a few hours later, the ringing of the telephone. It was someone from a television station asking if they could send a crew to film my comment on the countercoup. What countercoup? "Haven't you heard? King Constantine is leading an army against the junta."

We flew to the radio, just in time to hear the announcer say that the King was in Salonika, that the air force and the navy were following the King's orders, and that it was probable that much of the army would rally to him. The King had broadcast a message asking the support of the Greek people. Julie, Spiros, and I had a hurried conference. The television crew was on the way. What should I say? We all agreed that Constantine bore much of the blame for the coming of the junta, even if this particular one was not of his choice. We agreed that on April 21 he could have destroyed them, had he really wanted to. On that first day, to oppose them was to end them. Had he said: "I am against you, arrest me if you like," the whole coup would have collapsed. The United States, no matter what its wishes really were, could not have possibly supported the junta with the King under arrest.

Yet should I say any of this in my comment? Was it not more correct to hail any move against the junta, even if it came from the King? Julie thought not. He saw it as a battle between two cliques. He suggested that I say that I could not believe that the King was acting in the interests of democracy in Greece, that his undemocratic behavior in the past could not inspire such belief, that democracy would be restored to Greece by its people and not Constantine. Spiros and I, more European, more schooled to power politics, vetoed Julie. We could not imagine that the King would move without assurance of help from the Americans. Our attitude was, first things first. Let's get the junta out and then take up the fight for constitutional government. We kept the radio open, hoping for some news which would guide my comment. Nothing but unconfirmed reports. I finally uttered vague generalities of the need for unity in overcoming the dictatorship. I was interviewed about a half dozen times during the day, and kept repeating the same clichés. My interviewers were as disappointed with my statements as I was.

The royal fiasco is too well known for me to dwell on. In his radio broadcast on December 13, Constantine pounded his chest.

"I will not accept disobedience from now on—and it will be crushed without mercy. There will be no compromise."

By the next day, he had fled to Rome. His poor little abortion of a revolt was tragi-comic. It turned out that junta agents knew all of his plans in detail, as did an extraordinary number of people in Athens. It was no contest; a pitiful rout. There were no casualties. Not even a sprained ankle.

Perhaps the Greek people could have forgotten the travesty of the King's revolt and forgiven the defeat, had he shown a little more courage, but he was, as Clayton Fritchey put it:

> a king poised for flight even as he nervously blew an uncertain trumpet.

When this precipitate flight was questioned, Constantine replied that if he had stayed behind, he would have become the prisoner of the junta and "what purpose did that serve?"

Is it possible that he is so simple-minded? His arrest could have been very useful indeed. It would have given the Pentagon and the Johnson administration a very red face, and strong arguments to the junta opponents. He certainly could have had no fears that he would be tortured like any other ordinary Greek citizen. In his statement the King added:

> "Also I would be better able to speak freely to the world from a position outside of Greece."

Well, he's been away from Greece for more than three years now. What has he said to the world? Nothing. It all came to an end with a Sunday *Times* correspondent asking the King to comment on the London *Daily Mirror*'s description of him as: "Not a King but a mouse."

Constantine countered with a question. "What can I say? That I am not a mouse?"

His Majesty had a point. He could not say that he was not a mouse.

As long as Constantine was on his throne, the foreign powers were spared the embarrassment of recognizing the junta. Constantine was the titular head of state and all embassies were accredited to the monarch. But now what? When the State Department was asked if the junta would be recognized as the government of Greece, its spokesman, Robert J. Mc-Closkey had this to say: "Any comment might prejudice a highly complex situation."

Senator Stephen Young of Ohio, a member of the Senate Armed Services Committee saw things simply, and not complexly. He called on President Johnson to break diplomatic relations and recall the ambassador from Athens, but Old Faithful Sulzberger sent up a clarifying geyser:

The U.S. and other N.A.T.O. allies are in the anomalous position of having their envoys accredited to the King, who happens to be in Rome. [Sulzberger makes it sound like a holiday.] Yet since both Papadopoulos and Constantine still talk of the King's return, there has been no need to consider breaking diplomatic relationships.

(Okay Sulzberger, if that's the way you saw it, but the King's stay in Rome is going into its fourth year. I haven't read a piece by you asking for the ambassador's recall. How long do you think we ought to wait?)

The day after the King's coup, the pictures of King Constantine and Queen Anne-Marie were still on the Greek embassy walls. The press asked: "Will they stay?"

The spokesman answered: "I don't know, although they are very nice pictures."

Papadopoulos insisted that Greece was still a monarchy. Just to make sure there were no doubts, he found a stooge called Zoitakis and named him regent to the King. To make the farce complete, Zoitakis turned around and named Papadopoulos his Prime Minister, and as the colonel put it:

The Regent did me the honour of entrusting me with the formation of a new government.

The little dog laughed to see such sport, and the dish ran away with the spoon.

In the race to see who would be first to recognize the regime, Turkey came in first, closely followed by England and the United States. Turkey found the way to express its delight in the way the colonels strangled the Cyprus dream of Enosis.

The colonels had the dilemma of what to do with Andreas Papandreou. It would be awkward to kill him; too many people were watching. The Aspida case had collapsed like the vulgar frame-up it was, and world pressure for his release had never let up. They finally decided he was less dangerous to them abroad than within Greece. They let him out of prison and out of the country. Shortly after, he announced the formation of a resistance movement called PAK (Pan Hellenic Liberation Movement). Many people and organizations in the United States wanted to make contact with him. Julie was going to Paris to finish the editing of the documentary he made in Israel and was delegated to visit Mr. Papandreou. I was uneasy about his leaving, but thought it necessary. Besides, Spiros was with me. But it had become a pattern. Every time Julie went away, terrible things happened to me.

First there was the harbinger.

I was alone in my dressing room. The door opened just a crack and I saw Anna's eyes, big and frightened. "He's here. His brother is here."

I knew, without asking, whose brother he was. The Trappist monk. He pushed his way into the room. "My brother is dead. His last thought was of you."

I stared at him. The same face. The same black hands. There could be no mistake. It was the same man who had come the first time. There was no brother. This was a madman. "You're lying. You're not his brother. It was you who came before. What do you want?"

"My brother died. I shall carry on his work. I will take a vow of silence but I shall pray for you."

228

As he was led away, he kept repeating: "I will pray for you."
I am Mediterranean enough to know an evil omen when
I see one. When Spiros came to the theatre, I told him that
something was going to happen to us. He said it already had
happened. He'd been summoned to the Federal Bureau of
Investigation. To foreigners, the FBI meant one thing only.
It was the organization that tracked spies and Communists.
Were the Greek Consulate stories about us believed? Was I
considered a Communist? Were we going to be expelled from
the United States? Where could I go without a passport? And
why did this kind of thing always fall on Wednesdays, the
day of two performances? I'm pretty good at applying
make-up, but not that day. My hands shook too much. It was
Spiros who came back with the two handsome young men.
They had FBI credentials. "Miss Mercouri, we have information that an attempt is going to be made on your life."

The would-be assassin had been described to them. He was
of medium height. He had dark curly hair and he spoke English with a foreign accent. He had just come to New York and
had rented a room somewhere in the area of the theatre. The
local police would be called in, men in civilian clothes would
be placed in the audience. With this came a rapping at the
door that was so sharp, we all jumped. It was the stage
manager. "Curtain going up in five minutes."

In *Illya Darling*, I had a song to sing called "Piraeus, My
Love." It was one of the few moments in the show that had
not become a chore. I was alone on stage in a spotlight and
able to achieve intense concentration. When actors tell you
that they can become so steeped in their roles that they forget stage and audience, take it with a grain of salt. It rarely
happens. It did happen to me a number of times when I sang
"Piraeus, My Love." My concern for Greece, my longing to
see it again were stronger than actress or performance. It was
audience applause that brought me back to my stage sur-
roundings. And often the applause for that song had a wonder-

ful quality. The audience was telling me that they were sensitive to what I was feeling and that they cared about Greece too.

But that afternoon, all I could think of was a man of medium height and dark curly hair sitting in an aisle seat with a silencer on his black revolver. In that spotlight I was an easy target. It may have been a romantic way to die, but the idea had no appeal to me at all. It may have been comforting to see the gleaming badges of policemen in the wings, on each side of the stage, but it didn't help me to remember the words of the song. Some members of the cast, in costume and make-up, stood in the back of the theatre, ready to rush upon the Mediterranean John Wilkes Booth and tear him limb from limb, and dear Harry Lemonopoulos, our bouzouki player, came on stage and stood playing in the dark so that I could feel someone close to me. To put it mildly, the song was a flop. There was a tepid smattering of applause. The son of a bitch had not only scared me to death, he had also ruined my best number.

Julie moved up his departure from Paris, but in the meantime, he insisted that a private bodyguard should be added. This was arranged by my friend and lawyer, Joe Stratos. I began to feel like a character in a Keystone comedy. Each day I'd leave for the theatre surrounded by policemen, one next to the driver of the car, two on either side of me in the back seat and following closely, in his car, my private bodyguard. I was delivered like a parcel to the theatre where two other policemen received delivery. But what frightened me most of all was not the unknown assassin. It was my private bodyguard. He was smothered in revolvers and he wouldn't leave me alone for a minute. It was all I could do to get the door of the toilet closed.

After six weeks of this, the police said I was costing the City of New York too much money. They asked me to sign a paper releasing them and assuming responsibility for my own life.

I said that I was happy to let them go, but would not sign anything that relieved them of doing their duty. We compromised. The police wouldn't come to the theatre regularly, but they would make occasional checks. We kept the bodyguard on for two weeks after Julie's return. I can't say that I was sorry to see him go. Despo had devised ways for me to escape him from time to time. She thought I was invulnerable to anybody's bullet. In any case, she thought it worth the risk rather than have a nervous breakdown caused by the oppressive presence of the bodyguard. The fear had gone by now. Julie was back. Spiros was there and above all, there was stalwart, marvelous Despo. No assassin could get through her vigilant guard. One evening, Despo and I had managed a neat escape from my bodyguard. We went to a little restaurant in Greenwich Village. It was a merry place. There was a small orchestra stand, and anyone who felt like playing or singing just got up and did so. A group of actors who were rehearsing an off-Broadway play came to join us at our table. They were marvelously young and wildly funny. They improvised a hilarious parody of their rehearsals. I laughed wholeheartedly. Despo observed that it was the first time she heard me laugh that way since April 21. I realized that she was right. There is a wonderful Greek word, *palikari*. A *palikari* is a fighter, a warrior, but he's gay. He fights with kefi and can laugh at adversity. Despo used the word. "I like your fight. There's nothing else you can do. But I don't want to be depressed by you. I want you to give me courage. Fight—but like a *palikari*."

Right on, Despo, right on.

We were going to carry the fight to Europe. I was looking forward to the end of the run of *Illya Darling*. Acting was my life, but for the first time, my mind and heart were elsewhere.

Chapter Eighteen

If my destiny is in some mysterious way shaped by the number eighteen, I'll meet it halfway and make this eighteenth chapter the last. I've filled hundreds of little white cards with notes in Greek. I've talked for many hundreds of hours into a tape recorder in French and in English. Now, I yield to the translators. I understand that sometimes translators must adapt to the translated language. In this book, I give them free hand. What I ask to be kept literal, is my anger. My anger is the reason for this book.

If I had to thank all the people who worked for a free Greece, their names would fill this chapter, but how not to thank Victor Reuther for his aid in the creation of the United States Committee for Greek Democracy?* How not to thank the men who chaired this Committee, former attorney general,

* The initiators of the Committee were: Edward Albee, Joseph Clark, then Senator from Pennsylvania, Jack Conway, Ben Cohen, Jules Dassin, Congressman Don Edwards, John W. Edelman, the Honorable Kenneth Galbraith, Harry Golden, Maurice Goldbloom, Christopher Janus, Leon Keyserling, the Honorable Philip M. Klutznick, Archibald MacLeish, A. Philip Randolph, Victor Reuther, Leon School, Michael Straight, Joseph Stratos Jr., George Vournas, Rabbi Jacob, J. Weinstein, the Honorable G. Mennen Williams.

Francis Biddle and Congressman Don Fraser from Minnesota, and the man who chairs it today, Congressman Don Edwards from California?

The closing of a show is something like the end of a love affair. It is an occasion for sentiment and tears. I had made many friends in *Illya Darling*. We had lived and worked together for a year and a half. I loved them. They had helped me through many a bad moment. Yet on closing night I could not hide from them that I was glad it was over. Theatre and acting were not on my mind.

Now began a tour of American cities. Not everyone made us welcome. In Chicago, where I appeared with Andreas Papandreou, the police were alerted to search for bombs in our hotel and in the theatre where we spoke. When we arrived at the theatre, there was a vociferous picket line. Most, if not all, were Greek-Americans. They received us with obscenities and curses. Before the coup, this same kind of person used to receive me with song and flowers. Now they called me Communist and traitor. What had happened to them? What had happened to their minds that they could defend a dictatorship in Greece? I tried hard to find the answer.

Many of them, many of their parents, could not earn a living in Greece. They came to the United States and by hard work achieved material comfort. Was it enough to say the word Communist and in the furious clutchings of what they owned, stampede their judgment? If so, why is this not equally true of Greeks who emigrated to Canada, to Australia, to Germany? In those countries the pro-junta voices are few. I think the clue is to be found in the Greek's sense of patriotism. He is by nature a patriot. To him patriotism means love of country. The Greek who came to America and solved his economic problems transferred this patriotism to the United States. It is the golden land that gave him success. If the United States government supports the junta, then it is good enough for him. He can tolerate no criticism of the government. He has become "more royalist than the King." To give the full picture, the lower wage earners among Greek-Americans despise the junta. This is also true of the intellectuals and academicians. Most of the Free Greece committees in university cities were organized by Greek-American professors.

In March 1968, I was to leave for Europe. Shortly before, it had been proposed that I address a luncheon in Washington given by the Women's National Democratic Club. I hesitated to accept because my morale was low and I was tired to the bone. Then I read something that made me furious and restored my energy. The Honorable Dean Acheson, former Secretary of State, had written a letter that was published in the Washington *Post*. Mr. Acheson simply expressed the opinion that what Greeks needed was authoritarian rule. How not to answer that? Where better to answer than in Washington? I accepted the invitation. I had expected to meet with a small group of women, and hoped that some of the press be present. To my astonishment, I found some seven hundred people gathered in a huge room. The *Evening Star* reporter wrote that it was "the largest luncheon crowd in the Club's history." Another surprise was that many men were present, among them holders of important office. It was jokingly explained to me that the Women's National Democratic Club had political power and so the men had better come to their luncheons—or else. Some of our Washington Committee warned me that Mr. Acheson was one of the most respected men in the country, that he was held in particular esteem by most of the audience present, that he had influence in the Johnson administration and that to criticize him would be a tactical and political error. I replied that he was using his influence in a manner harmful to Greece and that was the precise reason for my coming to speak to this gathering.

I was nervous when I spoke. I made mistakes in grammar and in pronunciation, but the audience was forgiving and sympathetic until I came to speak of Mr. Acheson.

"In a letter to the Washington *Post*, Mr. Acheson expressed an opinion that authoritarian rule is what Greeks need. Now we all know that Mr. Acheson is an honorable man, yet he comes to bury democracy in Greece. Evil tongues say that Mr. Acheson had a pique against the former Greek government because they rejected his solution to the Cyprus issue. I must doubt this because Mr. Acheson is an honorable man. It is his honorable judgment that the people of Greece are ignorant and backward and not ready for democracy. I am only an unlearned actress and the honorable Mr. Acheson is a former Secretary of State, but I stand up to him and say: 'Mr. Secretary, you are wrong. We know the meaning of democracy. We invented it. We will refuse your counsel, Mr. Secretary. We will be free.'"

Suddenly I was talking in a refrigerator. The room became chill. I felt a little click of satisfaction that their coolness didn't matter. As an actress, I like to please, but what I felt was "the hell with the actress, you're a Greek who has something to say whether they like it or not." I had made a step forward. It freed me for other battles in the future.

My brother Spiros is Hercules. In less than six weeks, he organized a tour of eighteen cities in Europe (there's that number again). He dashed through Europe in his little Charlie Chaplin car, with the door falling off. He met with the heads of political parties, he arranged for the rental of theatres. Where there were no theatres available, he found banquet halls. Where there were no banquet halls, he begged for the use of university auditoriums. He arranged for hotels and haggled over rates. He scheduled press conferences and meetings with government leaders. He contacted exiled musicians from Mikis Theodorakis' orchestra and incorporated them into the tour. He flew back to New York for a six-hour meeting with me and Julie and then went right back to Strasbourg. He was Hercules, he was Tarzan, he was a Greek palikari. Jim Proctor marveled at Spiros' work. He said he himself would never

235

undertake such a job unless he had four months and the help of press agencies. We did have the help of one press agent in London, the precious help of Margaret Gardner. Dear, true, loving, loved Margaret Gardner. My friend, my guardian angel, my debt I never can pay. She would harangue journalists, take them by the throat to make them write about Greece. She vowed that the tour would be a success. She wrote letters by the ton. She spent days on the telephone. She flew from city to city. She gave her time, her money and her heart.

I worried about Despo. How would she live in America? Would she find work? She steadfastly refused to go back to the colonels' Greece.

"Me? If I can't talk, I'll die of frustration."

Despo, in Julie's words, "is an extraordinary dame." Her ancestors were heroes of the Greek revolution. Her immediate family was once immensely rich. When their fortune was lost in the war, Despo was sincerely relieved. It embarrassed her to be rich in Greece. She speaks six languages fluently. She has translated major literary works into Greek. She is perennially gay and optimistic. Wherever she goes, she's a fish in water. Nobody gets invited to more places, by more people, than Despo. "Don't worry about me. I can act. I can sing. I can write. I can wash dishes."

All true, and more.

It was time to say good-by to my American friends. It was not easy. To many of them, I had become deeply attached. And I said good-by to Julie. He was staying on to do his film on the black people.

Talk. Sing. Give interviews. Mass meetings. Planes. Cars. Theatres. Stadiums. Threats. Applause. Pack. Travel. Hotels. Rena taking the phone calls. Angeliki ironing a dress in a corner. Greek delegations sitting on the floor. Television cables coming up the window. Plane. Train. Memorize a speech while Maria Farandouris and Antonis Kaloyannis sing softly and beautifully, working out a harmony for a Theodorakis song.

236

Train stations. Airports. Greek refugees. Greek emigré workers. Tears. Laughter. Vienna. Press conference. Bruno Pitterman close by to help. The Konzerthaus. Emotion running through the audience like electricity. People coming up from the audience to crowd the stage and sing with us.

Headline: PAPADOPOULOS GIVES HIS WORD OF HONOUR AS AN OFFICER THAT HE WILL RESTORE DEMOCRACY IN GREECE.

Geneva. Cautioned not to say anything inflammatory. The Swiss speakers do it for me.

Headline: MARTIN LUTHER KING MURDERED.

England. Invitation to a reception at the House of Commons. Encouragement at Oxford. Lunch with the Dean. London. Help from England's greatest actors. God bless Vanessa Redgrave and her whole family. Help from Lord Snow, Lord Salisbury, Sir Maurice Bowra. How to be titled and progressive. Press conference. So nervous I couldn't think of the name Harold Wilson. Place a wreath at Lord Byron's statue. I am not arrested. In Athens at the same moment, Mr. Fraser, Member of Parliament places a wreath at Lord Byron's statue in Athens. He is arrested. His wreath carried the poet's words: "I dreamed that Greece may yet be free." Mr. Fraser is detained only a few hours. Released with apologies. But his wreath is removed. Trafalgar Square. Overflowing. Microphones set up to reach people in surrounding streets. Beside me as I speak, Aleka Paezi, friend of dramatic school, resistance fighter. It is Easter. Day of hope. It is April 21. Anniversary of shame.

Oslo, Helsinki. May Day in Stockholm. A procession of two hundred thousand people. Olaf Palme, future Prime Minister, offers me the honor of heading the parade with him. The largest stadium in Sweden. Fifty thousand people buy tickets. Directors, actors, artists perform. They act as ushers. They sell peanuts and programs. An enormous Greek flag, encircled by smaller flags. Another huge flag on the platform. Under it, Olaf Palme speaks. Anita Bjork speaks. I sing Mikis' "Metapo." Liberty or death. The impulse and the strength came to wave the flag. A storm of applause.

Dusseldorf. Munich. Essen. Centers of Greek emigré workers. Emotion. Money for prisoner families. Rage at news of my excommunication from the Greek church. In Essen eight thousand Greeks sing "Metapo" with me. Then in thunderous chorus: "We want guns."

Berlin. Anti-demonstration at my hotel. In Greek: "Red whore! Go to Moscow."

I send defiant kisses from a balcony.

"*Putana.* Go back to Moscow."

Other kinds of Greeks come to disperse them.

Headline: LEFTIST STUDENT RUDI DUTSCHKE ATTACKED. NEAR DEATH.

Amsterdam. The Hague. The creation of the International Greek Aid Fund. Mr. Van der Stoel, its chairman, indefatigable fighter for Greek freedom, *rapporteur* to the Council of Europe. He leads the fight to kick Greece out of the Council of Europe. He didn't succeed. Not exactly. Greece ultimately resigned in ignominy. They learned that expulsion would be voted.

Brussels. I am to speak in the university auditorium. The arrival of three busloads of rightist hoodlums. They smash the windows of the auditorium. Spiros and students fight them off with their fists. The meeting goes on. I speak well.

Paris. Help from Jean-Paul Sartre and Jacques Duhamel. Lunch at the French Actors' Union. Meeting at the Mutualité. Kindness from Alain Cuny and Pia Colombo and Sacha Pitoeff. Friendship and understanding from Eric Rouleau. La Salle Pleyel. Serge Reggiani solid as a rock. Meetings with Mendès-France, André Malraux, François Mitterrand, Daniel Mayer. Press conference interrupted by cries: "Those who are in Greek prisons deserve to be there." Answering cries. "*Foutez le camp!"* and *"Les fascistes dehors!"* The conference continues.

The tour ended in France. There was time to rest and reflect. The people of Europe were more aware of the dangers of a Greek dictatorship. They were closer. They had had first hand experience with fascism. They knew of its contagion. Their governments? That was something else again. Much talk, much lip service in defense of democratic government but business as usual, and competition with the Americans to sell arms to Greece. There were exceptions. The finest were the Scandinavian governments. The Swedes were great. There was no double-talk. Their government openly contributed money to PAK, the resistance movement created by Andreas Papandreou. Norway led the fight to oust Greece from NATO.

But we had no illusions. Greek freedom had to be won by the Greek people. That was the only truth and we had to face it. And I had to face the truth of my own situation.

It was fine to talk of democracy in public meetings. It was exciting to sing songs of freedom—and then what? More meetings? More songs? The tour had taught me that there were vast numbers of people ready to help—but how? By crying out to their deaf governments? By cheering at meetings and then returning to their homes? I understood that as time went on, the cheers would die down and that gradually the people would stop coming to meetings unless we gave them something tangible to support—and that meant a unified, active resistance force. That needed organization. It needed money. It would need blood. This was the bitter reality and I had to come to grips with it. There had been a romantic moment when I considered leaving the theatre and films until Greece was free. I would devote myself to political study and work. Now I realized that I could be most useful if I earned money and put it to good use. I accepted the first offer—a film in America. Before I returned to the United States, I witnessed an important moment of history, the May uprising in France.

It was directionless. It was glorious. It was quixotic. It was crushed. But it was a warning to the world.

Julie and I were in California, working in separate films, but our weekends were free. For the first time, I knew the joys of a five-day week. We swam, we loafed, we talked, we listened to music. The last years had seen so many separations, so much movement, so many heartaches that we felt little guilt in being happy and enjoying each other's company. The director of my film was Norman Jewison. He was tough, charming, and extremely gifted. His last film had been awarded an Oscar. Our first meeting was not quite a success. I was not mad about the script and foolishly told him that my main interest in the film was to make money to buy bombs. Perhaps he didn't take me too seriously but he was offended and had the right to be. In the end he forgave me and we became friends.

A cause for hope. Two men who are candidates for the presidency of the United States take a strong position against the Greek dictatorship: Eugene McCarthy and Robert Kennedy. I had met Kennedy twice, once at a delightful party in his home. The first impression—boyishness and charm. Then quickly the understanding that there was steel and sinew. It was a fun evening. Dancing and light-heartedness. Not much political talk, but enough to convince me that this young man with the irresistible smile had a driving need to identify himself with the most progressive in American life, a need to break the bonds of party machine prudence and reach out for the best a young America could create. There was a second meeting in New York. It was shortly before he announced his candidacy. He was still hesitant.

"You must run for the presidency," I had said. And he: "Do you want them to kill me too?"

June 4, 1968. I rushed back from the studio to hear the results of the democratic primaries in California. As the campaign developed, our hopes had mounted. It seemed sure that the Democrats would win the elections. There was a growing revulsion against the war in Vietnam. Johnson had announced he would not run again. Everyone felt that with either McCarthy or Kennedy, that monstrous war would be brought to an end, that a wave of liberalism would follow. We Greeks hoped that would mean the end of the colonels.

Angeliki had the television set turned on full blast. She yelled her greeting to me: "Kennedy! Kennedy has won!"

My heart leaped. I had enormous respect for McCarthy, but something I learned from my grandfather told me that he did not have the dynamism or the popular touch that could win him the presidency. The victory in the California primaries was decisive. I could foresee nothing that could keep Kennedy from the presidency. Angeliki and I fell into each other's arms. "Greece will be free."

Then came the assassin's bullets. Kennedy's face. That beautiful face, suffused in pain and infinite sweetness. A young life dying and something vital in America dying with it.

In Greece that August there was an attempt at another assassination. A young army officer, Alekos Panagoulis, tried to kill the tyrant Papadopoulos. The gods that wanted Kennedy dead, wanted Papadopoulos saved. Panagoulis was caught and imprisoned. He was tortured so mercilessly, he could barely stand in the dock at his trial.

"I believe that the finest testament of a fighter for freedom is death before the tyrant's firing squad. Violence breeds violence. I have failed, but others will follow."

I may not agree that death is the finest testament for a freedom fighter, but Greeks understood Panagoulis. He wanted his death to be useful. He was condemned to die. Pressure from everywhere, from the Vatican, from heads of governments, kept him alive. He now rots in a Greek prison cell. Sirhan Sirhan, the man who killed Kennedy, is in a jail in Los

Angeles. Two men who wanted to kill two other men. Should they be seen in the same light? Is Sirhan Sirhan a hero? Is Alekos Panagoulis a hero? Are they both criminals? Should Papadopoulos and Kennedy be seen in the same light? Was Kennedy a tyrant? Let the philosophers be impartial. I, as a Greek, wept for the death of Kennedy. I would not have mourned the death of Papadopoulos.

And yet another tragedy in that dark summer of 1968. The Russian army and its subalterns invaded Czechoslovakia. The spring of Prague, the dream of freedom, was crushed in the name of socialism. What hypocrisy. What brutishness. What heart-break. And what comfort it gave to some of the fine democrats in Washington. Oh, they branded the invasion for the crime it was, but they used it well to justify Vietnam, to justify aid to the Greek colonels.

The Democratic Convention watched by most of America on the television. In the streets, the Chicago police on a rampage, an orgy of violence against young demonstrators. Horrifying brutality. Skulls crushed, police faces deformed by hatred and a lust to kill. Young girls dragged by the hair and clubbed. And boys who cry out as they are being beaten: "The whole world is watching." Inside the Convention hall, the Chicago mayor sits smiling, watching the party power at work. Empty speeches, compromises. A noisy carnival to mock the ideals of a Eugene McCarthy who lost and a Robert Kennedy who died. Poor America.

The Republican Convention. Phony. Artificial. A greased political machine, rigged, smooth. Nowhere is felt the voice of the people. And Spiro Agnew chosen to run with Nixon. Agnew, Tom Pappas' man. Pappas, Greek-American, supporter and exploiter of the junta. Pappas, the CIA man has enough weight to influence the choice of a Vice-President. Poor America. Poor Greece.

I yearned to be back in Europe, to go anywhere and live with emigré Greek workers, so I was glad when our films were finished, Julie's and mine. Both were to be failures. I had not much hope for my film from the outstart and I could handle the failure. Not Julie. He put his heart into his film. He wanted so much for it. He believed it was needed, that it could contribute to America's understanding of the black man's agonizing struggle. He never let anyone see what failure did to him. But I live with him and I saw his heartbreak as a man and as an artist.

Strasbourg 1969. Hearings before the Council of Europe. Witness after witness testifying that they had been tortured in junta prisons. Sickening details. Anger. Anger and shame.

Rome. A speech to thousands of workers. Heartened by the will of the Italian people to help, to give money. Shock and despair to see open conflict between different Greek resistance organizations.

Stockholm. Begging leaders of resistance groups to compromise their differences and unite to create a single effective resistance organization.

Paris. Meeting with a man who has just come from Athens. He talks of the bitterness of the Greek people. He fears a sense of defeat and resignation. He talks about friends in prison. He is returning to Athens that same evening. He talks about the desperate need for money. The following day another Greek gentleman comes to speak to me. He claims he is sent by the Soviet embassy in Paris with an invitation to come to the Soviet Union, to make the same kind of speaking tour that I did in Europe and the United States. I talk of augmented Russian trade with Greece. He dismisses this as a hard reality of political life and assures me that if I come to the Soviet Union, I will see where their sympathies lie. I tell him I will go, but on condition that I be able to talk as freely as I did in the West—press conferences, radio, television, public meetings completely uncensored. He is certain that this condition will be met. He will relay this message to the embassy and get right back to me.

I never heard from him again.

London. I sit with a group of hunger strikers opposite the Greek embassy. The execution of Alekos Panagoulis was scheduled for the following day. Panagoulis' younger brother sits beside me. Runners come to tell us of a flood of protests sent to Greece. From the United States to Australia: from Picasso, from Jean-Paul Sartre, from De Gaulle, from the Pope. English passers-by offer encouragement to the hunger strikers. Technicians from BBC come with television cameras and rumors that the execution may be halted. When the news comes that Panagoulis will not be killed, his brother holds on to me and weeps.

Lausanne. Julie announces to me that we are engaged to do a film called *Promise at Dawn*. I am happy. It's a role I like and the film will give us money.

Boulogne. A film studio. Julie is shooting a scene that parodies silent movie making. I go to kiss Margot Capelier, our casting director. She has found "extra" work for dozens of Greek refugees. They have no work permits, but Margot exercised her charm and magic with the authorities.

Dole. A small town in France. It has been transformed to look like Cracow. It had been arranged to shoot in Poland, a contract had been signed, payments had been made. But while shooting in Nice, Julie had a bad fall. Bones were broken in both feet. The film had to shut down for five weeks. The Poles then declared that the delay made it impossible for them to receive us, and that they considered the contract null and void. It is my belief that the delay was a pretext. I believe that permission was refused because some administrator in Poland learned that Nina, the character I was playing, was Jewish, and was victim to persecution in Poland. I believe that permission was refused because Assaf Dayan, son of Israel's Prime Minister, was a member of our cast. I cannot prove any of this, but I believe it. I know people in Poland who could prove it.

While we were shooting in Dole, members of a Greek resistance organization were being tried by a court-martial in Athens. One night we returned from shooting to find a journalist waiting for Julie at our hotel. He asked Julie if he had a statement to make.

"About what?"

We were shown a newspaper. The dateline was Athens. Julie was charged with smuggling bombs into Greece together with manuals on the manufacture of explosives. He was to be tried in absentia under law 509 which meant he could be condemned to death. The journalist asked if the charges were true. I adored Julie's answer: "If I sent bombs, I would not admit it. If I did not send bombs, I'd be ashamed to say so."

Genoa. The port. It is dawn. The dockworkers come to work at six in the morning. I am there to invite them to a meeting that evening. They all promise to come. Julie, Spiros, Rena, and I stroll along the docks. There's a Greek merchant marine in the harbor. The sight of it moves me. I call out to the sailors. They gather into a group but do not speak. An officer close by glares at me. He disperses the group. Not a word has been spoken. As they leave, one of them furtively puts up his fingers in the sign for victory. I've had similar experiences at various airports with employees of the Greek Olympic Airways. Even outside of Greece they are afraid to speak to me, but with a sign, a look, they make me understand that they are friends.

Receiving threatening letters and telephone calls had become part of our lives. We just had to learn to live with them. That evening in Genoa, the threats were put into practice. On the stage of the theatre, there was a speaker's rostrum. Under the rostrum were nine pounds of plastic timed to explode at five minutes past eight. I was scheduled to speak at eight o'clock. I'm still around to tell this story because of Paola. I know little of Paola except for her blessed name. She was a member of the arrangements committee for the meeting. She came to the theatre a little early to see that everything was in order. It occurred to her to check the microphones. By chance her foot moved the small drapery that decorated the speaker's rostrum. She saw a package. It was wrapped in cellophane and ribbons. She decided it was a gift for me and took it into the wings. God willed that the doorman was an ex-partisan fighter and suspicious. The weight of the package troubled him. He sniffed at it, he bent his ear to it and leaped to the telephone to call the police. They came in a matter of minutes, followed by fire engines and trucks carrying sand. They rushed the beribboned package to an empty building site, the sand trucks were emptied, and they exploded the bomb.

It rocked the entire neighborhood. The police said that not only would it have killed everyone on the rostrum (among them Spiros, Julie and Rena) but that it had enough force to bring down the ceiling of the theatre. They calculated that the explosion and the resulting panic would have killed at least two hundred people. The reaction of the Italians was fantastic. In an incredibly short time, it seemed that all of Genoa knew about the bomb. Thousands came to throng the square where the theatre was located, in a spontaneous demonstration of solidarity. We went on with the meeting and my speech was beamed out to them. Needless to say, I departed from the text. The cheers of the people in the square could be heard in the theatre. The chairman of the meeting announced that a representative of the dockers' union had a few words to say. They were few but to the point.

"To protest this savage act, there will be no work on the docks tomorrow. I have been given the authority to tell you that tomorrow, we strike."

At the end of the meeting, hundreds walked beside our car until we reached our hotel. God bless them. God bless Paola. God bless the doorman. God bless the police and the firemen. God damn the fascists.

Mikis Theodorakis was free! —After three and a half years of prison and exile, he was in Paris. Never-ending world pressure and some last-minute able maneuvering by Jean-Jacques Servan-Schreiber secured his freedom. We had advance word and were on the airfield when his plane came down at Orly. That giant figure, tired, strained, bewildered, descending from the plane, his dazed recognition of friends on the field, his emotion, ours, images that will stay with me forever.

He rested a few days and has been active ever since. He came from Greece with one message, one will—all Greeks, whatever their political opinions, must unite in a single front against the dictatorship, up to and including King Constantine. This proposition has caused friction among many in the resistance groups. The young people particularly oppose the idea of uniting with the ultraconservatives whom they judge to be anti-junta only because they themselves want the power. They reject out of hand the notion of trusting Constantine. They cannot forgive the damage he has done. But Mikis and others insist that this unity is a political imperative. They make the point that much of the military hates the junta—not the younger officers whom Papadopoulos has bought by tripling their salaries—but the thousands who have been purged from the army, the NATO-trained people and those who were in the higher echelons.

I myself am torn. I realize the need for unity, yet I fear betrayal. I know the junta must be destroyed, but I would wish a deeper unity, based on a common ideal for the future of Greece. I am uneasy about a unity that is worked out around a table by people who are wary about each other. I believe that Greece needs a unity that is organic, that is formed in struggle. I believe in those Greeks who, day and night, work actively to bring down the dictatorship. Such Greeks will inevitably meet and work together.

I am finishing this final chapter in January 1971. Easter will come again in April. It will mark four years in the life of the military dictatorship, a life granted and sustained by the American CIA and State Department. A year ago, Eastertime, Colonel Patakos made a speech to U.S. officials and newspapermen. He was euphoric in his gratitude:

> A new star shines in the Western skies, the American star. Europe should accept its bright light without any jealousy or reservations. American wisdom may be identified with the modest wisdom of Euripides.

(Word of honor, it's a direct quote.)

And this coming Easter, Patakos can rejoice in the resurrection of full military shipments from Washington. The State Department, to justify this scandalous decision, announced that "the trend towards a constitutional order is established," and the State Department knows that:

> Martial law is still in force.
> There are continued arrests, condemnations and imprisonment without trial.
> Habeas Corpus does not exist for political prisoners;
> The Red Cross has been refused permission to visit Greek prisons;
> Every Greek institution is under direct military control; this goes for sports organizations; this goes for universities; this goes for the rewriting of history books; this goes for the theatre where an army commissar is the arbiter for the choice of plays and the way they are cast; this goes for the church where they actually created a post, "Archpriest of the Armed Forces." In effect, that simply means that a major general exerts a tight military grip on the church.

The State Department knows all of this and has the gall to say that the colonels are moving toward constitutional order. In the words of Dimitrios Papaspyrou, last President of the Greek parliament (no red, he):

> The State Department knows all of this perfectly well. Hence its assertions about the evolution of the Athens' regime toward democracy constitute proof of its complicity in the fraud.

248

(That's telling them, Mr. President.)

Senator Fulbright, in a hearing before the Senate Foreign Relations Committee, expressed his disgust that the Americans should support what he called "this disgraceful regime." The principal witnesses at the hearing were Deputy Assistant Secretary of State for Near Eastern and South Asian Affairs, Davies, and Robert J. Pranger, Deputy Assistant Secretary of the Defense. Senator Fulbright asked a leading question.

MR. FULBRIGHT: Can you say categorically whether or not we had anything to do with the overthrow of the previous administration?

MR. DAVIES: Mr. Chairman, the way things are organized within our government and from my knowledge of our actions in adjacent areas, I would think it highly unlikely that there was any connivance whatever. In fact, I would say categorically, I am certain there was not. I believe that I can relay your question back to my superiors and provide confirmation of that assurance.

MR. FULBRIGHT: Under oath?

MR. DAVIES: I am under oath.

To Mr. Fulbright, I humbly suggest a list of questions. It would be interesting to hear the answers—under oath.

In 1961, did Mr. Laughlin Campbell, head of the American CIA in Athens, put pressure on Andreas Papandreou to accept changes in Greek election laws that were prejudicial to the Center Union Party?

Did Mr. Campbell ask Andreas Papandreou to arrange a meeting between himself and George Papandreou on this subject?

When Andreas stated his father's opposition to these changes, did Mr. Campbell say: "You tell your father we get what we want."?

In the same year, did the Center Union Party protest the interference of the American ambassador in the internal political life in Greece?

Why?

Was it the system to pay American funds directly to the Greek intelligence service without any control of the Greek government?

In 1965, a number of deputies deserted the ranks of the Center Union Party. Were any of them given money by the CIA to do so?

If so, how much?

Was a Greek girl given fifty thousand drachmas by the CIA to depose against Andreas Papandreou in the Aspida case?

Were two army officers offered bribes of one hundred thousand dollars each to testify against the Papandreous in the Aspida trial?

Did a third officer accept a bribe of one million drachmas and turn state's evidence?

Did the CIA finance the right-wing newspaper, Eleftheros Cosmos?

Was Paul Totomis, the Junta's Minister of Public Order, a member of the CIA?

Was Tom Pappas, heavy investor in Greece, partner of Standard Oil Company of New Jersey, sponsor of Spiro Agnew, a member of the CIA?

How did Colonel Papadopoulos get his hands on the NATO Prometheus Plan?

Did the CIA have positive knowledge of the coup? Did they know the scheduled date?

These are only a few of the questions. I can suggest many more. But finally I rage against myself and all the Greek people who know that the United States has controlled Greece for twenty-five years and haven't lifted a finger in protest. Oh, every once in a while, somebody lets off steam. He makes an indignant speech about foreign powers, industrial military complexes, NATO, and then, exhausted by this righteous effort, takes the weekend off. We condemned the German people for permitting the rise of Nazism. Should we not be condemned for permitting a fascist government in Greece? Is it not conceivable that we have the government we deserve? In the final analysis, who is more guilty, the exploiter or the exploited? Those who rule by terror, or those who are intimidated? Who sinned more against God, those who turned on the gas in the death chambers, or those who marched to those chambers, unresisting? I know all the pat answers. The oppressors have the guns and the tanks. They have the computers, the press and the airwaves; but let's tell the truth. Who shoulders their guns? Who drives their tanks? We do. We collaborate with the enemy; we work for him; we make him rich. We give him our children to fight his wars. We allow him to divide us, to paralyze our minds, to buy our souls for refrigerators and television sets. One truth is inescapable. They are the few and we are the many. Despite their computers and their guns we are infinitely stronger and yet we let them make us cowards. We hide behind the slogan "One must live," though it really means "One must live shabbily."

And yet I swear I am optimistic. Because everywhere in the world, young people are taking a stand. They are more courageous than we are. They are wiser. They are not for sale and they are militant. They may not yet have a plan or a perfected social program, but they reject the lies of the West and the betrayal of the East. The revolution they are preparing is more than scientific or technological. They demand that life be meaningful. They demand that life be lit by some large vision of beauty and goodness and truth. They are American; they are French; they are Italian; they are Greek. They are everywhere. By repudiating our fears and our values, they make us better, they love us more. They will lead us to a free and beautiful world. I believe this with all my heart.

Dear Dora, Dear Iannis,

Cross your fingers. We're on the final revisions. Julie and Robbie are meeting with M.B. in Paris in two weeks. If he likes the screenplay, we'll have the money for the film. We're hopeful. But if he doesn't like it, we'll knock at other doors. We're determined to make it.

We listened to your tapes again, all day yesterday. It's a shame we can't use all of it. Impossible. Do you realize that you, Iannis and Kitty took twelve hours to tell your story. We've got to reduce it to two hours for the film. But I do think we have the heart of it and the meaning. For the scenes where you are questioned at the Security, we are using your recording, word for word. Neither animals like Lambrou nor his dialogue could be invented. I think Robbie and Yorgos have resolved the problems of the torture scenes. No audience could withstand seeing what you went through. They have found images that may surprise you, but the use of the soundtrack is ingenious, very powerful, very effective. Dora, please tell Kitty that the scene in the prison cell with the stout woman is just as she told it, nothing added, nothing taken away. And Iannis, I think the film will be what you wanted. It will be more than your story, it will be an act of resistance.

The final scene: Lambrou and the guards taking Dora to the quarry. Seen from the car, the streets of Athens, landscapes, the sea and faces, faces. On the soundtrack, Ritsos' words:

> How did our vineyards and our doors become locked
> How did the light thin over the roof and the trees
> Who will tell that one half of them is under the earth
> And that the other half is in iron?
> > (It is at this point we bring in Mikis'
> > music, softly at first.)

With so many leaves the sun sends its greetings
With so many banners the sky is agleam
And these Greeks are closed in iron
And these other Greeks are in the earth
Hush, any minute now
The bells will ring out
This soil is theirs and ours
Beneath the soil, in their crossed hands
The dead hold the bell's rope
They await the hour
They wait to sound the resurrection
This soil is theirs and ours
No one can take it from us
Hush, any minute now
The bells will ring out
This soil is theirs and ours.

Get well quickly, Dorula, and cross your fingers, hard. Do
you know when we want to start shooting? Easter.

Love,
Melina